Library of Congress Catalog Number: 2011032103
ISBN: 978-1-4128-4623-3
Printed in the United States of America

Library of Congress Cataloging-in-Publication Data

Wong, Kam C.
    One country, two systems : cross-border crime between Hong Kong and China / Kam C. Wong.
        p. cm.
    Includes index.
    ISBN 978-1-4128-4623-3
    1. Criminal justice, Administration of—China—Hong Kong. 2. Criminal justice, Administration of—China. 3. Law enforcement—China—Hong Kong. 4. Law enforcement—China. I. Title.
        KNQ9392.4.W66 2012
        345.5125'05—dc23
                                                                        2011032103

For my sister Rose, a study in kindness

# Contents

# Foreword

With billions of dollars of ransom money at stake and a notorious gang boss allegedly at the heart of a scheme embracing kidnappings, murder, and explosives smuggling, the criminal charges against Cheung Tse-keung—aka the "Big Spender"—in the People's Republic of China (PRC) culminated in what legitimately can be considered as a leading contender for "trial of the century" laurels. On rare occasions, criminal trials transcend the courtrooms in which the interplay of lawyers, judges, witnesses, case-specific facts, and black-letter rules of law results in verdicts that embody the legal system's best approximation of justice. Involving far more than the fate and fortunes of the involved parties, some trials are at the vortex of such powerful social and political forces that they are engulfed by them, threatening to reduce the actors within court to little more than proxies for those overarching themes. And sometimes, an observer and bard comes along who is positioned by virtue of talent and insights not only to ensure that the sociolegal drama will be faithfully reported, but who additionally helps elucidate its deeper meaning.

Professor Kam C. Wong's careful and evocative depiction of the trial of Cheung Tse-keung in the PRC for sensational crimes committed largely in the Special Administrative Region of Hong Kong, reflects all of the above ingredients, and more. *One Country, Two Systems* is a meticulously documented exposition of how this dramatic case became a canvas on which the emergent legal and political ties that would bind these dual cultures was imprinted.

The PRC assumed sovereignty over Hong Kong—previously under British colonial rule—in 1997. Under the "one country, two systems" principle characterizing this new arrangement, Hong Kong's political system, including its common law-based judicial system, was to retain a "high degree of autonomy" vis-à-vis the PRC, even as Hong Kong acquired the status of city-state within mainland China. The "Big

Spender's" 1998 trial was based primarily on conduct that took place in Hong Kong and that preceded the 1997 transfer of sovereignty. The trial nevertheless was held in the PRC, according to its vastly different laws. As compelling as the principal defendant and his alleged crimes were, the case simultaneously put on trial the "one country, two systems" premise defining the nascent political relationship between the PRC and Hong Kong.

We are accustomed to the uncertainties that surround and help precipitate criminal trials, to the conflicting accusations and denials made by the prosecution and defense, and to the inevitable gaps between a perfect reconstruction of past events and the evidentiary presentations made in court. Yet we are conditioned to accept, and for the most part we do accept trial verdicts as producing a final resolution of even highly contentious disputes. At some point, the involved parties and the community unsettled by the conduct at the base of the contested allegations must move forward, relegating what happened in the past to the past with a measure of finality. Not so with trials such as the "Big Spender's" which, as Professor Wong so vividly illustrates, invite (and perhaps demand) a new round of profound and lingering questions that take on a life of their own.

*One Country, Two Systems* exposes and explores these larger questions after first artfully describing the fascinating plot line established by the arrest and prosecution of Cheung Tse-keung for masterminding the spectacularly grand crimes at issue. Then, using the trial and its culmination as a springboard, Professor Wong moves on to analyze the underlying legal, political, and policy dimensions of the case and their vitally important implications for the meaning of "one country, two systems" for the PRC and Hong Kong. He is uniquely well qualified to integrate and make sense of the factual, legal, and social underpinnings woven into the fine tapestry comprising this volume.

Formerly an Inspector of Police in Hong Kong, Professor Wong pursued higher education in the United States, earning his undergraduate and law degrees from Indiana University, and a Ph.D. in criminal justice from the University at Albany. In addition to his impressive policing credentials, he was a practicing lawyer for several years. Currently on the faculty of the Department of Criminal Justice at Xavier University, he is renowned as a demanding and inspiring educator. His distinguished academic accomplishments include the publication of multiple books and scholarly articles. He is recognized internationally for his contributions to comparative law, the sociology of law, policing, and other subjects, focusing on legal and political systems in the United States as well as in China.

I have been privileged to have been on the receiving end of many peregrinations of Professor Wong's wide-ranging and creative intellect when our paths joined for a few years at the University at Albany. This volume is continuing evidence of his abiding and triumphant commitment to his scholarly craft. *One Country, Two Systems* is richly informative and theoretically elegant.

The pages within this book reveal and then thoughtfully probe the numerous fundamentally important legal, policy, political, and cultural issues stemming from the trial of Cheung Tse-keung. The "Big Spender" was reputed to have lived much of his life substantially outside of the law. Ironically, the prosecution of his case raises the specter of a governmental regime being willing to operate similarly, bending if not breaking rules of law in pursuit of objectives perceived as more urgent. Professor Wong explores the short term and likely enduring significance of the machinations surrounding this fascinating case for the PRC, the Special Administrative Region of Hong Kong, and the "one country, two systems" principle. He persuasively argues that "[t]he 'Big Spender' case is not only a test case over the meaning of law; it is a litmus test on the legal culture of the Chinese and Hong Kong people."

This book is equal parts classic courtroom drama and scholarship of the highest and most penetrating order. It anticipates and offers cogent analysis of issues that are as timely and important as they are destined to recur; issues that are fundamental within the PRC and Hong Kong, and redolent with implications for other lands and in other contexts, as well.

James R. Acker
Distinguished Teaching Professor,
University at Albany

# Preface

On July 1, 1997, Hong Kong, a British Colony since 1841, was returned to China as a Special Administrative Region (HKSAR). To facilitate a smooth transition, Deng Xiao-ping fashioned the "one country, two systems" principle ("Principle"). The Principle was designed to allay political anxiety, absorb cultural shock, and grandfather vested interests of the Hong Kong people for a period of fifty years. Since 1997, there were a number of high-profile cases exploring the meaning and testing the limits of the Principle.[1] This book reports on the "Big Spender" case. The "Big Spender" case is the first time a Hong Kong legal resident (Cheung Tse-keung) was prosecuted, tried, and executed in China under the PRC Criminal Law for criminal conduct largely perpetrated in Hong Kong. As such, it tests for the first time the criminal jurisdiction boundary between the PRC and Hong Kong under "one country, two systems."

I have a threefold interest in researching the "Big Spender" case. First, I was born in Hong Kong. My roots are in Hong Kong. As a Chinese saying goes: "Falling leaves eventually return to the roots." I am also emotionally bonded. As another Chinese saying goes: "Looking up I see the bright moon; looking down I think of my old home." I am instinctively interested in and naturally concerned about what transpired in Hong Kong. I write this book because I love and care about Hong Kong. Second, I was an Inspector of Police with the Hong Kong Police (HKP) and now serve as its trainer and consultant. The "Big Spender" is one of the biggest criminal cases in HKP history, in seriousness, audacity, notoriety, and impact. I have a professional interest in the origin, development, and resolution of the case. Third, I am a comparative legal and policing scholar. My lifelong pursuit is to explore the similarities and differences of Chinese versus Western jurisprudential thoughts, in theory and practice. The "Big Spender" case offered a unique opportunity to explore contrasting images of law, order, justice, and control on West versus East.

In writing the book, I have the following objectives: The first objective is to inform on how the PRC criminal system and process operates in principle. The second objective is to inform on how the PRC criminal justice system works in practice. The third and final objective is to provide a methodical and detailed presentation of the facts, circumstances, law, and process of the case in order to facilitate informed discussion, sound analysis, enlightened debate, and balanced resolution over many of the legal and policy issues raised in the case, particularly as they relate to the meaning and application of the Principle.

Besides "one country, two systems" constitutional and policy issues, some of the comparative legal issues to be discussed in the book include:

1. How are criminal cases initiated in the PRC versus Hong Kong? For example, in China, case initiation (*lian*) is a duty of citizens as well as responsibility of police. Hong Kong victims and the public have no obligation to report a criminal case.
2. How long can a criminal suspect be detained for investigation? According to Article 57 of the PRC Criminal Procedure Law, custody for investigation in theory can last for thirty days, but in practice ("Big Spender") custody length averages two months and six days. There is a huge disparity between theory and practice.
3. Where should the "Big Spender" case be tried? This is a legal jurisdiction versus trial venue debate.
4. How is the PRC criminal procedure different from that of Hong Kong, as in the case of particularization and specificity of charges? Charging practices raise issues with notice (due process) and appeal (check and balance).
5. Is there a right to remain silent? Article 67 of the PRC Criminal Law encourages voluntary cooperation and truthful confession to the police with the maxim: "leniency to those who confess their crimes and severity to those who refuse to" ("*tan bai cong huan, kang ju cong yan*").
6. What is the standard of proof in a criminal trial in China? Article 162 of the PRC Criminal Procedure Law provides that guilt or innocence is to be decided when "the facts of a case are clear, the evidence is reliable and adequate" ("*anjian shishi qingchu, keshi, chongfen*"). What then is the standard, quantum, and burden of proof?

I came upon the "Big Spender" case quite by accident. My exposure to the—moral, legal, and political—issues raised long preceded my professional involvement with the case as a media consultant, legal advisor, public intellectual, and academic scholar. I returned to

Hong Kong in 1984 and remained until 1987, holding a position in Hong Kong as a public law lecturer with the Chinese University Hong Kong. At that juncture, the British and Chinese governments were negotiating for the transfer of Hong Kong sovereignty to China. I had a front row seat to observe the unfolding saga. I followed the private negotiation, engaged in public debate, and wrote on many of the "Big Spender" issues diligently. As a Hong Kong person, my position then, as now, is that we (Hong Kong people) need to accept the transfer of sovereignty as a "historical"[2] fact. But we need to do what we can to secure the welfare and interests of the Hong Kong people. Then, I was skeptical of the feasibility of the Principle. I made my position known in *South China Morning Post*, White Hall, the Hong Kong Government, and many public forums.

My professional involvement with the "Big Spender" case was in 1998, as a law professor, public intellectual, and legal consultant. I entered the fray as the Director of Chinese Law Program at Chinese University of Hong Kong. In such a capacity I was invited to speak, write, and debate on many of the 1997 issues anticipated by the 1984 negotiation, but now surfaced in more concrete and contentious terms with the "Big Spender" case.

After ten odd years, in fits and starts, and after much procrastination and delay, I finally finished this project. Much like running an exhaustive marathon, a lot of thoughts went through my mind, during and especially after the (running) writing:

First, I reckoned that every individual involved in the "Big Spender" case is in agreement: all parties to the "Big Spender" debate are losers. The Hong Kong Government (HKSAR) lost some of its hard-earned political independence and with it much public confidence when it chose to hand over Cheung Tse-keung without a fight. The PRC lost some of its credibility in interfering with the HKSAR justice administration by catering to the special interest of Li Kar Shing, father of the kidnapped person. The incident also shows clearly that the PRC is not above using political pressure to force the hand of the HKSAR when circumstances call for it, e.g., dispensing "substantive justice" with "Big Spender."

Second, we observe that the conflict of "one country, two systems" is a conflict between two entirely different political, social, and economic systems having to live and work with each other within a confined ideological spectrum and limited legal space as envisioned under the

Principle and as provided for by the Basic Law framework. In such a case, much like odd couples with big egos sharing a crowded room, there are going to be explosive confrontations between the PRC and HKSAR. Thus observed, legal disputes and constitutional litigations under the Basic Law are here to stay. They are normal, rather than exceptional.

Third, conflicts between the PRC and HKSAR are healthy and should be welcomed. They expose/clarify ingrained misconceptions and reveal/release deep hidden tensions to an uneasy but budding relationship. If constructively handled, i.e., disputes being viewed as necessary conflicts between friends (in Mao's term, "contradictions within people") and not as intentional animosities between enemies ("contradictions between enemies"), such conflicts can contribute immensely to the improvement and cementing of a lasting and rewarding relationship. Joint effort in problem-solving promotes mutual understanding, leading to a better appreciation of each other's values, an enhanced respect for each other's position, a growing willingness to accept each other's needs and wants as one's own, and an increased accommodation of each other's interests and welfare.

Lastly, we observed that the Basic Law is designed in such a way for the PRC and HKSAR to negotiate their differences. People should keep in mind that the larger purpose of the Basic Law is to bring Chinese nationals (the PRC and Hong Kong) together to plan the future of Hong Kong and not in setting the PRC and HKSAR residents apart. PRC political leadership and Hong Kong legal professionals should keep in mind the aforesaid intent and spirit of the Basic Law when they confront each other over the Principle, under circumstances of "fire and fury" on another occasion, which is sure to come as Hong Kong turns another unexpected corner.

In beginning this book, it bears to repeat the obvious. The Basic Law should be used to resolve conflicts and not to create disputes; this is for the betterment of all and not the benefit of some. Hong Kong gaining at the expense and to the detriment of the PRC or vice versa is not the intent of the Principle. The suggestion here is that Basic Law disputes need not be conceived as a zero-sum game. If properly dealt with, i.e., with patience and understanding, Basic Law disputes can in fact be win–win situations for all concerned.

In finishing this book, I have many intellectual debts to pay, and still more persons to thank. First, I would like to thank my colleagues and students at the HKP who freely gave me their time and supplied me with information in my investigation into the case. I regret that I cannot disclose their names due to the sensitiveness of our discussion. Without their cooperation, this book could not be written. Second, I would like to thank the students and faculty (Joseph Cheng, Andrew Wong, Byron Wang, Peter Lee, Michael Davis, Cheng Chek Yim) at Department of Government and Public Affairs, Chinese University of Hong Kong, for helping me in developing this book. Third, I would like to thank the many Hong Kong officials who helped me in thinking through many issues in this book. There are too many of them to recognize by name. Fourth, I would like to thank Distinguished Professor Jim Acker at Albany who mentored me through the years, and graced this book with an elegant Foreword. Finally, and most importantly, I would like to thank my wife, Rainbow Wong. Without her constant encouragement and support, I do not think I could have ever completed this intellectual project, much delayed.

This book is dedicated to my sister Rose Wong, a kind and affectionate person, on the date of her sixtieth birthday in Seattle, Washington.

Kam C. Wong
August 8, 2011

## Notes

1. Joseph R. Crowley Program Report, "One Country, Two Legal Systems?" *Fordham International Law Journal* 23, no. 1 (1999): 1–119.
2. What the PRC described as "problem left over by history" meaning two things: (1) The "unequal treaty" (Treaty of Nanking, August 29, 1842) and with it the national disgrace of a bygone era has come to past. (2) Hong Kong, as with Taiwan and Macau, must be reunited with the motherland.

# 1

# Introduction

Tuesday, October 20, 1998, was an eventful day for Hong Kong. It was the day Cheung Tse-keung,[1] also known as the "Big Spender,"[2] and thirty-five other alleged accomplices went on trial in China for a host of criminal charges,[3] ranging from murder to kidnapping to smuggling of explosives, committed in Hong Kong and China[4] from 1991 to 1997. The case attracted worldwide attention and aroused public imagination in part as a result of the flamboyancy of the legendary gang boss "Big Spender"[5] and in part because of the unprecedented amount of ransom money involved.[6] Cheung Tse-keung demanded and obtained HK$1.38 billion for the kidnapping of Cheung Kong Company's deputy chairman Victor Li Tzar kuoi on May 23, 1996, and HK$0.6 billion from Sun Hung Kai Company's chairman Walter Kwok Ping-sheung on September 29, 1997.

More significantly, the "Big Spender" case made legal history in Hong Kong and China. It was the first time a Hong Kong legal resident was prosecuted, tried, and executed in China under the PRC Criminal Law[7] for criminal acts largely perpetrated in Hong Kong, thus testing for the first time the limits of "one country, two systems."[8] For this reason, Mr. Ivan Tang, the Hong Kong defense lawyer for "Big Spender," openly challenged the "legal basis for holding the trial of a Hong Kong resident on the mainland when most of the alleged crimes were said to have been committed in the SAR."[9]

The "Trial of the Century" ended on November 12, 1998, with the court of the first instance, Guangzhou Intermediary People's Court, finding Cheung (and all other defendants) guilty as charged.[10] The court of the second instance, Guangzhou Higher People's Court, rejected Cheung's appeal and confirmed his verdict on December 5, 1998, proclaiming: "We have sufficient witnesses and evidence to show Cheung Tse-keung took a mastermind role in the crime . . . And it did not appear the offences only took place in Hong Kong."[11] Cheung Tse-keung was immediately executed.[12] The case ended as dramatically, momentously, and controversially as it had began.[13] Cheung's defense lawyer in Hong Kong, Mr. Ivan Tang, claimed that "this is not only a death sentence for Cheung Tse-keung but also a death sentence for 'one country, two systems.'"[14] The PRC's official newspaper in Hong Kong insisted that "justice has been done and people are satisfied."[15] The Chief Executive of the HKSAR, Mr. Tung, called for an immediate review of the judicial cooperation between the PRC and the SAR.[16]

The "Big Spender" might have been convicted and executed, but lingering legal,[17] political, and policy issues remain.[18]

As a policy matter, should HKSAR have prosecuted Cheung Tse-keung, notwithstanding the lack of cooperation from the victim's family, e.g., failure to report a crime? Should HKSAR have frozen Cheung Tse-keung's ill-gotten gains, if there was not enough evidence to prosecute him for kidnapping in the first instance? Should HKSAR have prosecuted Li's family for not reporting the crime and failure to cooperate with the kidnapping investigation? Should HKSAR have asked for the extradition of Cheung Tse-keung, before, during, or after the trial? Should HKSAR have defended the legal rights of the PRC to try the case? Should HKSAR have insisted on trying the "Big Spender" case in Hong Kong courts, notwithstanding PRC's competing jurisdiction claim? Should HKSAR have assisted the PRC in prosecuting Cheung Tse-keung by sending an officer to China as an observer? Should HKSAR, in any future negotiations with the PRC over rendition, insist on the nonwaiver of capital punishment as a material condition?

Legally, what was the jurisdictional reach of the PRC Criminal Law? Does the PRC Criminal Procedure Law[19] apply to Hong Kong residents who have committed preparatory crimes in China but carried out the main corpus of the crime in Hong Kong? How should the conflict between Article 6 of the PRC Criminal Law (which allows the prosecution of criminal conduct, including preparatory crimes, committed in China before the PRC courts) and Article 18 of the Basic Law (which asserts that Hong Kong courts have exclusive jurisdiction over Hong Kong crimes) be resolved?

In the end, the "Big Spender" case forced the HKSAR and PRC politicians, government officials, and the public to come to terms with cross-border crime's legal and policy issues, which have thus far escaped public scrutiny and political debate. In spite of the pressing need for cross-border cooperation and judicial assistance, no formal rendition or criminal judicial assistance agreement was reached. As a result, the PRC and HKSAR had to cooperate with each other on an informal basis before and after July 1, 1997. In this regard, the secretary for justice observed:

> Though we do not have a formal SFO [Surrender of Fugitive Offenders] arrangement with the Mainland, there exists an administrative arrangement whereby Hong Kong residents are returned from the Mainland to the HKSAR for investigation or trial if they have committed crime solely in Hong Kong, and if they have also committed offences in Mainland, they are returned after proceedings in the Mainland have been completed, and the sentences have been served.[20]

The "Big Spender" case was the first to test the limits of the "one country, two systems" formula.[21] As a test case, the "Big Spender" case crystallized the issues, galvanized the opponents, captured the attention of the public, and finally set the stage for a public debate over the future handling of similar and other cross-border crime cases.[22] In this regard, the legal debate has already transformed itself into a political contest in the HKSAR over the viability of the "one country, two systems" formula, as envisioned by Deng and as provided under the Basic Law,[23] in securing a "high degree of autonomy" for the Hong Kong people.[24] This sentiment was aptly expressed by Ronny Tong of the Hong Kong Bar:

> The issue is whether, putting aside the possible kidnapping charges, the fact that Hong Kong Government made no attempt to seek the return of some of these defendants in relation to possible robbery or firearms charges may give people the false impression that the Judiciary and the rule of Hong Kong is somehow *subordinate* to that of the rest of China, and thus indirectly cast a question mark over the concept of 'one country, two systems.'[25] (Emphasis mine)

Simply put, the major issue was whether the Basic Law was adequate to protect Hong Kong people from PRC's criminal jurisdiction for crimes being committed in Hong Kong. The collateral issue was whether Hong Kong security and legal officials have been diligent in protecting Hong Kong people's legitimate interests and legal rights under the Basic Law.[26] These two questions reflected a still larger concern of whether the PRC has any intention of honoring the Basic Law.[27] As a subplot, and by no means insignificant, the public was most concerned with the perceived erosion of the "rule of law" in Hong Kong after 1997, since the "Big Spender" case suggested a "two-tier" legal system at work: one for the rich and the other for the poor.[28] Other concerns were raised by academicians, who were worried about the structural implications and systemic effects of allowing multiple criminal jurisdictions to coexist in close proximity, which might give rise to judicial "forum shopping" by the police[29] or "fugitive sheltering" for the criminals.

This book is intended to be a working-policy paper for deciding important legal policy issues raised in the "Big Spender" case, in a broader sociopolitical context. It is also meant to be an academic treatise for interested scholars who want to understand cross-border crime and related jurisprudential issues.[30]

The book begins by analyzing and discussing various legal and policy issues raised by the "Big Spender" case in a broader historical, richer factual, and deeper legal context, than what has been attempted to date. The book ends with a framework of analysis outside the realm of law and politics. The book offers lessons learnt from the "Big Spender" case, with a view to anticipating similar cases in the future.[31]

The rationale and contributions of this study are many, and all too apparent. Conflicts of criminal jurisdiction are embedded within a "one country, two systems" constitutional framework. As a result, they are structural in nature and enduring in kind. In essence, they are inevitable and recurring problems. As such, they should be resolved earlier than later, reflectively than reactionary, and comprehensively more so than in an ad hoc manner. There is also a dire need and urgency to find workable solutions to "concurrent jurisdiction,"[32] "police cooperation,"[33] and "judicial assistance"[34] problems in order to better facilitate ongoing cross-border crime control and multijurisdictional justice administration.[35] The rationale of such a study is no better stated than by Barrister Martin Li, LegCo member and founding chairperson of the Hong Kong Democratic Party (1994–2002): "This is not an isolated case . . . Until there is an acceptable arrangement governing the rendition of offenders between Hong Kong and mainland China, the one country, two systems cannot be administered."[36]

This book is divided into eight chapters. After this "Introduction," Chapter 2 "Background" presents a brief factual background to the "Big Spender" case. It elaborately discusses Cheung's life experience, personal character, criminal career, and the investigation, prosecution, and adjudication of the "Big Spender" case. Such background information helps us to put the case in context, hopefully enabling the readers to see Cheung the person and the case by itself in a different light. We begin to see that the PRC officials had other compelling reasons to try Cheung in China, rather than to deliberately undermine the HKSAR judicial system.

Chapter 3 "Chinese Criminal Justice Process" gives a general overview of the PRC criminal justice process as it dissects the anatomy of the"Big Spender" case. Specifically, the chapter analyzes the legal proceedings—facts, charges, verdict, and appeal—of the "Big Spender" case.[37] In order to perform this analysis, the chapter presents translations of the judgment of the courts from the original Chinese documents. In the process, many controversial and unsettled legal issues raised in the actual disposition of the "Big Spender" case are discussed. Through this thorough examination of the anatomy of the "Big Spender" case, readers can more effectively understand and process the operations of the PRC criminal justice system. It also helps us to understand why the Hong Kong people were disturbed and concerted about having Cheung tried in China.

Chapter 4 "One Country, Two Systems" outlines in detail the debate in Hong Kong over the "Big Spender" case—what are the issues involved and who are the stakeholders. In the process, it describes "Big Spender" as a "test" case and the public's reactions—politicians, press, and public—to it.

Chapter 5 "Cross-Border Cooperation: HK versus the PRC" provides a brief historical account of PRC–HKSAR cross-border police cooperation and judicial assistance negotiations. How were cross-border crimes between HK and the PRC dealt with in the past? What was the magnitude of the cross-border crime problem—for law enforcement and justice officials? What has been the impact of such cross-border crimes on Hong Kong and Chinese criminal justice systems? How critical and/or urgent was the cross-border problem? Is the Cheung Tse-keung case unique as a kind of cross-border crime? Given information on how such cross-border cases have been dealt with before, why has cooperation between the PRC and the HKSAR governments not been more forthcoming?

Together, the first five chapters contextualize this case study. They provide a necessary background for a balanced understanding and informed discussion of the "Big Spender" case.

Chapter 6 "Legal Analysis" is devoted to the legal analysis of the case in light of the legal positions held by the PRC and HKSAR and as informed by existing scholarship on the subject at that time. The literature on legal issues on Hong Kong and China cross-border crimes is sparse and mostly in Chinese. This chapter provides a systematic, comprehensive, and in-depth analysis of the applicable Chinese, British, Hong Kong, and international law, bearing on the disposition of the "Big Spender" case. It then outlines in detail the respective position of various parties to the dispute, i.e., Hong Kong, China, British, and the international community, before commenting on the merits of each of them.

Chapter 7 "Policy Analysis" provides a new framework to analyze the "Big Spender" case. It advances the proposition that the "Big Spender" case is not a dispute over law as much as it is a debate over policy and contest of will in politics. With that said, the "Big Spender" case touches upon matters that deeply concern Hong Kong people in the time of transition, i.e., vested interests and entrenched values of the pre-1997 period.

The correct analysis and satisfactory resolution of the "Big Spender" debate ultimately rests on the adoption of a proper frame of reference in response to the question: "How should a functional political relationship between the PRC and HKSAR be structured and an administratively workable solution to cross-border crimes be arrived at under the rubric of 'one country, two systems' formula?" This chapter observes that the taking of a "rule of law" approach to the analysis and resolution of the legal issues involved in the cross-border crime conflict is ill-informed in theory and not helpful in practice. This proposition is supported by three arguments. First, the exact meaning of the Basic Law, e.g., "high degree of autonomy," was not determined when formulated and not determinable when applied, with certainty and exactitude. Second, the "Big Spender" case is a debate over interests and an argument over policy, not law. Third, the "Big Spender" case is a contest over values and a battlefield of politics, not law. The chapter concludes with a discussion on how the "Big Spender" case was reflected in the form and content of Hong Kong's post-1997 legal culture.

Chapter 8 offers some "Final Reflections" on the study. Particularly, it provides some observations of the state of rule of law in Hong Kong as revealed by the settlement of the Cheung Tse-keung case. It concludes with the observation that politics not law, culture not rationality, and more importantly, feelings not thinking set the stage, influenced the process, and decided the outcome of the Cheung case.

## Notes

1. "Cheung Tse-keung" can also be translated as "Cheung Chi-keung" in Cantonese or "Zhang Zi-qiang" in Mandarin (*Pinyin*). I have used "Cheung Tse-keung" throughout this book since this is the name most often used. I have used "Big Spender" to refer the case and "Cheung Tse-keung" or sometimes just "Cheung" to refer the person.

2. "Big Spender" is a pseudonym of Cheung Tse-keung. In the local language, it actually is a translation of "da fu hao," which literally means "big boss." For the lifetime exploits of the legendary Cheung Tse-keung, the "king of thieves," see *Next Magazine*, November 6, 1998, 38–58. See also the highly acclaimed TV documentary on the life experience and criminal career of Cheung Tse-keung on November 19, 1998, 8:30 p.m.: "Looking Closer Today" (an investigative report program), *Asian Television (ATV)*, Chinese channel, Hong Kong; the documentary "King of Thieves of the Century: The Final Chapter" produced by PRC Phoenix Station; and "King of Thieves of the Century – Cheung Tse-keung" (Shiji Zhi-wang), VCD produced by People's Liberation Army Television Broadcast Centre, ISRCCN-A57-98-0126-0/V.E7 (two discs).

3. Tommy Lewis, "Trial of Big Spender to Start Next Week," *South China Morning Post (SCMP)*, Internet ed., October 17, 1998; Ng Kang-chung, "Troops on Alert for Start of 'Big Spender' Trial," *SCMP*, October 20, 1998. For a summary of the prosecutor's case, see "The Prosecutor's Case," *SCMP*, November 6, 1998. For a list of defendants and specification of charges, see "The Case against Cheung Tse-keung," to Part One, *infra*.

4. There is no question that Hong Kong is within the territorial ambit of the People's Republic of China (hereinafter the PRC or China). However, whether Hong Kong is within the criminal jurisdiction of China is one of the major issues raised by the "Big Spender" case. See Zhang Xin, "The Content of 'Lingyu' (Territory) in Chinese Law," *Hong Kong Economic Journal*, November 28, 1998. (The Secretary for Justice, Ms. Leung, suggested that "lingyu" in Article 7 of the PRC Criminal Law meant "jurisdiction." The position is not a tenable one.) For the purpose of this chapter and ease of reference, I have used the PRC or China to refer to the PRC government as a distinct legal qua political entity, excluding Hong Kong. I have used Hong Kong Special Administrative Region (hereinafter HKSAR or SAR) to refer to Hong Kong as a distinct legal qua political entity. I have used Mainland to refer to the territorial limits of the PRC excluding Hong Kong. I have used Hong Kong to refer to the territorial limits of HKSAR. For a superlative discussion on the geo-political boundary of the PRC versus HKSAR see, Roda Mushkat, *One Country, Two International Legal Personalities* (Hong Kong: Hong Kong University Press, 1997), esp. chap. 2, 44–84, esp. 44–45.

5. According to one account, Cheung Tse-keung, wired with explosives, went to Li Kar-shing's home to negotiate with him over the ransom and release of his son. See *Next Magazine*, November 6, 1998, cover story on the "Big Spender," 51. A local prominent newspaper, *Ming Bao*, headlined the case as the "Trial of the Century" (*Shiji Shenpan*) in its daily reporting of the case. *Wen Hui Bao* reported Cheung Tse-keung's final appellate verdict in

full under the caption "The 'Biggest Crook of the Century' to be Executed" ("'Shiji dadao' fufa"), December 6, 1998, A4. No sooner had Cheung Tse-keung been convicted and executed, two movies on his exploits were released: "Operation Billionaires" (CD released by Universal Laser & Video Co. Ltd., Hong Kong) and "Big Spender" (Glenlord Limited).

    For a sample of international news coverage, see Martin Lee's interview with Michelle Han, "Cheung Tse-keung's Case," 9:45–10:00 p.m., December 9, 1998, CNN, Hong Kong; "Crook Left Final Letter, Not Treasure Map," *Yazhou Zhoukan* (Asia Weekly), December 14, 1998. See also *Next Magazine* and *Ming Bao Daily News*; all have international circulation in overseas Chinese communities.

6. Anthony Spaeth, *Time*, November 9, 1998 (The payoffs—$70 million for Kwok and $134 million for Li—are destined to be in the record books.)

7. *Criminal Law of the People's Republic of China* (adopted at the Second Session of the Fifth National People's Congress on July 1, 1979, and revised at the Fifth Session of the Eighth National People's Congress on March 14, 1997) was promulgated by Order of the President of the People's Republic of China, No. 83, and entered into force as of date of promulgation (Beijing: China Procuratorial Press, 1998) (hereinafter PRC Criminal Law).

8. Editorial: "Slippery Slope," *SCMP*, October 20, 1998. ("even more than the Big Spender case, the decision to try Li in Shantou represents the start of a slippery slope that could erode Hong Kong's legal autonomy.")

9. Ceri Williams, "Fresh Attempt to Move Case," *SCMP*, October 27, 1998; Ng Kang-chung and others, "Mainland Law Doesn't Apply, Lawyers Argue," *SCMP*, October 27, 1998. (The lawyers for the defense argued in their closing arguments to the Guangzhou Intermediate People's Court that PRC's law is supposed to protect Mainland citizens, not non-Mainlanders outside the Mainland.) Personal conversation with Ivan Tang, October 27, 1998, Radio Television Hong Kong.

10. "Guangdong Sheng, Guangzhou Shi, Zhongji Renmin Fayuan, Xingshi Panshu (1998) Wei Zhong Fa Xing Chu Di 468" (Guangdong Province, Guangzhou Municipality, Intermediary People's Court, Criminal Verdict [1998] Guangzhou, Intermediary, Legal, Criminal, Initial, No. 468). Published in full in *Ta Kung Pao* on November 13, 1998.

11. See Billy Wong Wai-yuk and Clifford Lo, "Abundant Evidence to Reject Appeal," *SCMP*, December 6, 1998, 2.

12. See Wong Wai-yuk, "Big Spender Shot After Plea Barred," *SCMP*, November 6, 1998, 1 (MPS official Zhu Entao announced Cheung Tse-keung's death at 11:15 a.m., while Xinhua News Agency officially announced the carrying out of the execution at 11:48 a.m.).

13. The battle line was drawn. Cheung's lawyer wanted to appeal to the international community for justice. "Chueng's Wife Decided to Appeal," *Ming Bao*, November 13, 1998. The PRC thought that justice had been done and Hong Kong people were happy. "The Public Said: 'Most Satisfying to the People,'" *Ta Kung Pao*, November 13, 1998. *Hong Kong Economic Journal* editorial called for reforming and improving upon the PRC–SAR judicial cooperation system and process—"Plug judicial cooperation loophole, prevent criminals from using the gaps."

14. "Big Spender Case Legal Dispute," *Apple Daily*, November 13, 1998, A4.
15. *Ta Kung Pao*, A9.
16. "Judicial Cooperation between the Two Places, the Chief Executive Urged Prompt Actions," *Ming Bao*, November 13, 1998. See also "Pledge to Speed up Extradition Talks," *SCMP*, November 12, 1998.
17. "Jurisdiction Issues Must Be Discussed Say Democrats," *Hong Kong Standard*, December 6, 1998, 3. (The Democratic Party stressed that the execution of Cheung does not mean that it is the end of the issue—on the contrary, this is just the beginning.)
18. Wang Ziyan, "The Agenda for 'One Country, Two Systems' Left Behind by the 'Big Spender' Case," *Hong Kong Economic Journal*, December 7, 1998. (The "Big Spender" case raised issues of securing fairness for Hong Kong residents who are tried for committing crimes in China, the returning of political prisoners to China, and the lack of a clear policy on the death penalty by the HKSAR.)
19. *Criminal Procedure Law of the People's Republic of China* (adopted at the Second Session of the Fifth National People's Congress on July 1, 1979, and revised in accordance with the Decision on Revising the Criminal Procedure Law of the People's Republic of China at the Fourth Session of the Eighth National People's Congress on March 17, 1997) was promulgated by Order of the President of the People's Republic of China, No. 64, on March 17, 1998, and entered into force as of date of promulgation. (Beijing: China Procuratorial Press, 1998) (hereinafter PRC Criminal Procedure Law).
20. "LegCo Panel on Security: Arrangements with Mainland on Surrender of Fugitive Offenders," December 3, 1998.
21. Richard Cullen and H. L. Fu, "How the "Big Spender" Case Has Exposed the Limitations of the Basic Law" ("It is the rule rather than the exception for the criminal law of most jurisdictions to have some level of extra-territorial reach."). Paper presented at the PRC–HK Law Seminar on *Legal Issues in Cross-border Crimes: Looking into the Future*, November 27, 1998. See also Wang Zhiyan, "A Higher Degree of Autonomy is Not God Given," *Hong Kong Economic Journal*, November 9, 1998. (The "Big Spender" case is the first time the Mainland court tried such a cross-(district) border (*kua qu*) crime under the "one country, two systems" context. "Hong Kong people governing Hong Kong" is confronted with a challenge.)
22. Christ Yeung, "Return of Suspected Poisoner Ruled Out," *SCMP*, November 10, 1998; Jimmy Cheung, "Grey Areas Over First Legal Move," *SCMP*, November 9, 1998. ("The question of who should be the first one to exercise [criminal jurisdiction in cross-border crime] needs further co-ordination.") Editorial: "After Conviction Still More Work to Do," *Apple Daily*, November 13, 1998, A6.
23. The Basic Law of the Hong Kong Special Administrative Region of the People's Republic of China (April 1990) (Basic Law). (Adopted on April 4, 1990, by the Seventh National People's Congress of the People's Republic of China at its Third Session.) Article 2 provides: "The National People's Congress authorizes the Hong Kong Special Administrative Region to exercise a high degree of autonomy and enjoy executive, legislative and independent judicial power, including that of final adjudication, in accordance with the provisions of the law." Article 8 provides: "The laws previously in

force in Hong Kong, that is, the common law, rules of equity, ordinances, subordinate legislation and customary law shall be maintained, except for any that contravene this law, and subject to any amendment by the legislature of the Hong Kong Special Administrative Region." Article 18 provides: "The laws in force in the Hong Kong Special Administrative Region shall be this Law, the laws previously in force in Hong Kong as provided in Article 8 of this Law, and laws enacted by the legislature of the Region. National laws shall not be applied in Hong Kong Special Administrative Region except for those in Annex III to this Law. The laws listed therein shall be applied locally by way of promulgation or legislative by the Region." Article 19: "The Hong Kong Special Administrative Region shall be vested with independent judicial power, including that of final adjudication. The court of the Hong Kong Administrative Region shall have jurisdiction over all cases in the Region, except that the restrictions on their jurisdiction imposed by the legal system and principles previously in force in Hong Kong shall be maintained." Article 22: "No department of the Central People's Government and no province, autonomous region, or municipality directly under the central Government may interfere in the affairs which the Hong Kong Special administers on its own in accordance with this Law."

24.  Wang Ziyan, "How is 'a High Degree of Autonomy' Being Manifested?" *Hong Kong Economic Journal*, November 23, 1998. ("'High degree of autonomy' issue has engendered discussion" over the sanctity of the "one country, two systems framework in protecting Hong Kong's freedom and autonomy.")

25.  Christ Yeung, "The Case that Threatens our Autonomy," *SCMP*, November 14, 1998. ("A clear demarcation was seen as crucial to the viability of the "one country, two systems" experiment . . .")

26.  Letter to editor, S. C. Gladys Li, "Alarmed by Top Officials' Lame Excuse," *SCMP*, October 28, 1998. ("The consequences of the HKSAR officials not maintaining this interpretation [Criminal Law of PRC has no force or effect in HKSAR] . . . is chilling. Any activities in Hong Kong, whether lawful or not under Hong Kong law, and whether done before or after July 1, 1997, can be made the subject of criminal proceedings in the mainland if there is a breach of PRC law." See also Audrey Parwani, "Police Morale 'Hit by Lack of SAR Hearing,'" *SCMP*, November 9, 1998. ("How can [police] trust . . . [Secretary for Security] . . . if the case has been investigated but not put up for trial for political reasons?")

27.  Editorial: "The Case of Cheung Tse-keung: Central (government) Interferes and Damages One Country, Two Systems," *Next Magazine*, October 30, 1998. (Notwithstanding the fact that there was no extradition agreement in the past, 128 criminals have been returned to Hong Kong. It is hard to believe that none of these violated Hong Kong criminal laws, thereby foreclosing their eventual return to the Mainland. In this case, Cheung was not returned because of decisions made by leaders at the highest level.)

28.  It was widely rumored that the "Big Spender" case was tried in China because Li Kar-shing, the father of the victim, Victor Li, was rich, powerful, and well-connected in China. He was able to ask President Jiang to try the case in Guangzhou instead of Hong Kong. Editorial: "The Case of Cheung Tse-keung," *Ming Bao*, October 10, 1998, A5. (The handling of the Cheng's case showed that there were two systems of justice—one

for the rich and the other for the poor.) See also "Public Interpretation: Two Big Bosses?" *Ming Bao*, October 10, 1998, A5 (Mr. Cheng: "One 'Big Spender' committed a crime, the other 'Big Spender' Mr. Li allowed Cheung Tse-keung to stay in his house for two days and failed to report a crime, this is also illegal"); "The Mystery of Li Kar Shing 'Getting Mad,'" *New Magazine*, no. 460, January 1, 1999 (On December 9, 1998, at a LegCo meeting, Martin Lee openly faulted Li Kar-shing: "If people petitioned the imperial government to arrest criminal suspects, this showed distrust for the HKP . . . I feel that Li Kar-shing is wrong in handling the case this way. This sets a bad example for the public"), 41. Notwithstanding the uproar, Li Kar-shing had declined to comment. "Li Kar-shing Talk about Cheung Tse-keung's Case: I Respected the Police Department Very Much," *Shidai Chao* (Contemporary Tide), 1998, no. 15, 38 (Li: "I have said before. I did not talk yesterday. I am not talking today. I will not talk in the future.")

29.    The author was informed by serving police officers that it was best to try the case in China since there were less procedural impediments and stringent penalization. This attitude, however, justified in this case, may be a time bomb waiting to explode. HKP might be tempted to allow the PRC police to "take care" of some of their most troublesome cases, e.g., cases difficult to prove. Kam C. Wong, "A Reflection on the Prosecution of 'Big Spender,' PRC," *Chinese University Student* (Zhongda Xuesheng), no. 111, 12–13.

30.    There is a continued debate over the relevancy and utility of social science research findings to policy makers. Scientific research is directed toward facts. Policy formulation is driven by values and determined by interests. These are different enterprises serving different social functions. James Gilsinan, "Public Policy and Criminology: A Historical and Philosophical Reassessment," *Justice Quarterly* 8, no. 2, 201–6.

31.    As the "Big Spender" case was being tried in the PRC court of law in secrecy and debated in the Hong Kong court of opinion publicly, another similar case was looming on the horizon. In what has come to be known as the "fung shui master" case, a fung shui master Li Yuhui, a Chinese national, poisoned five women in Telford Gardens, Kowloon Bay, Hong Kong, before he fled to China with the $1.3 million ill-gotten gain. The Deputy Director of Guangdong Public Security, Hou Tongfen, said that Li would be tried in China under Chinese criminal law as a Chinese national committing crimes abroad. Cindy Sui and Cliff Buddle, "Mainland to Try Fung Shui 'Master' for Poisoning Five," *SCMP*, October 10, 1998.

32.    "LegCo Panel on Security: Arrangements with Mainland on Surrender of Fugitive Offenders" (December 3, 1998). ("We do not wish to see the HKSAR becoming a haven for fugitive criminals. The recent case of Li Yuhui has also highlighted the need for a rendition arrangement in certain situations of concurrent jurisdiction.")

33.    Wu Zhiqiang, *HKP* (Guangdong renmin chubanshe, 1996), 368. (Hong Kong and Macau should not be a "shelter" for Chinese criminals.)

34.    Leung Mei-fen, "Observing the Problem of China-Hong Kong Judicial Assistance through the Cheung Tse-keung Case," *Hong Kong Economic Journal*, October 27, 1998. (China and Taiwan have already entered into judicial assistance agreement and Hong Kong should follow suit.)

35. Wang Changyin (Editor-in-Chief), *Analysis of Criminal Cases Involving Foreigners and Hong Kong and Macau in the Shenzhen Special Economic Zone* (Shenzhen Jingji Tequ She-wai She-Kang-Aou Xingshi Anli Pingxi) (Beijing: Renmin fayuan chubanshe, 1990); "PRC-Hong Kong Governments Need a Formal Agreement and Structural Arrangements to Deal with Cross-border Crimes," Chris Yeung, *SCMP*, November 26, 1998. (HKSAR to jump-start negotiation with the PRC over the rendition of fugitives.)

36. Ceri Williams, "Basic Law Fears in Big Spender Case," *SCMP*, November 2, 1998. In the aftermath of the "Big Spender" case, the secretary for justice, after consultations with the legislative council and executive committee, was prepared to negotiate with the PRC on judicial assistance. "Six Religious Representatives Plead Over Cheung Tse-keung's Death Sentence," *Apple Daily*, November 24, 1998, 4.

37. In order to limit the scope of the study, I have focused my discussion on issues pertaining to Cheung Tse-keung type of cases, i.e., cross-border crime cases involving Hong Kong residents committing crimes in Hong Kong as well as in China.

# 2

# Background

**Introduction**

The "Big Spender" case was debated among the public as a constitutional, i.e., the interpretation of the Basic Law, and criminal law problem, i.e., the determination of the jurisdictional reach of the PRC Criminal Law, with far-reaching policy implications, i.e., the viability of the "one country, two systems" framework, and still broader political ramifications, i.e., the autonomy of the HKSAR. However, behind the heated constitutional debate and sterile legal analysis and beyond the tumultuous political bickering and calculated policy posturing lies a fascinating and absorbing, if at times messy and chilling, human saga of good and evil. It is a story about human ambition run amok and social control agents tested to the limit.

The obscured human drama beneath the "Big Spender" case provides connecting tissues and communicating nerves between legal evidence and sociological fact. These networks of tissues and nerves, like the undergrowth in a tropical rain forest, never get to see the light of day, especially when examined in close range as in the court room[1] or looked at from afar as in the social science laboratory.[2] Connections between human tissues and nerves, invisible to the naked eye are essential constitutive parts of social life and legal reality. They impart bare social facts with vibrant life and give legal evidence rich meaning. In so doing, they contribute to a comprehensive and holistic understanding of disputed legal issues or social problems.

It was Justice Holmes who once said: "The life of law has not been logic but experience." In another context, Bradley, the philosopher, had the occasion to remark: "At every moment my stage of experience, whatever else it is, is a whole of which I am immediately aware. It is an experienced non-relational unity in one."[3] In both instances, we are told that "living" the experience is better than "understanding" it. Living an experience allows us to "appreciate" things we otherwise cannot see, feel, or touch. To take the imagery further, going into the rain forest in search of the essence and spirit of the forest through experience is much more productive than looking at the canopy from afar (in abstraction) or examining the individual tree up close. Applying this lesson to the task on hand, our study of the "Big Spender" case cannot be limited to legal analysis of an issue here or policy review of a problem there. Such an approach is fragmented and piecemeal, not to mention missing much information that should have been considered.

Thus, a true and comprehensive understanding of the "Big Spender" case must start with "experiencing" the case in its totality of circumstances, starting with investigating the contextual background of the case. Who was Cheung Tse-keung? How and why did the "Big Spender" case happen?

A comprehensive understanding of the case, away from the case-specific legal issues and particular public concerns, helps us to see the case in a different light. We begin to see that the PRC officials had other compelling reasons to try Cheung in China. They did not try to undermine the HKSAR judicial system, still less its political autonomy.

## The Background of the "Big Spender" Case

### Cheung's Background

Cheung was born on April 7, 1955,[4] to a poor farming family in the mountainous area of Zhaoxing Yunan County in Guangdong province[5] in southern China, a stone's throw from Hong Kong, also in the same province. In 1960, China, in general, and Cheung's resident county, in particular, were hard hit by famine brought about by Mao's ill-conceived but zealously executed "Big Leap Forward." Cheung's family was not spared; no one was. His sister died of starvation, as did many, many others during that time. Cheung's father decided to smuggle his family into Hong Kong to find a living. Cheung inherited the rugged spirit and perseverance of the mountain people. He learned from his father the need to struggle in order to survive and be successful in life.

When Cheung's family first came to Hong Kong, they settled in Causeway Bay. Their life was poor. Cheung attended a few years of primary school in Hong Kong between the ages of six and eleven. He was bright, hard working, and excelled in school. However, the school Cheung attended was not particularly a good school. Cheung was constantly harassed in school because he was a new immigrant from

Mainland China. He learned that in order to survive he had to fend for himself. He realized early in life that "might is right." He soon earned his place as the leader of his gang by being tough.

In the meantime, Cheung's father opened a Chinese "herbs" drink shop in Temple Street at Yaumati.[6] Yaumati, then as now, was a place for criminals, gangsters, and hoodlums who engaged in all kinds of petty crimes and vices. Cheung's father operated a "zifa" (illegal lottery) stand to supplement his income. Cheung quit school and helped his father attend to the shop and lottery.[7] Cheung received his education on the street corners of Yaumati. He soon was exposed to all kinds of vices, bad company (*he dao*), and corrupting influences.[8] This was his initiation into the criminal world.[9]

At the young age of sixteen years, Cheung was already a 14K triad society member and was arrested for the first time. Between the ages of sixteen and twenty, he was arrested no less than fifteen times for assault, theft, robbery, conspiracy to robbery, and a host of other minor offenses. Cheung was labeled a hardened offender and treated as such.[10] In time he took pride in such a "big brother" street image of himself.[11] All the while, Cheung considered criminal conduct as normal, acceptable, and appropriate for his neighborhood[12] and with his associations.[13]

When Cheung was twenty years old and after he was released from jail, he made one final attempt to be successful in a legitimate business. With the help of his father he understudied to be a tailor at Yang Ke Tailors. The stint at Yang Ke Tailors changed Cheung's life. He met two important persons there. He met his wife and later partner in crime, Luo Yin-fang (Maggie).[14] They were married in 1987. He also met Wang Feng-qi, a co-worker, who convinced him that the only certain way to get rich was to engage in an illegitimate business: "In order to get rich one has to resort to illegitimate means (*pianmen*) and also to do so with detailed planning, much like when we are tailoring clothes, making it tight (*tianyi wu feng*)."[15]

At the ripe young age of twenty-three years he was in the company of another 14K member, later to become one of the biggest drug kingpins in Hong Kong, Liu Guo-xiong, alias "stir shit Xiong." This was to be his "ticket" to the real underworld.[16] In 1978, with the financial support of "stir shit Xiong," he started an illegal gambling store in Mongkok. He was not successful. In 1985, he started a loan shark business. He was fairly successful in that venture.

Cheung gathered one valuable lesson from this early part of his life: "money means everything" in life. Later when he was interrogated by the PRC officials with regard to the kidnapping charges, he made the following revealing remark:

> My tenet (*xintia*) in life is this: I cannot be poor in this world. Life to me is very short and fragile (*cuiruo*). I am already 40 odd years old. I cannot labor like other people. I have neither the patience nor time to earn money by engaging in legitimate (*zhengdang*) business. In order to be rich I have to use break-through [extra-ordinary] (*tupo*) means.[17] In this world money is God.[18]

Cheung was now ready to embark on his criminal career!

### Cheung's Character Profile

Cheung exhibited the following characteristics that made him a successful "king of thieves."[19]

The first characteristic was that Cheung was an independent, logical, and methodical thinker. As described by one PRC investigative author: "Meticulous planning, excelling in the use of the brain, knowing how to employ strategy, being familiar with the law, these are major characteristics of Cheung Tse-keung's type of intellectual criminal gang."[20]

After the Rolex robbery, Cheung was nominated as the gang leader.[21] He set forth the "Big Spender" gang's goals, objectives, and principles and defended them in a coherent, systematic, eloquent, and persuasive manner.[22]

> I have been thinking about this for a long time. [The purpose of the gang. The role of the leader.] Our organization should not be a disorderly band (*wuhe zhi zhong*). We should have organization, discipline, and purpose. Only then can we achieve big things . . . I think our goal should be to make money and be all "big bosses." We should not engage in indiscriminate killings and harmful activities like local ruffians (*dipi*) and hooligans (*liumang*), thereby causing troubles and commotions without real benefits in return. These kinds of thankless activities (*chili bu taohao*) we will not engage in. That is why I have to declare a few gang rules: (1) Our organization is called "da fu hao." (2) We are absolutely against committing murder, arson, rape, harassing and robbing of common people. I have sworn that even as a bad person, I will not kill or take advantage of common citizens. Whoever violates these prohibitions, I will not hesitate to punish him with impartiality and incorruptibility (*tiemian wu si*). (3) Our targets are people from the high society (*shangliu shehui*). They are all the big bosses in Hong Kong (*di fu hao*). We will rob their properties to enrich ourselves. (4) We should follow strict orders and not act separately on our own. Here, I want to explain our gang rules and clarify my reasoning. Why is the organization called

the "big bosses" ("da fu hao")? Because I want you all to remember the primary purpose of the organization. Our purpose is money, to be rich so that every one can be a big boss and to live a high society life. We are all poor by origin. We have suffered too much of poverty and hard life. Can we engage in legitimate business or employment? No. In this world the most important thing is money and treasure. Beyond money and treasure, there is nothing that concerns me . . . I do not approve of murder and arson, harassment of common folks, raping of women, and robbing the public. These are my personal principles and also meeting our "da fu hao" organization's survival, development, safety, goal achievements' needs. All of you should know, the charge of robbery is not as serious as murder and arson? If we kill a person and cause disorder to society, it is like contracting leprosy, we will never have a day of peace. This will attract the police to pursue us daily. How can we do big things? I do not approve of harassing the common people and robbing the public. This is also reasonable. Hong Kong has many people; most of them are common people. If we do not hurt them, they will not hate and guard against us . . . If we hurt the public, they will hate those who hurt them and want to eliminate them as soon as possible. They will work with the police to punish them. I want to be a bad person but not hated by the public. This is what I mean. Besides, how much can we get by robbing the poor? This goes against our "da fu hao" ideal and should be strongly opposed. As to why [I] do not approve of raping women. This also deserves explanation. The two main reasons are stated above. Also, we all have father, mother and sisters. If our sisters were raped, would we not seek revenge? . . . Why should we target the big bosses? That is because they possess all the world's money and also their money came from exploiting the people. We can only get rich by seeking out the big bosses. We will have no remorse in getting their money. The richer the person, the more the person is fearful for his life. If you do not take their life, they will turn over the money willingly. To give an example, if you take away 200 million dollars from a big boss with one billion dollar net worth, there is still 800 million dollars left.[23]

The second characteristic was that Cheung was an intelligent person. He was a self-learner. He was a fast learner.[24] He learned to speak English sufficiently enough to communicate with his lawyer while he was imprisoned for the Kai Tak Airport robbery. He learned to read the PRC Criminal Law and Criminal Procedure sufficient to discuss legal strategy with his PRC lawyer, Tung Jian-hua, when he was held by the PRC police. His PRC lawyer described him thus:

He likes to learn. He has high IQ. He is not an average criminal. Before his arrest he did not understand much about PRC law. While in prison he asked me to send him some law books to read.[25] He then had much more understanding of the mainland law. Finally, he was able to propose his own defense viewpoint.[26]

The third characteristic was that Cheung was a philosopher. He was a follower of Nietzsche (1844–1900).[27] In this regard, observing Cheung at close range, one finds that he shared much of Nietzsche's personal dispositions and philosophical beliefs. For example:

1. According to Bertrand Russell: "He (Nietzsche) attempts to combine two sets of values which are not easily harmonized: on the one hand he likes ruthlessness, war, and aristocratic pride; on the other hand, he loves philosophy and literature and the arts, especially music."[28] Cheung was also a complicated man of many contradictions: on the one hand, he was ruthless and daring; on the other hand, he was gentle, polite, and generous to people. As one 14K member remembered him: "He ("Big Spender") did not like to use guns and knife, unless he has to. Ordinary when you are with him, he spoke politely and seldom used foul language. But once he is mad, he is very fierce. I have been around for so long, even I was frightened when being looked at."

2. Nietzsche has his own sense of right or wrong, good or evil, that cannot be understood in conventional terms or by the common people. In his book *Beyond Good and Evil*, Nietzsche observed thus: "I abhor the man's vulgarity when he says 'What is right for one man is right for another'; 'Do to others that which you would not that they should do unto you.' . . . The hypothesis is ignoble to the last degree: it is taken for granted that there is some sort of *equivalence in value between my actions and thine*."[29] (Italics in the original.) Cheung also had his own sense of personal right or wrong not shared by others and otherwise not conforming to conventional norm. As evident from above, his idea of robbing the rich but not the poor was a perfect example of his unconventional moral compass.

3. Nietzsche believed in Spartan discipline and the capacity to endure as well as to inflict pain for important ends. "I test the *power of a will* according to the amount of resistance it can offer and the amount of pain and torture it can endure and know how to turn to his own advantage . . . The object is to attain that enormous *energy of greatness* which can model the man of the future by means of discipline and by means of annihilation of millions of bungled and botched . . ."[30] To Cheung, disciplining of the mind and body for great end was the true mark of a superior person and fearless leader. Cheung constantly reminded his gang followers the need for self-discipline in order to survive in the business as a gangster. "If we kill a person and cause disorder to society, it is like contracting leprosy. We will never have a day of peace. This will attract the police to pursue us daily.

How can we do big things?"[31]  Cheung's PRC lawyer was amazed at how he could face death with calmness: "I have seen him 10 times in jail. I sensed that he has a strong will to live. Even so, he maintained a relatively calm composure up until he was shot."[32]

4.    Nietzsche did not believe in the State. He was a passionate individualist and a believer in the hero of self.[33]  Likewise, Cheung exhibited self-confidence to the point of being conceited:

In Hong Kong, in order to kidnap those rich people, I am the only one who can do it. Other people cannot do such a big thing! I am very smart. There is nothing I cannot learn.[34]

The fourth characteristic was that Cheung was a born competitor and driven to success. When asked at his trial why he did not stop after making millions with the kidnapping of Li, Cheung remarked:

The kidnapping of rich people is similar to the best professional mountain climbers. They will be happy after conquering a peak. After a while, they will be unsatisfied and seek another challenge. My purpose in kidnapping is about money. This can never be completely satisfied.[35]

The fifth characteristic was that Cheung was obsessed with getting rich. For example, Cheung had a big "M" letter, which stands for MONEY, on his bed headboard.[36]  When he formed the "Big Spender" gang, he said "Our purpose is money, to be rich so that every one can be a rich person and to live a high society life . . . In this world the most important thing is money and treasure. Beyond money and treasure, there is nothing that concerns me . . ."[37]

The sixth characteristic was that Cheung resented government authority.[38]  His resentment was built-up over the years and through his various encounters with the police. For example, Cheung felt abused when his wife, one of the few persons he loved, was tortured by the police to elicit incriminating evidence against him after the Kai Tak robbery.[39]  Cheung felt abused by the police and prison officials when he was arrested and jailed over the Kai Tak robbery. When he won his appeal and was released from jail he had an informal press conference:

Q: What do you think of police arresting you?

A: Hong Kong should be a society of rule of law. The citizens' human rights should be protected. They [police] arrested me without any evidence and sent me to prison for 14 years. This is clearly against the law. I feel very angry.

Q: How did you fare in the last three years? Have the police mistreated you?

A: You see (Cheung lifted his shirt and showed his scars), these were the treatments I received during imprisonment. The police, in order to frame me, in order to get credit, promotion and salary increase for early detection of the case even used inhuman means to treat law abiding and innocent citizens. They kicked, punched, slapped me. They whipped me with belts and hit me with sticks in order to force a confession out of me and give them what they consider as evidence. But I am a law-abiding citizen, what can I tell them? I have scars all over my body, this tells people what their police really are like? What kind of law enforcement is this, I believe that all people with a conscience and sense of law will yell at them. They are a bunch of rascals, they take the taxpayers' money, they were useless against real criminals, allowing them to break the law with impunity but treat the innocent citizens with atrocity.[40]

His resentment of the police and correction authorities led him and his gang to ram the prison guardhouse twice, followed by threatening letters to Lai Ming, then the head of the Correctional Service Department (CSD). He even planned to firebomb Lai Ming's house and kidnap the Chief Secretary Ansen Chan in order to show his contempt.[41]  In all, it is clear that he had little respect and still less fear of the Hong Kong government authority.

The seventh characteristic was that Cheung was a born leader. He was loyal to his friend. For example, in April 1996, Cheung learned that the Hong Kong CSD was mistreating his friends in prison, including Yip Kai-fun. He stole a tractor and rammed the CSD prison, leaving a message as a warning to the prison authority not to mistreat prisoners.[42]  For example, in 1994, when he learned that one of his jail mates had family difficulties, he asked his wife to take care of the fellow prisoner's family.[43]  Cheung took care of his men. When Yip was injured and arrested by the police, he sent money to his relatives in China. Even though Yip was injured and did not participate in the kidnapping of Li, he nevertheless got his share of $750,000.[44]  When his gang members came out of jail, he was the first to receive them by car. Cheung was generous with his colleagues and friends.

The eighth and final characteristic was that Cheung was a professional. He conducted his crime like a business. His crimes were all well planned. For example, Cheung planned for his wife to gather intelligence for the two robberies. He accosted Yip Kai-fun, known for his ruthlessness, to come to Hong Kong to carry out the kidnapping of Li. He was principle minded and disciplined in conducting his criminal activities. For example, when planning for the Rolex robbery he instructed his men to "(1) only to rob goods and not to harm people[45]; (2) only fire as a last resort[46]; (3) if there should be a struggle, they should try to escape and not stay for the fight[47]; (4) if anyone is arrested, they should not confess, the other gang brother will try to rescue them from outside."[48] He took calculated risks. He went alone to Li Kar-shing's residence to negotiate for the release of his son, calculating correctly that Li Kar-shing would not risk his son's life in reporting him to the police. He was calculative in dealing with the police. He knew his rights and law. For example, he seldom broke down in interview, even when induced or coerced. He refused to volunteer information unless he had to.[49]

In all, Cheung exhibited psychopathic antisocial personality.[50] Cheung's nickname was "biantai lao" (perverted or abnormal person). Cheung intentionally, deliberately, and openly challenged the police, and correction and legal establishments in Hong Kong.[51] He showed no remorse for his crime and wrongdoings.[52] He felt that his criminality was justified.[53] He held different and unconventional moral values. According to the *Diagnostic and Statistical Manual of Mental Disorders*,[54] antisocial personality is defined as follows:

> The term is reserved for individuals who are basically unsocialized and whose behavior pattern brings them repeatedly into conflicts with society. They are incapable of significant loyalty to . . . social values. They are grossly selfish, callous, irresponsible, impulsive, and unable to feel guilt or to learn from experience and punishment. Frustration tolerance is low. They tend to blame others or offer plausible rationalization for their behavior.

### *Cheung's Past Criminality*

Cheung's serious brush with criminality occurred in 1990. Cheung decided to rob the Rolex Company (HK) Limited. He carefully and meticulously planned for the robbery which later became his modus operandi (MO)and claim to notoriety. He had his wife infiltrate the Rolex Company (HK) Limited to gather the necessary intelligence to stage the robbery. On February 22, 1990, he robbed the armored car transporting Rolex watches in thirty seconds. He got away with thirty-six million dollars.

On July 12, 1991, he robbed a Guardforce armored car carrying US$17.5 million and HK$35 million for the Republic National Bank of New York. This was the largest in Hong Kong's history of robbery.[55] Cheung Chi-fung, Chan Shue-hon, Wu Chai-shu, Wu X, and Wang X were key participants in the robbery. Cheung Chi-fung, Chan Shue-hon, and Wu Chai-shu later played a key role in Cheung's kidnapping schemes. The Bank put up a US$2 million reward for the information leading to the arrest and conviction of the offenders. In July 1991, the Hong Kong Police (HKP) sought the assistance of the PRC police for the arrest of Cheung Chi-fung, Wu Chai-shu, Wu X, and Wang X.

On September 12, 1991, Cheung Tse-keung was arrested, charged, convicted, and sentenced to eighteen years for the robbery. He successfully appealed against the conviction; the security guard who initially identified him later changed his stance.[56]

### The Investigation of the "Big Spender" Case

To the PRC and HKP, the "Big Spender" referred to the Cheung Tse-keung and Yip Kai-fun gangs together.

The core members of Cheung Tse-keung's gang were Wu Chai-shu, Cheung Chi-fung (Zhang Zhi-feng), Kam Wing-keung (Gan Yong-qiang), and Chan Shue-hon (Chen Shu-han).

1. *Wu Chai-shu* and Cheung were the core members of the "Big Spender" gang. Wu Chai-shu met Cheung through Wang Feng-qi, a co-worker at Yang Ke Tailors. Wu Chai-shu was also known as "fu shu" ("rat bat"), "lao huli" ("old fox"), or "lai fu" ("old fu"). He used the false identity of Chen Shu-guan. The first two described his mind, i.e., crafty, the last described his appearance, i.e., white haired. He was forty-seven years old. He was born in Donguan, Guangdong province. He was a Hong Kong resident. He had a primary school education. Before meeting Cheung, he had a string of criminal records, including robbery, use of counterfeit money, and usury. He was Cheung's real mentor to organized criminality.[57] In 1987, Wu was introduced to Cheung by Wang Feng-qi, Cheung's co-worker from the tailoring shop days.[58] He participated in both the February 22, 1990 Rolex Company and July 12, 1991 Kai Tak Airport robberies. He was given HK$7 million, the same as Cheung, for the Rolex Company robbery.[59] He was given HK$310 million for the Kai Tak robbery. He was wanted for the Kai Tak robbery and escaped to Cambodia where he invested in a restaurant, casino, nightclub, and state TV.[60] He came back to Hong Kong to help plot Li's kidnapping.

2. *Cheung Chi-fung* was introduced to Cheung by Wu Chai-shu. He was fifty-three years old. He was a Hong Kong resident born in NanHai, Guangdong province. He had a junior high school education. He was arrested earlier by the HKP for possession of a false passport.

Cheung Chi-fung was Cheung Tse-keung's close friend for over twenty years. He participated in the 1990 Rolex and 1991 Kai Tak robberies. For the latter crime, he was placed on the wanted list by the HKP. The HKP sought the PRC public security's assistance in August 1991.[61] He (and Wu Chai-shu) helped plan the July 1997 kidnapping of Kwok.[62] He was responsible for keeping observation over Kwok. He was paid thirty-one million for the kidnapping.[63]

3.  *Kam Wing-keung* was introduced to Cheung by Wu Chai-shu. He was forty-seven years old. He was a Hong Kong resident born in Huadu. In 1975, he was arrested for the robbery at St. Teresa Hospital and was imprisoned for eight years. In 1985, he was arrested for robbing Zhongxin Watch Company. He was later released for lack of evidence.[64]

Cheung's alter ego in Hong Kong, and sometimes partner in crime, was Yip Kai-fun. Both set records for criminal offences in Hong Kong. Both earned their place in the annals of Hong Kong crime history for their daring and sensational exploits: Cheung for making some of the largest ransom demands for kidnapping Li and Kwok, and Yip for his largest robbery and fearless firefight with the police. Both openly challenged the police in Hong Kong. Both were not arrested as a result of HKP investigative efforts. Cheung was arrested in China by public security officers. Yip was arrested "accidentally" when a HKP constable confronted his gang while on routine duty. Both were household names to the people of Hong Kong, making millions for the media and entertainment business.

The core members of Yip Kai-fun's gang consisted of Yip Kai-fun (Ye Ji-huna), Chan Chi-ho (Chen Zhi-hao), and Ma Shan-chung (Ma Shang-zhong).

1.  *Yip Kai-fun* was born in Haifeng county, Guangzhou province, on June 20, 1961. He was stubborn and naughty as a kid. He was smart but did not perform well at school. He left school after primary three and followed the profession of his father as a carpenter. In 1978, at the age of seventeen years, he left for Hong Kong illegally. In 1979, he robbed a jewelry shop and was arrested. He was released for insufficient evidence. On October 10, 1984, he robbed the King Fook Jewelry shop in Tsim Sha Tsui of HK$1 million. On October 26, 1984, he robbed Dickson Jewelry in Central of HK$8 million, firing ten odd shots. On December 28, 1984, he was arrested while trying to sell the "hot" property to an undercover police officer.[65] On October 8, 1985, Yip Kai-fun was convicted by the High Court for possession of illegal weapons and resisting arrest, and was sentenced to Stanley Prison for eighteen years. On August 24, 1989, he escaped

from custody after feigning sickness. In 1991, he returned home (China) and got married. On June 9, 1991, he and his gang—Chan Chi-ho, Ma Shan-chung, Chu Yuk-sing and others—robbed five goldsmith shops in Kungtong, getting away with $5 million. In the process, they entered into a firefight, using AK47 rifles, with the pursuing police in broad daylight. In all, over one hundred rounds were fired, with forty shots by the police and the rest by the gang. On March 10, 1992, Yip Kai-fun, Chan Chi-ho, and other gang members again robbed two jewelry shops in Shamshuipo, getting away with $1 million. Again, they entered into a firefight with the police. The HKP put up a million-dollar reward for his arrest. He and his gang returned to China. In 1993, Yip Kai-fun and his gang kidnapped a Hong Kong businessman in Foshan, Guangzhou, for HK$4 million. He used the money to invest in properties in Guangzhou and opened up a karaoke. The case was never reported. On January 14, 1994, Yip Kai-fun together with Chan Chi-ho and Ma Shan-chung decided to rob the Tianjin Materials Trading Centre, Shenzhen office. They accidentally killed the manager (Li Chen-xi). On November 27, 1995, Yip Kai-fun discovered that one of his men, Choi Chi-hung (Cai Zhi-xiong), was an informant for the HKP and killed him in Shenzhen.[66] (See Table 2.1.)

2. *Chan Chi-ho*, alias "ah qi" ("number seven"), was thirty-six years old. He was born in Haifeng county, Guangzhou province. In 1980, he was smuggled into Hong Kong and worked as a casual laborer. He had a criminal record in Hong Kong for criminal intimidation.[67] He was a close friend of Yip Kai-fun. In June 1991, he was arrested for the armed robberies in Kungtong. There he met Cheung Tse-keung. Later he introduced Cheung to his crime boss, Yip Kai-fun. In 1994, he participated in robbing the Tianjin Materials Trading Centre, Shenzhen office.

3. *Chu Yuk-sing*, alias "gao lao" ("tall guy"). He was forty-two years old. He was born in Guangzhou, Chaozhou. He participated in the two jewelry shop robberies in Hong Kong in 1991 and 1992. He was involved in the kidnapping of Li in May 1996.

4. *Ma Shan-chung*, also known as "lao Ma" ("old Ma"), was born in Hebei province, Qin Huang Dao County. He was thirty years old. In 1991, he was recruited from the Chinese People's Armed Police (*Wujin*) (PAP) where he served as a platoon leader, and was known for his audacity.[68] He did not use a head mask and was captured on TV having a shootout with the police.[69] When asked during the "Big Spender" case whether he was afraid to shoot, he said: "Why would I be afraid of firing a weapon? I was a PAP before. I've had a lot of opportunities to shoot."[70] Ma helped Yip to purchase two AK47 rifles to be used in the June 9, 1991 Kungtong robberies of the five goldsmith shops. Ma was injured on the leg in the ensuing firefight with the police. He was smuggled back into China to treat his wound.[71] In 1997, Ma was sentenced to eleven years of

**Table 2.1**
**Yip Kai-fun's Criminal Career**

| Year | Events |
| --- | --- |
| 1979 | Smuggled into Hong Kong. |
| 1979 | Arrested for robbery. Released for insufficient evidence. |
| 1983 | Served one year for loitering offense. |
| 1984 | October 10—robbed King Fook Jewelry for $1 million. October 26—robbed Dickson Jewelry for $8 million. |
| 1985 | December 28, 1984—arrested for selling "hot" (stolen) property. Convicted of possession of stolen goods and use of illegal firearms. Sentenced to sixteen years of imprisonment. |
| 1989 | August 24, 1989—escaped from prison. |
| 1991 | On June 9, 1991, he and his gang—Chan Chi-ho, Ma Shan-chung, and others—robbed five goldsmith shops in Kungtong, getting away with $5 million, entering into a firefight with the police. |
| 1992 | On March 10, 1992, Yip Kai-fun, Chan Chi-ho, and other gang members again robbed two jewelry shops in Shamshuipo, getting away with $1 million. Again, they entered into a firefight with the police. |
| 1993 | Kidnapped a Hong Kong merchant in Foshan for a ransom of $4 million. |
| 1994 | On January 14, 1994, Yip Kai-fun together with Chan Chi-ho and Ma Shan-chung robbed the Tianjin Materials Trading Centre, Shenzhen office, and killed the manager (Li Chen-xi). |
| 1995 | On November 27, 1995, Yip Kai-fun killed Choi Chi-hung (Cai Zhi-xiong), an informant for the HKP, in Shenzhen. |
| 1996 | Conspired with Cheung for the kidnapping of Li in Guangzhou, Dongguan, and Shenzhen. |
| 1996 | Shot by police for smuggling weapons into Hong Kong. |
| 1997 | Convicted of smuggling of firearms. Sentenced to thirty years. Conspired with Cheung and escaped from prison, sentenced to forty years. |

*Source:* Extracted from Lao Tang, *Cheung Tse-keung Zhuan* [Biography of Cheung Tse-keung] (Guangzhou: Huaren Wenhua Chubanshe, 1998), 143–44; *Tian Di* [Heaven-Earth], no. 48 (January 1999), 47.

imprisonment for supplying arms and ammunition for another robbery. He was serving time at Ping Shi prison when the "Big Spender" case happened.

In 1991, while serving his soon-to-be-quashed sentence in the prison, Cheung met Chan Chi-ho who introduced him to Cheung. Cheung was then in China to avoid the HKP. The new "Big Spender" gang was a match made in heaven: Cheung masterminded the criminal plan (kidnapping of Li and Yip) and used his courage to put the plan in practice. Together, they made a "dream team."[72]

Cheung and Yip's gangs committed the following robberies and crimes in Hong Kong:

In February 1990, Cheung's gang robbed the Rolex armored escort of $30 million valuable watches.

On June 9, 1991, Yip's gang (Yip, Ma, and Chan) using AK47 rifles robbed five goldsmith and jewelry shops in Kungtong, getting away with $10 million. In the process, they had a firefight with the HKP in broad daylight.[73]

In July 1991, Cheung's gang robbed the Republic National Bank of New York's armored car escort of HK$170 million, the largest in Hong Kong's history of robbery.

In January 1994, Yip's gang robbed the Tianjin Municipality Comprehensive Trading Centre in Shenzhen, killing a manager in the process.

With the transfer of sovereignty, the HKP formed a task force with a plan to decommission the "Big Spender" gang. The HKP Criminal Intelligence Unit set up a special task force to investigate Cheung and his gang. The task force was headed by Senior Superintendent of Police Liu Jin Min and Superintendent Lian Jiaming.

The criminal exploits of the "Big Spender" gang came to the attention of the PRC political leadership at Zhongnanhai, independently and through the HKP.[74] The seven members of the Political Bureau of the Central Committee of the Communist Party China met and conferred over the matter. They concluded that the "Big Spender" gang must be stopped, lest it disrupt the stability and prosperity of Hong Kong. The directive to bring the "Big Spender" gang members to justice came from President Jiang Zemin personally. The PRC and HKSAR police were specifically instructed to work with each other to eliminate the gang and to serve as a warning for the Hong Kong–Macau criminals.[75]

The above facts, if true, show that the initiative to investigate and prosecute the "Big Spender" gang came from Zhongnanhai, particularly Jiang. But the instruction to act was based on three real concerns. First, the PRC was concerned with runaway criminality by intelligent and ruthless gangs, such as the "Big Spender" gang. Second, the PRC was concerned with the state of law and order in the Guangdong area, particularly Macau and Hong Kong. Third, the PRC and HKP considered the "Big Spender" gang a continued menace to law and order and enemy number one of Hong Kong.

The "Big Spender" case was hardly the first time the PRC and HKP joined hands to bring criminal elements of concern to justice. It was perhaps the only time we know of that an "official order" for fighting a specific crime came from the Chinese and Hong Kong political leadership at the highest level. If that should be the case, the command and control at the political level, and cooperation and coordination at the execution level of the "Big Spender" case could only be achieved by Chinese political authority and not by the Hong Kong government administrative officials. Hong Kong as a Special "Administrative" Region of China was very much a junior "partner" of a national effort to capture Cheung and eliminate his "Big Spender" gang for national interests. More simply put, national security trumps local order, a touchy, but real concern post-1997 and under "one country, two system" regime.

Two years into the transition of sovereignty, the "Big Spender" case set the stage for a test (to some, showdown) of the "one country, two systems" principle—national (the PRC) sovereignty versus local (Hong Kong) autonomy, and collective interest in safety (Chinese people) versus individual entitlement to legal process (Cheung); the former is a classical constitutional qua philosophy of governance question, the latter an emerging clash of civilization made apparent. The former attracts protracted debate over values. The latter leads to a ferocious fight over interests. To such issues and concerns with the implementation of "one country, two systems," let us familiarize ourselves with the "Chinese Criminal Justice System" so alien to most of the people in the world, including those from Hong Kong. This then could tell us why the Hong Kong people objected to prosecuting Cheung in China. We now turn to this subject.

## Conclusion

After Cheung's trial began (October 20, 1998) and before it was completed (November 12, 1998), Cheung's mother, Deng Xi-mei, wrote a letter to the HKSAR Chief Executive, Mr. Tung, to intervene on her behalf:

> Chief Executive:
>
> Please pardon me for writing this letter to you. I have heard that you are particularly thoughtful of old people and young children.
>
> I am 64 years old. I am the mother of Cheung Tse-keung. I have experienced the war, riot in 66. I have seen a lot of big things in my life. I am a strong person. I thought that I would not cry anymore after my husband passed away.
>
> In January this year, my son suddenly disappeared. I did not know where he went. Not only was there no letter, there was not even a telephone call. Some said that he has been detained by the gongan (PRC public security). I do not know where he was detained. As you know, Chinese people love to see each other and have a happy family gathering during this New Year. I remember seeing my grand children this New Year. They said that their father have not given them any "leisi" (red package of "lucky money"). I dare not cry in front of them. New year passed away silently with me worrying.
>
> Chinese people worried away having older one sending younger ones to grave. In my eyes, Cheung Tse-keung is a very filial pious person. He also loves his children. I sincerely hope that the Chief Executive considers me and my two grand-children . . . (in seeking for the return of the Cheung Tse-keung . . .)
>
> November 9, 1998<br>Deng Xi-mei[76]

The chief executive intervened on her behalf but it was of no avail.

After the death sentence was announced in November, Cheung's wife wrote a letter (petition) to the PRC National People's Congress asking for a reprieve on grounds that her husband, Cheung Tse-keung, was unfairly treated and did not deserve to die. The petition read:

> National People's Congress,
>
> I am the wife of Cheung Tse-keung. I write this letter on behalf of Cheung Tse-keung, myself and my two children to sincerely ask of you to relieve my husband Cheung Tse-keung of his death penalty.
>
> 1. I personally believe what my husband's lawyer had told me, the adjudication committee's sentencing decision has a problem of excessive punishment. My husband's lawyer informed me, during

the first day of court hearing it was revealed that my husband has only engaged in the trading of explosives in Macau and Hong Kong. He has not committed any crime in China. According to Hong Kong law, even if the (alleged) crime were proven, my husband would get no more than 14 years imprisonment. He could not be sentenced to death. Alternatively, the party (seller) who was convicted of illegal trading of explosives was only sentenced to a fixed term of 10 years, my husband was sentenced to death unfairly.

2. Unlike other death sentence offenders, my husband never killed any person.

3. When there was no rendition system established between HKSAR and the PRC, there is a legal grey area, with respect to my husband—a person who was sentenced to death for crimes committed in Hong Kong and Macau, it is not fair.

4. I love my husband dearly. I have children three and seven years old. My husband has shown filial piety to his mother and was generous to friends. He has helped untold number of people. For example: while my husband was imprisoned in Hong Kong, he discovered that a prisoner's father was not taken care and he asked me to think about giving some money to him.

5. I only hope that the PRC government should relieve my husband of the death sentence based on humanity and respect for life principles.

Ever since January of this year when I last saw my husband, I was not able to see him again alone. I hope that I and my children can be given the opportunity to see my husband. Lastly, on behalf of myself, my children and my mother-in-law, I would like to extend my appreciation to you for your effort in seeking a reprieve for my husband Cheung Tse-keung's death penalty from the PRC.

Lo Yim-fong (Luo Yin-fang)
Date: November 24, 1998.[77]

## Notes

1. Lawyers will object to the irrelevancy of Cheung's upbringing and background in considering his legal responsibility.

2. Social scientists will continue to debate the criminogenic conditions giving rise to Cheung's criminality, e.g., is it genetics or differential association?

3. See Alfred N. Whitehead, *Adventure of Ideas* (New York: MacMillan, 1956), 229.

4. The "background" is reconstructed from official (People's Liberation Army documentary film) as well as unofficial (Hong Kong and PRC investigative reports) data. Except when necessary to highlight certain sources, the following source materials are used. Official source: "King of Thieves of the Century – Cheung Tse-keung" (Shiji Zhi-wang), VCD produced by People's

Liberation Army Television Broadcast Centre, ISRCCN-A57-98-0126-0/ V.E7 (two discs). Unofficial sources: Lao Tang, *Cheung Tse-keung Zhuan* [Biography of Cheung Tse-keung] (Guangzhou: Huaren Wenhua Chuban-she, 1998), 294. (A first person account of Cheung's life from childhood to final execution. The information was gathered from "insider" information from press, police, and judiciary.); "'Big Spender' Road to Thiefdom," *Next Magazine*, November 6, 1998, 38–70 (A summary account of Cheung's criminal career); "Big Spender" retribution chapter, *Next Magazine*, December 11, 1998, 50–58 (A brief account of Cheung's earlier years); *Tian Di* [Heaven-Earth], no. 48, January 1999, 1–96. (A detailed account of Cheung's criminality leading to PRC judicial intervention—investigation, prosecution, conviction, and appeal.) "Major Crime Investigation," *South Literature* (Nanfang Wenxue), January 1, 1999, 55–58. (A summary account of Cheung's criminal exploits leading to his final demise.)

The biggest problem with reconstructing the "background" of the "Big Spender" case was establishing the authenticity and reliability of source information. The most reliable source was the official (People's Liberation Army) VCD documentary of the "Big Spender" case: "King of Thieves of the Century – Cheung Tse-keung" ("Shiji Zhi-wang"). However, being official and widely circulated in the Mainland, the documentary tends to reconstruct the case from an official (propaganda) point of view. Even then, according to one seasoned Hong Kong TV reporter, much of the publicly available information on the "Big Spender" case was shared. For example, it was evident that some footage in the made-for-TV documentary "King of Thieves of the Century – Cheung Tse-keung" was lifted from the acclaimed Hong Kong TV documentary on the life and criminal career of Cheung Tse-keung—"Looking Closer Today" (an investigative report), Asian Television (ATV), Chinese channel, Hong Kong, shown on November 19, 1998, 8:30 p.m. Likewise, the article "Big Spender" retribution chapter, *Shida Chao*, 1988, no. 15, 12–19 was a reprint of an article of the same title in *Next Magazine*, December 11, 1998, 5–28.

Inasmuch as reliability of the information reported above on the "Big Spender" case cannot be independently validated and any cross-collaboration may just be the result of the "blind leading the blind," the "background" should be read with care. The only known and proven facts in this case are those investigated by the police and proven in court, i.e., facts concerning the bare essential of the commission of crimes. Even then, one wonders how reliable PRC judicial information was.

5.  "King of Thieves of the Century – Cheung Tse-keung" (Shiji Zhi-wang), VCD produced by People's Liberation Army Television Broadcast Centre, ISRCCN-A57-98-0126-0/V.E7 (disc one); Tang, *Cheung Tse-keung Zhuan*, 7–84; *Tian Di*, 90, chap. 3, 31–40; "Big Spender" retribution chapter, 51.

6.  Tang, *Cheung Tse-keung Zhuan*, 31. (The name of the "herb" tea shop was called "Zhang Ji Yu Lin Zuzhuan Herb-tea shop.")

7.  Richard A. Cloward, "Illegitimate Means, Anomie, and Deviant Behavior," *American Sociological Review* 24 (1959): 164–76. (Lower-class people be-came criminals not only because they have limited access to legal means but also because they have easy access to illegal opportunity, as in the case of Cheung.)

8. Robert E. Kapis, "Residential Succession and Delinquency," *Criminology* 15, no. 4 (February 1978): 459–86 esp. 461–64. (Based on Shaw and McKay's social ecology theory of crime, Kapis proposed a cultural transmission of crime thesis. High delinquent areas are characterized by a breakdown of the normal kind of social relations and organizations such that criminal and delinquent behaviors are allowed to emerge. Those behaviors got supported over time by values and norms, so that the area develops a criminal or delinquent culture that was durable and transmitted.)

9. Tang, *Cheung Tse-keung Zhuan*, 30 (When Cheung saw how his mother was being sexually harassed by her boss, he remarked: "Being a bad person without money would not be taking advantage of.")

10. Howard Becker, *Outsiders – Studies in the Sociology of Deviance* (New York: Free Press, 1963), 32–33. (Official agencies create criminals through labeling them as criminal in formal status degradation ceremonies, i.e., arrest and conviction.).

11. Albert K. Cohen, *Deviance and Control* (Englewood Cliffs, NJ: Prentice-Hall, 1966), 98 ("The self is built up in the process of interacting with others. In doing business with them, we discover what we are—i.e., the categories to which we have been assigned . . .").

12. Clifford R. Shaw, *The Jackroller* (Chicago, IL: The University of Chicago Press, 1930), 172. (Delinquent grew up "in a social world in which [delinquency] was an accepted and appropriate form of conduct.") See also Shaw, *Brothers in Crime* (Chicago, IL: The University of Chicago Press, 1938). (Delinquency was considered as play activities in socially disorganized, economically depressed, and culturally deviant neighborhood.)

13. Albert K. Cohens, *Delinquent Boys: The Culture of the Gang* (New York: The Free Press, 1955).

14. Cheung's wife provided valuable insider's information for the first two robberies: 1990 Rolex robbery and 1991 Kai Tak robbery.

15. Tang, *Cheung Tse-keung Zhuan*, 55. See also *Tian Di*, 33. Cheung's initiation to criminality validates Sutherland's theory of differential association. Cheung learned from Wang both the drives (to get rich illegally) and techniques (to plan for crime) to be a criminal. H. Edwind, *Sutherland Criminology*, 4th ed. (Philadelphia, PA: Lippincott, 1978), 80–81. (Criminal behavior is learned. "When criminal be is learned, the learning includes (a) techniques of committing crime . . . (b) the specific directives, drives, rationalizations, and attitude . . ."). The frequency and intimacy of association with Wang also assured that Wang has more influence over him than his parents.

16. Liu Guo-xiong was sent to prison for a drug offense in 1990 for five years. Cheung shared the same prison facility with him while serving time for the Kai Tak robbery. Tang, *Cheung Tse-keung Zhuan*, 140–42. Liu introduced Cheung to Yip Kai-fun through Chan Chi-ho.

17. Robert K. Merton, *Social Theory and Social Structure* (Glencoe, IL: Free Press, 1968). (Crime results from severe strain in cultural values. (1) Culture places a disproportionate emphasis on achievement of monetary goal. (2) Social structure effectively limits the opportunities of groups of people (poor immigrants) from achieving cultural goals through institutional means. The mismatch between socially exhorted ends and

approved means is called "anomie" that causes people to embark on criminal activities.)

18. *South Literature*, 12. This is by far the most often quoted statement and was used to depict Cheung's central character trait. See "Big Spender" (Glenlord Limited). See also Tang, *Cheung Tse-keung Zhuan*, 139. (The comment was made while negotiating with Kwok's family over ransom.) Cheung provides a classical case study for anomie. Cheung's socially induced ambition (making money) is not matched with readily available economic opportunities (good jobs), notwithstanding his demonstrated intelligence and proven industriousness.

19. Cheung did not share a "typical" street gang culture or mentality, i.e., toughness (masculinity, endurance, strength, etc.); smartness (skill at outsmarting the other guys; "street sense" and "street wise" rather than just with plain high IQ); excitement (the constant search for thrills, as opposed to just "hanging around"); fate (the view that what happens to people is beyond their control, and nothing can be done about them); and autonomy (resentment of authority and rules). See Walter B. Miller, "Lower Class Culture as a Generating Milieu of Gang Delinquency," *Journal of Social Issues* 14, no. 3 (1958): 5–19. Cheung was beyond that street culture. Cheung established a whole new way of thinking about doing crime, with a philosophy to match.

20. *Tian Di*, 58. *South Literature*, 7. (Cheung is filled with criminal intelligence. He operated in a most careful and meticulous manner.)

21. In attendance were Cheung Tse-keung and Wang Feng-qi.

22. Tang, *Cheung Tse-keung Zhuan*, 105–6. The statement was attributed to Cheung in first person form. I could not find any collaboration from other sources. The statement, though consistent with Cheung's background and utterance, should be read with care. The author said that the original data is authentic and firsthand. He has taken efforts to make the story come to life fitting that of a novel. Ibid., 2.

23. In criminology theoretic terms, the speech consisted of a series of "neutralization" techniques. Denial of responsibility: "We are all poor by origin. We have suffered too much of a poor and hard life." Denial of injury: "To give an example, from a 1 billion dollars worth of super-rich, if you take away 200 million dollars, there is still 800 million dollars left." Denial of victims: "Why should we target the super-rich? That is because they possess all the world's money and also the money came from exploiting the people." Appeal to higher loyalties: "I want to be a bad person but not hated by the public." Ibid.

24. This led his PRC lawyer Tung to conclude that he could be successful in legitimate business if he applied himself. *Tian Di*, 17.

25. *Xingshi Xusong Shiwu Quashu* (Compendium of Criminal Procedural Practice) and *Zhonghua Renmin Gongheguo Xianxing Falu Fagui Ji Sifa Jieshi* (Compendium of PRC Contemporary Law, Regulations, and Judicial Interpretation.)

26. *Tian Di*, 7. (In answer to the question: Can you talk about the Cheung Tse-keung you know?)

27. "Big Spender" retribution chapter, 51. (When HKP searched Cheung's residence in 1991 in connection with the Kai Tak robbery, they found

that he liked to read philosophy books, particularly those of Nietzsche [1844–1900].)

28. Bertrand Russell, *A History of Western Philosophy* (London: Counterpoint, 1961), 729.
29. Ibid., 730.
30. Ibid., 730–31.
31. Tang, *Cheung Tse-keung Zhuan*, 105–6. The statement was attributed to Cheung in first person form. I could not find any collaboration from other sources. The statement, though consistent with Cheung's background and utterance, should be taken with care. The author said that the original data is authentic and firsthand. He has taken efforts to make story come to life fitting the novel style. Ibid., 2.
32. *Tian Di*, 17.
33. Russell, *History of Western Philosophy*, 731.
34. *South Literature*, 12.
35. *Tian Di*, 26; Tang, *Cheung Tse-keung Zhuan*, 139. (Comment made in reply to interrogation by PRC public security.)
36. Tang, *Cheung Tse-keung Zhuan*, 289.
37. Ibid., 105–6.
38. *Tian Di*, 35.
39. Tang, *Cheung Tse-keung Zhuan*, 135. (The HKP—Organized Crime Bureau—humiliated and tortured Cheung's wife, leaving a knife wound 25 cm long.)
40. Ibid., 136–37.
41. Ibid., 285.
42. Ibid., 231–33.
43. Ibid.
44. Ibid., 212.
45. This reduces any unnecessary resistance. Cheung observed that security guards are paid employees. They will not risk their life to protect property, particularly when they are all insured.
46. This reduces violence and injury, making the case more serious in the eyes of the police and attracting attention from the public.
47. This reduces the chances of arrest. The longer the stay, the more likely the police intervention and/or public involvement.
48. This reduces the chance of gang members telling on each other to gain favor from the police.
49. See the interrogation record of the HKP with Cheung over the Kai Tak robbery. Tang, *Cheung Tse-keung Zhuan*, 134. See also the interrogation record of the PRC police after Cheung was arrested in the PRC over the Li's kidnap. *Tian Di*, 86.
50. Not all antisocial personality types are criminals. Some criminals are not antisocial. Samuel B. Guze, *Criminality and Psychiatric Disorders* (New York: Oxford University Press, 1976, 35–36.
51. *Tian Di*, 35. (In March 1996, Cheung stole a tractor and rammed the CSD guard station in the midnight. Weeks later he sent threatening letters to the Chief Secretary Ansen Chan and secretary for security.)
52. *Tian Di*, 35; (Q: Did he (Cheung) show remorse? His PRC lawyer Tung answered: He shed no tears.), 7.

53.     Viewed in criminology theoretic terms, the speech consisted of a series of "neutralization" techniques. Denial of responsibility: "We are all poor by origin. We have suffered too much of a poor and hard life." Denial of injury: "To give an example, from a 1 billion dollars worth of super-rich, if you take away 200 million dollars, there is still 800 million dollars left." Denial of victims: "Why should we target the super-rich? That is because they possess all the world's money and also the money came from exploiting the people." Appeal to higher loyalties: "I want to be a bad person but not hated by the public." *Tian Di*, 26.

54.     *Diagnostic and Statistical Manual of Mental Disorders* (Washington, DC: 1968), 41.

55.     The old record was set on August 5, 1975, with the robbing of a Hang Seng Bank armored car carrying HK$75 million. *Tian Di*, 43.

56.     See Tang, *Cheung Tse-keung Zhuan*, 143–44; *Tian Di*, 47.

57.     Tang, *Cheung Tse-keung Zhuan*, 81.

58.     Ibid., 105–6.

59.     Ibid., 56.

60.     *Tian Di*, 58.

61.     For a copy of the wanted notice, see *Tian Di*, 43.

62.     Ibid., 27–58. (The first planning session was conducted over Cheung Chi-fung's new-born child party.)

63.     Ibid., 58.

64.     Ibid., 59.

65.     Ibid., 47.

66.     Ibid., 50 (The PRC Xinhua News Agency reported the case on July 22, 1998, in association with Cheung Tse-keung's case.)

67.     Ibid., 60.

68.     Ibid., 53. (In February 1991, Chen Li-xin who was in the PLA introduced Ma Shan-chung, his platoon leader, to Yip Kai-fun.) See also Tang, *Cheung Tse-keung Zhuan*, 166–69.

69.     Tang, *Cheung Tse-keung Zhuan*, 151.

70.     Ibid., 169.

71.     *Tian Di*, 54–56.

72.     Tang, *Cheung Tse-keung Zhuan*, 169.

73.     Ibid., 151.

74.     *South Literature*, 10. (HKP informed the PRC MPS of the "Big Spender" case at the end of 1997. The MPS forthwith sought instruction from the Central Party and government leadership.)

75.     Ibid., 10.

76.     For a copy of the letter to the HKSAR chief executive, see Tang, *Cheung Tse-keung Zhuan*, 284–85.

77.     For a copy of the petition, see Tang, *Cheung Tse-keung Zhuan*, 292–93. The letter was simultaneously sent to the Xinhua News Agency, PRC Hong Kong Foreign Diploma Office, and Jiang Zemin.

# 3

# Chinese Criminal Justice Process

## Introduction

This chapter provides an overview of the PRC criminal justice process as it conducts an in-depth anatomy of the "Big Spender" case. Such an overview and anatomy are necessary for three reasons.

First, the overview is necessary to inform the uninitiated readers on how the PRC criminal system and process operate in theory, e.g., what were the pertinent PRC Criminal Law and PRC Criminal Procedure Law provisions governing various substantive and procedural aspects, and/or legal issues in the "Big Spender" case?

Second, the anatomy is necessary to inform the more sophisticated readers on how the PRC criminal justice system works in practice, particularly in relation to the processing and disposition of the "Big Spender" case, e.g., what were some of the more salient legal obstacles standing in the way of Cheung in challenging the jurisdiction of the PRC courts?[1]

Third, a methodical and detailed presentation of the facts, circumstances, and the law and process of the case is necessary in order to lay a proper foundation for a meaningful discussion and analysis of the case. In this regard, it is useful to observe that thus far public discussion of the "Big Spender" case in Hong Kong has been driven more by opinion than facts, emotion than reason, conviction than reflection, ideology about the rule of law than application of the law.

To this end, this chapter seeks to correct the public record in order to facilitate an informed discussion, sound analysis, enlightened debate, and balanced resolution of many of the legal and policy issues raised in the case, e.g., whether the PRC court has over-reached in prosecuting the "Big Spender" case in China?

35

In light of the above, this chapter provides a summary of the legal process involved in the "Big Spender" case: from case initiation (*lian*) by the public security to public prosecution (*qisu*) by the Procuracy to final judgment (*panju*) by the court of the first instance and appeal (*shang su*) by the court of the second instance to finally sentence execution (*jixing*). In the process, the chapter will discuss some of the more salient PRC criminal law and procedural issues raised by the "Big Spender" case. The legal process of the case is reconstructed from the Bill of Prosecution ("Qixushu"),[2] the Criminal Judgment ("Xingshi panshu"),[3] and the Appellate Decision.[4]

## The Initiation of a Criminal Case

### *Legal Process*

In the PRC, a criminal case starts with the discovery of a crime.[5] Article 83 of the PRC Criminal Procedure Law provides in pertinent part: "The public security organs upon discovering facts of crimes or criminal suspects, file the cases for investigation within the scope of their jurisdiction." In most cases, this means the filing of a crime report with the public security organ by the citizen.[6] In this regard, the PRC Criminal Law requires the citizens to report all crimes. Article 84 of the PRC Criminal Procedure Law provides that: "Any unit or individual, upon discovering facts of a crime or criminal suspect, shall have the right and duty to report the case or provide information to a public security organ, a People's Procuratorate or a People's Court."[7]

After a crime is reported, the public security organ has to open a case file, a process known as *lian*,[8] if the report is substantiated. Article 86 of the Criminal Procedure Law requires the public security organ to open a criminal case file "If it believes that there are facts of a crime and criminal responsibility should be investigated."

After a case file is opened, the public security organ "shall carry out investigation, collecting and obtaining evidence to prove the criminal suspect guilty or innocent or to prove the crime to be minor or grave."[9]

After the investigation is completed, a preliminary inquiry will be conducted to determine whether a crime has been committed, whether the suspect has committed the crime, and whether a criminal charge is warranted. Thus, Article 90 of the PRC Criminal Procedure Law provides that "the public security organ shall start preliminary inquiry into a case for which there is evidence that supports the facts of the crime, in order to verify the evidence which has been collected and obtained." After a preliminary inquiry ("*yusheng*"[10]) as per Article 90, a preliminary-inquiry report ("*yusheng zhongjie baogao shu*") is prepared, which forms the basis of recommendation for prosecution.

The preliminary-inquiry report should include: (1) personal background and conditions of the defendant; (2) whether coercive measures have been used and the reasons supporting such measures; (3) verified facts and circumstances of the case; (4) verified facts and circumstances of the defendant's confession; (5) verified facts and circumstances pointing to the absence of crime or lack of criminality; (6) verified facts and circumstances suggesting lack of or insufficient evidence; (7) the defendant's confession attitude[11]; (8) recommendation on how to dispose of the case based on articulated facts and particularized PRC Criminal Law and PRC Criminal Procedure Law; (9) in cases of joint criminality, the role and responsibilities of each and every joint-defendant should be separately listed; (10) in cases of alternate disposition of related parties in the case, their alternate dispositions should be made clear; and (11) the disposition of seized property should be accounted for.[12] If the public security organ concludes that a crime has been committed and certain offenders are responsible, it has to make a recommendation for prosecution. In this regard, Article 129 of the PRC Criminal Procedure Law provides:

> After a public security organ has concluded its investigation of a case, the facts should be clear and the evidence reliable and sufficient and, in addition, it shall make a written recommendation for prosecution, which shall be transferred, together with the case file and evidence, to the People's Procuratorate at the same level for examination and decision.

In terms of procedure, the transfer of the case file is accompanied by a "written recommendation," i.e., the "*qixu*[13] *yijianshu*" (Recommendation for Bill of Prosecution). The recommendation should contain: (1) title and case number; (2) the defendant's background information; (3) facts and circumstances of the case; (4) reasons and basis for prosecution, including nature of criminal conduct, motive, purpose, danger, and legal basis; and (5) the concluding part, i.e., transfer to identified people's Procuracy, date and time, detention place, and seal.[14]

The transfer of a case file with written recommendation for prosecution marks the conclusion of the phase of police investigation of a criminal case. The people's Procuracy has to review the case for prosecution. Article 136 of the PRC Criminal Procedural Law provides that: "All cases requiring initiation of public prosecution shall be examined for decision by the People's Procuratorate."

### Case Initiation

On May 23, 1997, Cheung kidnapped Victor Li, a Hong Kong tycoon's son. On September 29, 1997, Cheung kidnapped Walter Kwok, a Hong Kong tycoon. In January 1997, Cheung transported substantial amount of explosives into Hong Kong. Cheung's major criminality—kidnappings and transportation of explosives—was not *officially* reported to the Hong Kong or PRC police. The HKP was made aware of Cheung's kidnappings unofficially and after the incident had occurred.[15] The police discovered Li's kidnapping after his car, with a window broken, was found in the middle of the road near his home. They found out the illegal transportation and storage of explosives in Hong Kong through undercover investigation.[16]

Cheung escaped to China on January 15, 1998. Before he made good his escape, he had been under the surveillance of the HKP. In fact, the HKP was on the lookout for Cheung when he was caught on video transporting the boxes (of explosives) into the storage area in Hong Kong. HKP was aware of Cheung crossing the border into China, but did not have sufficient evidence to arrest him at that point. Subsequently, HKP searched and found the explosives in Cheung's hideout on January 17, 1998. Cheung was then put on the INTERPOL wanted list with the PRC police being informed.[17]

Cheung's criminality in China and Hong Kong was not reported to the PRC police. According to an unconfirmed investigative report, Cheung became the focus of the PRC police as a result of Li Kar-shing's personal relationship with PRC President Jiang Zemin. On the basis of the report, President Jiang instructed the PRC Ministry of State Security to arrest Cheung. An "Operation Catching Tiger" was launched in Guangdong for the arrest of Cheung, headed by the PRC Ministry of State Security and assisted by Guangdong public security.[18]

### Discussion

How the kidnapping came to the attention of the HKP was a hotly debated factual question that had a bearing upon the "proper" disposition of the case. As reported earlier, the families of the two kidnapped victims did not report to the HKP before or after the incidents. Some of the unresolved factual questions in the "Big Spender" case include: (1) How and when did the HKP come to know about the kidnappings? (2) Did the HKP possess sufficient evidence to arrest Cheung for kidnapping or explosive charges before he left for China on January 15, 1998? (3) Could the kidnapped victims be legally compelled to cooperate in the investigation of a crime? (4) How and when did the PRC Police come to know about the kidnappings? (5) Why did the HKP not take the initiative to follow-up with the investigation of the case and prosecution of Cheung after he escaped to China?

The answers to the first three questions determine whether Cheung could have been brought to justice in Hong Kong, thus sidestepping the jurisdictional dispute with China. The last two questions inform upon the issue of whether Li Kar-shing had used undue personal influence to have Cheung "properly" dealt with in China, thus raising concerns regarding equal justice under the law in Hong Kong.[19]

It is interesting to observe that under the "one country, two systems" political settlement, the HKP and the PRC Public Security are expected and allowed to differ in many ways on how they handle suspected or alleged criminality. The divergence of approaches reflects the fundamental and material differences in political ideology, jurisprudential thinking, and criminal justice philosophy separating the two regimes. First, in Hong Kong, which is fashioned after a liberal democracy,[20] the citizens do not have a legal obligation to report a crime, although it is illegal to affirmatively assist criminals in covering up a serious offense, i.e., being an accessory after the fact in a felony. In the PRC, every citizen has a legal "right and duty" to report a crime.[21] Second, the HKP plays a much more reactionary role in the uncovering and investigation of a crime than their counterparts in the PRC. In Hong Kong, the police await the report and the testimony of the citizens before acting upon suspected criminality. Though theoretically the HKP can and should take proactive action to expose crime, e.g., victimless (e.g., vices) or investigative crime (e.g., murder), they rarely do so with most of the minor and routine crimes (e.g., gambling). In any event, the crime investigation and prosecution by HKP is subjected to the outstanding policy of not opening a criminal investigation without the active and continued cooperation and support of an aggrieved and willing victim, whose assistance is deemed necessary in the successful investigation of a crime and prosecution of a criminal.

The differences in approach to criminal investigation between the Chinese public security and the HKP can be explained in ideological and philosophical terms. In a Communist regime and a Socialist State, there is a strong sense of community and collective interest in fighting established crime and suppressing incipient criminality. In a Communist State, which is a closed society, there is a much shared idea of what is right and wrong. With socialist citizens, their commitment toward an ideal State is much stronger. The Communist State has a strong sense of purpose and an overriding sense of mission to achieve an utopian State. A crime is not only a private wrong, but also a challenge to the State in achieving its ideal. The socialist government, of and by the people, is obliged to take affirmative action to protect the people in furthering the common interests of the collective. What harms the individual is a challenge to the collective.

Whatever be the legal differences between the "two systems," one should be prepared to ask the question whether such and other noted differences between the two jurisdictions translate itself into observable sociological differences. More pointed is the question how does the law "behave" (Black, Behavior of Law [1976]) in real terms and at the street level? If we should pose this question, we will find that there are more similarities than differences between the "two systems" in terms of organizational behavior of the police and cultural disposition of the people. First, organizationally and bureaucratically, law enforcement officers are not given to assertively searching out for crime because of a number of reasons. There are more crimes than the limited law enforcement resources made available. In essence, they are too busy. Second, the law enforcement officers will not reach out for crimes that they know cannot be easily solved. In essence, they are not inclined to make work for themselves. Third, the law enforcement officers are offered little incentives to unearth the crimes that they might not be able to solve. This will show up their incompetence as unsolved cases.[22] In essence, they are not inclined to discover unsolvable crimes. Culturally, people from different countries, particularly Chinese of common heritage (PRC Chinese and Hong Kong Chinese), are not interested in reporting crime to the police. They find it to be too much of trouble, i.e., in terms of time and effort, and not worth their while to do so, i.e., the loss is too little (pickpocket) or irreversible (rape), and the police can do nothing about it (unidentified criminal, as in the case of burglary).

### *The Defendants in the "Big Spender" Case*[23]

### The Defendants

In total, there were thirty-six defendants in this case:

1. *Cheung Tse-keung*, forty-three, Hong Kong; kidnapping, illegal trading of explosives, and smuggling of arms and ammunition.
2. *Chan Chi-ho*, thirty-six, Hong Kong; kidnapping, illegal trading of explosives, smuggling of arms and ammunition, murder, and robbery.
3. *Ma Shan-chung*, thirty-three, Hong Kong; illegal trading of explosives, smuggling of arms and ammunition, murder, and robbery.
4. *Liang Fei*, thirty-two, Mainland; kidnapping, illegal trading of explosives, smuggling of arms and ammunition, murder, and robbery.
5. *Qian Han-shou*, forty-two, Mainland; illegal trading of explosives.
6. *Chuk Yuk-sing*, forty-two, Hong Kong; robbery, kidnapping, and smuggling of arms and ammunition.
7. *Li Wan*, forty-one, Hong Kong; robbery, kidnapping, and smuggling of arms and ammunition.
8. *Yu Honjian*, thirty-three, Lufeng; robbery.
9. *Cai Zhijie*, thirty-four, Mainland; robbery.
10. *Lau Ding-fun*, forty-seven, Hong Kong; illegal trading and transport of explosives.
11. *Luo Ji-ping*, thirty, Xiaoguan; kidnapping and smuggling of arms and ammunition.
12. *Zhang Huaqun*, twenty-three, Haifeng; kidnapping and smuggling of arms and ammunition.
13. *Wu Chai-shu*, forty-seven, Hong Kong; kidnapping.
14. *Wong Wah-sang*, thirty-six, Hong Kong; robbery.
15. *Or Yin-ting*, forty-seven, Hong Kong; kidnapping.
16. *Ye Xinyu* (female), twenty-nine, Shantou; robbery.
17. *Chin Hon-yip*, forty-three, Hong Kong; illegal transport of explosives.
18. *Kam Wing-keung*, forty-seven, Hong Kong; kidnapping.
19. *Tang Lai-hin*, forty-seven, Hong Kong; kidnapping.
20. *Chen Lixin*, thirty, Shantou; illegal trading of arms and ammunition.
21. *Wang Yinde*, fifty-two, Heifei; illegal trading of ammunition.
22. *Ho Chi-cheung*, fifty-four, Hong Kong; kidnapping.
23. *Yu Chuan*, forty-six, Shantou; illegal trading of explosives.
24. *Wang Wenxiong*, twenty-seven, Shantou; illegal trading of explosives.
25. *Lau Kwok-wah*, twenty-nine, Hong Kong; illegal trading of explosives.

26. *Cheung Chi-fung*, fifty-three, Hong Kong; kidnapping.
27. *Wang Yi*, twenty-six, Hunan; robbery.
28. *Jiang Yongchang*, forty-six, Shantou; illegal trading of explosives.
29. *Chan Shue-hon*, forty-seven, Hong Kong; kidnapping.
30. *Hon Fa*, twenty-four, Hong Kong; illegal trading and transport of arms and ammunition, smuggling of weapons and ammunition.
31. *Jiang Chaigu*, twenty, Shantou; illegal trading of explosives.
32. *Chen Huiguang*, twenty-eight, Shantou; illegal transport and hiding of arms and ammunition.
33. *Luo Yue-ying* (female), twenty-six, Xiaoquan; illegal transport and storing of arms and ammunition.
34. *Yip Kai-chung*, thirty, Haifeng; hiding stolen property.
35. *Yip Kai-yuk*, thirty, Hong Kong; hiding stolen property.
36. *Liu Ganyong*, twenty-seven, Haifeng; hiding of arms and ammunition.

*Discussion*

In Hong Kong, there were repeated questions being asked as to why only some and not all the defendants implicated in the "Big Spender" case were being prosecuted—particularly, why the suppliers of arms, weapons, ammunitions, and explosives were not investigated and prosecuted? The suppliers of such lethal goods were guilty of as serious, if not more serious, criminality as that of Cheung and the other offenders being charged in the "Big Spender" case. The failure to prosecute such yet-to-be-identified fugitives at large raised troubling questions about the efficacy of the PRC criminal justice system in preserving the rule of law and securing equal justice for all. It otherwise fueled continued mistrust in the integrity of the PRC criminal justice system. For example, conspiracy theorists have suggested that China did not want Hong Kong to investigate and try the "Big Spender" case because she did not want the identity, background, and criminality of the people who were responsible for supplying the arms, ammunitions, and explosives in China revealed in public. The open investigation and public prosecution of the "Big Spender" case in Hong Kong might prove to be embarrassing to the PRC as they might reveal corruption in high places (those who covered up for Cheung in return for bribe) and criminality involving the military (those who supplied the arms and explosives).

On a larger compass, it is precisely such lack of trust by the Hong Kong people in the PRC criminal justice system that underscored the jurisdiction dispute in the "Big Spender" case[24] and accounted for the lack of a PRC–HKSAR rendition agreement in spite of its demonstrated necessity and urgency, and which, if existed, could have served to short-circuit the present dispute.[25]

*Investigative Detention*

## The Legal Process

In the PRC, most criminal investigations can be conducted without the suspect being ever placed under investigative custody. By law, custodial investigation is the exception rather than the norm. Custodial investigation is reserved only for the more serious offenders deserving punishment or dangerous criminals posing potential risks for the community. Ordinary criminal suspects are usually subject to community surveillance, i.e., they are allowed to reside at home to be closely watched by their neighbors in the community and co-workers at the workplace.[26] Community surveillance is possible in pre-reformed China and still with most backwater areas in China because the population is relatively stable and the community closely knitted. Local people are all meticulously registered[27] and placed under stringent administrative control. Outsiders and strangers are being kept under close scrutiny by the public security with the help of the people.[28] In effect, there is little need for police detention.

Investigative detention, if allowed, is to be used under limited and well-defined situations.[29] Article 61 of the PRC Criminal Procedure Law provides the following grounds for detention before investigation:

> Public Security Organ may initially detain an active criminal or a major suspect under any of the following conditions:

1. if he is preparing to commit a crime, is in the process of committing a crime or is discovered immediately after committing a crime;
2. if he is identified as having committed a crime by a victim or an eyewitness;
3. if criminal evidence is found on his body or at his residence;
4. if he attempts to escape after committing a crime or he is a fugitive;
5. if there is likelihood of his destroying or falsifying evidence or tallying confessions;
6. if he does not tell his true name and address and his identity is unknown; and
7. if he is strongly suspected of committing crimes from one place to another, repeatedly, or in a gang.

Furthermore, criminal investigative detention cases and persons are regulated by Article 69 of the PRC Criminal Procedural Law[30]:

> A public security organ which finds it necessary to arrest a person already detained shall, within three days after the detention, submit a request to the people's procuratorate for approval. Under a special circumstance, the time limit for submitting the request for approval may be extended by one to four days.

From examination of the legislative history, intent, language, and spirit of the PRC Criminal Procedural law, it is clear that investigative detention is for emergency purposes and is to be imposed selectively based on necessity, temporarily, and shortest duration principles.[31] For example, Article 12 provides that a person is innocent until proven guilty by the court.[32]

When first promulgated, the "Regulations *on* Arrest and Detention of the People's Republic of China" (1954) only allowed for twenty-four hours of investigative detention. The twenty-four-hour period was extended to the current three days' detention with four days' extension, i.e., a total of seven days, with the approval of the Procuratorate and in 1979 with the promulgation of the then new "Regulations *on* Arrest and Detention of the People's Republic of China" (1979).

On May 14, 1998, the Ministry of Public Security (MPS), due to perceived investigative needs of roaming migrants, issued "Regulations on Public Security Process in Handling Criminal Cases" providing (Article 112) for prolonged (thirty days) detention of suspects who refuse to reveal their name, address, or background to the investigators. The time for ascertaining such an extended detention (ED) starts with the proper ascertaining of name, address, and background of a suspect. In effect, the MPS regulations allow for unlimited detention of suspects based on investigative needs. The MPS provision (Article 112) was justified as a necessary and exceptional measure, and later incorporated in Article 16 of the PRC Criminal Procedural Law.

With regard to major suspects committing crimes from one place to another, repeatedly committing crimes, or committing gang crime, the time limit for submitting requests for approval may be extended to thirty days.

This brief excursion into the history of investigative detention shows that "investigative detention" is to be selectively employed and only under the most exceptional circumstances. Routine detention is never the goal.

**Table 3.1**
**Status of Criminal Detention with the**
**Public Security Agencies**

| Investigated Cases | No. of Cases | Detain versus Free Cases/Total Investigated Cases (%) | No. of Persons | No of Persons/ Total People Investigated (%) |
|---|---|---|---|---|
| No detention | 69 | 9.58 | 108 | 11.36 |
| Detention | 651 | 90.42 | 843 | 88.64 |
| Total | 720 | 100 | 951 | 100 |

*Source:* Zhang Cao, "Investigation report on criminal detention term enforced by the police" ("公安机关实施刑事拘留期限状况调查报告"), *Journal of China Lawyer and Jurist* 6, no. 3 (2007): 1–12, Table 1, p. 4.

As to how extensively over-extended investigative detention was used, in November of 2006, Professor Zhang Coa of Wuhan Law School conducted an empirical study of criminal investigative "extended detention" in a central China city.[33] The research is one of the very few scholarly studies that empirically investigates into the subject matter of ED. The research found clear and compelling evidence of substantial ED as it conclusively demonstrates a consistent pattern of police compliance with Procuratorate supervision and rule of law.[34]

One of the key findings of the research is that investigative detention is the standard operational procedure (SOP)of the police. In analyzing the data (Table 3.1), it is clear that investigative detention is preferred in 90.52 percent of the cases and 88.64 percent of the suspects. Only in a small minority of cases, the suspects were allowed to be free from detention while being investigated (9.58 percent).[35] Police investigative detention, contrary to letter and spirit of PRC Criminal Law, is the norm and not the exception. Such a routine detention practice does not appear to be justified by legitimate investigation needs, and is more likely to be an accepted police practice, either due to ease demand on police resources or to serve other illegal purposes, e.g., detention as punishment without due process, or detention as a coercive means to leverage commercial settlement.[36]

*Discussion*

It is not clear from the court records why Cheung was detained in the first place, instead of being subjected to other lesser compulsory measures, e.g., residential surveillance (Article 57 of the PRC Criminal Procedure Law). Applying Article 61 to the facts of this case, Cheung could have been detained for the following reasons. First, he was a dangerous criminal. Second, he had committed serious crimes. Third, he was the principal offender of a major criminal gang. Fourth, he was without a permanent residence. Fifth, he was a fugitive from justice wanted by the HKP. Sixth, there were good reasons to suspect that Cheung would try to escape or otherwise obstruct justice, such as by destroying evidence.

It is also not clear from the court records why Cheung was first detained on January 26, 1998, but the approval for his formal arrest was only sought very late, some five months and twenty-five days later, i.e., on July 21, 1998.[37] The prolonged detention was over and above the legal limit of thirty days when arrest approval must be sought from the people's Procuratorate for criminals under detention for investigation by the PRC public security. A plausible explanation for such an over-extended detention, as offered by the investigating PRC officials, concerned the fact that when Cheung was arrested he tried to disguise his true identity, claiming himself to be "Chen Xing-wei" instead.[38] Specifically, Article 128 of the PRC Criminal Procedure Law allows for the "indefinite" investigative detention of a criminal if his/her true identity cannot be ascertained: "If the criminal suspect refuses to disclose his true name, address, and identity, the period under which he can be held in custody starts from the date the identity is clarified."[39] In light of this explanation, two more questions can be asked of this case. First, whether Article 128 was applicable to the facts and circumstances in this case. By all accounts, the PRC police knew, very early on in the investigation, that the person they arrested (Chen Xing-wei) was in fact Cheung Tse-keung, notwithstanding his incredible denial. They were just waiting for Cheung to confess to the details of his crime.[40] Even if the PRC police did not know the true identity while arresting Cheung, the police could have easily ascertained his identity through DNA/fingerprint matching[41] and or eyewitness identification.[42] In essence, it was not a case whereby the PRC police had no clue as to the suspect's identity. After all, Cheung was the target of a high-profile investigation ordered by the President of the PRC. The police task force should have had all the identification documents in case of an arrest. Second, even if Article 128 is applied, there is still a factual–legal question as to why Cheung was not formally approved for arrest when he had confessed to his true identity in the mid of June 1998.

In fact, almost all the criminal defendants in the "Big Spender" case were detained beyond the statutory limits. If we take one month as the optimal period of investigative detention before an approval must be sought, twenty-six out of the thirty-six defendants were detained over thirty days without an approval for arrest. The average detention for all thirty-five criminals was two months and nine days. This ranged from the maximum of five months and twenty-five days to two days. (See Table 3.2.)

**Table 3.2**
**PRC Public Security Investigative Detention of the "Big Spender"**

| Defendant | Detained | Arrest Approval | Approved Arrest | Time Detained |
|---|---|---|---|---|
| Cheung Tse-keung | January 26, 1998 | July 21, 1998 | July 22, 1998 | Five months and twenty-five days |
| Chan Chi-ho | April 27, 1998 | July 21, 1998 | July 22, 1998 | Two months and twenty-four days |
| Ma Shan-chung | Imprisoned for other offense | Imprisoned for other offense | Imprisoned for other offense | Imprisoned for other offense |
| Lian Fei | June 19, 1998 | July 21, 1998 | July 22, 1998 | One month and ten days |
| Qian Han-shou | July 6, 1998 | July 21, 1998 | July 22, 1998 | Fifteen days |
| Chu Yuk-sing | May 2, 1998 | July 21, 1998 | July 22, 1998 | Two months and nineteen days |
| Li Wan | May 7, 1998 | July 21, 1998 | July 21, 1998 | Two months and fourteen days |
| Lau Ding-fun | April 11, 1998 | July 21, 1998 | July 21, 1998 | Three months and ten days |
| Ye Xin-yu | June 26, 1998 | July 28, 1998 | July 30, 1998 | One month and two days |

*continued on next page*

**Table 3.2** *(continued)*

| Defendant | Detained | Arrest Approval | Approved Arrest | Time Detained |
|---|---|---|---|---|
| Wong Wah-sang | May 1, 1998 | July 28, 1998 | July 29, 1998 | Two months and twenty-seven days |
| Qian Han-ye | May 3, 1998 | July 21, 1998 | July 22, 1998 | Two months and twenty days |
| Or Ying-ting | May 29, 1998 | July 21, 1998 | July 22, 1998 | One month and twenty-three days |
| Luo Ji-ping | June 2, 1998 | July 21, 1998 | July 22, 1998 | One month and nineteen days |
| Zhang Huan-qun | June 17, 1998 | July 21, 1998 | July 22, 1998 | One month and four days |
| Wu Chai-shu | January 26, 1998 | July 21, 1998 | July 22, 1998 | Five months and twenty-five days |
| Wang Ying-de | July 21, 1998 | July 29, 1998 | July 29, 1998 | Eight days |
| + | January 27, 1998 | July 21, 1998 | July 22, 1998 | Five months and twenty-five days |
| Kam Wing-keung | May 9, 1998 | July 21, 1998 | July 22, 1998 | Two months and twenty days |
| Tang Li-hin | May 10, 1998 | July 21, 1998 | July 22, 1998 | Two months and nineteen days |
| Ho Chi-cheung | June 6, 1998 | July 21, 1998 | July 22, 1998 | One month and fifteen days |
| Yu Chuan | July 14, 1998 | July 28, 1998 | July 29, 1998 | One month and fourteen days |
| Jiang Yongchang | July 10, 1998 | July 28, 1998 | July 29, 1998 | Eighteen days |

*continued on next page*

**Table 3.2 *(continued)***

| Defendant | Detained | Arrest Approval | Approved Arrest | Time Detained |
|---|---|---|---|---|
| Jiang Chai-gu | July 10, 1998 | July 28, 1998 | July 29, 1998 | Eighteen days |
| Wang Wenxiong | August 20, 1998 | August 22, 1998 | August 26, 1998 | Two days |
| Lau Kwok-wah | April 10, 1998 | July 21, 1998 | July 21, 1998 | Three months and eleven days |
| Yu Hong-jian | July 14, 1998 | July 28, 1998 | July 29, 1998 | Fourteen days |
| Wang Yi | July 9, 1998 | July 28, 1998 | July 29, 1998 | Nineteen days |
| Chan Shue-hon | April 12, 1998 | July 21, 1998 | July 22, 1998 | Three months and nine days |
| Chen Hui-guang | May 4, 1998 | July 28, 1998 | July 30, 1998 | Two months and twenty-four days |
| Luo Yue-ying | June 2, 1998 | July 28, 1998 | July 29, 1998 | One month and twenty-six days |
| Chen Lixin | June 25, 1998 | July 28, 1998 | July 30, 1998 | One month and three days |
| Liu Ganyong | May 30, 1998 | July 28, 1998 | July 30, 1998 | Two months and twenty-nine days |
| Yip Kai-chung | June 24, 1998 | July 28, 1998 | July 30, 1998 | One month and four days |
| Yi Kai-yuk | May 1, 1998 | July 28, 1998 | July 29, 1998 | Two months and twenty-seven days |
| Total | | | | Eighty months and six days |
| Average | | | | Two months and six days |

*Source:* Extracted from Bill of Prosecution, 1–9.

*The Criminal Charges*

**The Legal Process**

Article 137 of the PRC Procedure Law instructs the people's Procuracy to examine a criminal case transferred to it by the public security with a view toward public prosecution:

> In examining a case, a People's Procuratorate shall ascertain: (1) whether the facts and circumstances of the crime are clear; whether the evidence is reliable and sufficient and whether the charge and the nature of the crime has been correctly determined; (2) whether there are any crimes that have been omitted or other persons whose criminal responsibility should be investigated; (3) whether it is a case in which criminal responsibility should be investigated; (4) whether the case has an incidental civil action; and (5) whether the investigation of the case is being lawfully conducted.[43]

Article 141 of the PRC Criminal Procedure Law further provides that the People's Procuratorate should initiate a criminal prosecution if the facts and evidence warrant it.

> After a People's Procuratorate considers that the facts of a criminal suspect's crime have been ascertained, that the evidence is reliable and sufficient and that criminal responsibility should be investigated according to law, it shall make a decision to initiate a prosecution and shall, in accordance with the provisions for trial jurisdiction, initiate a public prosecution in a People's Court.

The "*Qixushu*" (Bill of Prosecution) starts the public prosecution of a crime in the PRC courts. Substantively, the Bill of Prosecution is made up of three essential parts:

1. *Introduction part*: This part provides information on the nature of the case and particulars of the parties to the case, i.e., the name of the Procuratorate office; title of the document; case number; the background information of the accused (name, sex, age, nationality, ethnicity, place of birth, cultural level [education], profession [work unit, job], address, prior record, and coercive measure status [detention, etc.]); and origin of the case.
2. *Main part*: This part details the facts and circumstances, law and legal provisions, and criminal charges, including investigated and verified facts and circumstances of the case; confirmed criminal evidence against the accused; legal basis and reasons supporting prosecution (including summary of facts on the criminal, brief statement of the danger and punishment for the crime, a clear description of criminal

conduct, and applicable laws for prosecution and punishment); and any associated civil proceedings.

3. *Concluding part*: This part provides information on the legal status and process of the case. "This is forwarded to XX People's Court," Procuratorial official capacity, name, date/time, and seal.[44]

## *The Bill of Prosecution*

### Initial Part

Defendant Cheung Tse-keung, alias Chen Xing-wei, alias 'Big Spender' (*da fu hao*),[45] 'abnormal guy' (*biantai lao*), male, 43 years old, Guangxi, Zhuang Autonomous Region person, senior middle school cultural (education) status, resided in 10 Nanwan Rd, Flat 1(H), Ya Jing House, Hong Kong. Hong Kong I.D. Card No.: D123744 (7). Detained on January 26, 1998, arrest approval sought on July 21, 1998 to the Guangdong Province People's Procuracy office, arrest approved on July 22, the same year.

This is a case of defendant Cheung Tse-keung ... (and other co-defendants). ... engaging in illegal trading of explosives, smuggling of arms and ammunition, kidnappings, murder, robbery, illegal trading of arms and ammunition, illegal concealment of arms, and concealment of loots.[46] The case was uncovered by the Guangdong Province Public Security Bureau and transferred to Guangdong Province People's Procuracy office,[47] the said office petitioned this Court for prosecution and adjudication ...

### Main Part

Specifically, Cheung Tse-keung was charged with the following offenses:

This office is of the opinion: Defendant Cheung Tse-keung disregarded state law and illegally traded, transported, and stored explosives. His conduct violated Article 125, paragraph one of the PRC Criminal Law and thus guilty of the crime of illegally trading, transporting, storing of explosives under serious circumstances and should be punished severely; (Cheung) avoided custom control in the smuggling of arms, ammunition and explosives, his conduct already violated Article 1 to the Standing Committee of National People's Congress "Supplemental Regulations Regarding Severe Punishment of Smuggling Offenses"[48] made applicable by Article 12 of PRC Criminal Law[49] and is guilty of smuggling of weapons and ammunition under specially serious circumstances, and thus should be severely punished in accordance with the above applicable regulations; (Cheung) in kidnapping people for the purpose of extorting money, his conduct has violated the Article 2(3) to the Standing Committee of National People's Congress "Decision Regarding Severe Punishment of Criminals Abduct to Traffic and Kidnapping of Female and Young Children"[50] and Article 239 of the PRC Criminal Law.[51] In accordance with Article 12 of the PRC Criminal Law (on force and effect of applicable law), Article 239 of the PRC Criminal Law is the applicable law (in effect at the time), (Cheung) is guilty of kidnapping under serious circumstances and should be punished severely. According to Article 64 of the PRC Criminal Law before revision and Article 69 of the (current) PRC Criminal Law, defendant Cheung Tse-keung should be punished separately for different offences.[52] Cheung Tse-keung conspired with others and assumed a principal role in organizing and directing many joint offences,[53] and was a principal offender according to Article 23 of the PRC Criminal Law before revision and Article 26 of the (current) PRC Criminal Law,[54] and should be punished more severely for all the crimes he organized and directed.[55]

### Discussion

The pleading and criminal charges raised a number of interesting legal questions and perplexing policy issues in the "Big Spender" case that have not been explored or discussed in the Western press:

### 1. The issue of proper venue

Under normal circumstances, Article 19 of the PRC Criminal Procedure Law provides that: "The Primary People's Courts shall have jurisdiction as courts of first instance over ordinary criminal cases. . . ." However, according to the Bill of Prosecution, the "Big Spender" case was initiated in the Intermediary People's Courts (34). The Bill of Prosecution did not explain why there was a need to prosecute the case in the Guangzhou Intermediary People's Court.

The Guangzhou Intermediary People's Court, and not the Primary People's Court, assumed initial jurisdiction as the court of the first instance over this case because this is not an "ordinary criminal case." Rather, it is a major, complex, and serious case, i.e., a capital crime involving multiple defendants and different jurisdictions (PRC–HKSAR). According to Article 20 of the PRC Criminal Procedure, the Guangzhou Intermediary People's Court is the proper court to initiate the prosecution. Article 20 provides for *mandatory* removal of a serious case:

> "The Intermediary People's Courts shall have jurisdiction as courts
> of first instance over the following cases: . . . (2) ordinary criminal
> cases punishable by life imprisonment or the death penalty . . ."

In this case, since Cheung was charged with life and capital offenses—smuggling of arms and ammunition, being a principal criminal
in kidnapping and transportation of explosives—his case *must be* tried
in the Intermediary People's Courts.

Alternatively, if the case had been initiated in the Primary People's
Court, it would have been removed by that court to the higher court
as allowed by Article 23 of the PRC Criminal Procedure which provides for the *discretionary* removal of major or complicated cases to
a higher level:

> When necessary, People's Courts at higher levels may try criminal
> cases over which People's Courts at lower levels have jurisdiction as
> courts of first instance; If a People's Court at a lower level considers
> the circumstances of a criminal case in the first instance to be major
> or complex and to necessitate a trial by a People's Court at a higher
> level, it may request that the case be transferred to the People's Court
> at a higher level for trial.

The PRC Criminal Procedural Law does not make clear what a
"major and complex" case is that allows for discretionary removal on
petition of the lower people's court. However, there is little doubt that
the "Big Spender" case qualified, less so on the more serious of charges,
but as a first case involving "one country, two systems" dispute.

Lastly, an interesting legal–policy issue can be raised about whether
Cheung should be tried in the Intermediary People's Courts as a
"foreigner" because he was a Hong Kong citizen, enjoying special legal
protection under the Basic Law. Article 20 of the PRC Criminal Law
provides for mandatory removal of a foreigner's case: "The Intermediary
People's Courts shall have jurisdiction as courts of first instance over
the following cases: . . . (2) criminal cases in which the offenders are
foreigners." The PRC judicial authorities, however, have taken the
view that Hong Kong residents are PRC nationals, not "foreigners."
A case can be made for the discretionary removal of a Hong Kong
resident's case from a Primary People's Court to an Intermediary
People's Court on two grounds: (1) Substantively, criminal cases
involving Hong Kong residents potentially raise conflict of law and
jurisdiction issues which the lower people's court is ill-equipped

to deal with. (2) Symbolically, a Hong Kong resident case, as with a foreigner's case, raises sensitive political ("one country, two systems") and international (treaty obligations under the Joint Declaration[56]) issues that must be decided by a higher court. (3) In terms of judicial administration, the lower court, being more close to local interest and concerns, cannot be trusted to fully protect the rights of the Hong Kong residents, e.g., a Shenzhen[57] People's Court trying Hong Kong criminals.

### 2. The specificity of the pleadings

The Bill of Prosecution is structured in such a way that the facts and circumstances in the case were recited in detail (9–19) before the specific criminal charges were specified. It is not clear on the face of the Bill of Prosecution as to how each respective charge and corresponding elements of the offenses were supported by particularized facts and evidences. Correspondingly, it is not apparent which factual events relate to which charge or elements of an offense.[58] The Bill of Prosecution allowed the facts to speak for themselves and parties and observers to draw their own conclusion. This kind of "fact pleading" raised issues of notice and fairness.

In the "Big Spender" case, e.g., the first charge in the Bill of Prosecution was for illegal trading, storing, and transportation of explosives (19). The charge could have referred to the October 1997 incident when Cheung Tse-keung asked Qian Han-shou to orchestrate the purchase of explosives in China. It could also refer to the Spring 1997 incident when Cheung and Chen Zhihao directed and assisted others to smuggle arms, ammunition, and explosives to Hong Kong (11). Likewise, the third charge summarily concluded that Cheung was guilty of kidnapping(s) (20) without further specifying whether Cheung was being charged with and was found guilty of one or more kidnapping charges, and what facts alleged in the Bill of Prosecution supported which kidnapping charges, e.g., Mr. Li's kidnap (12) versus Mr. Kwok's kidnap (13). Finally, the last charge alleged that Cheung was a principal criminal in a number of joint-offenses (20). It was not clear what alleged facts were used to support which joint-offenses. This failure of specification of charges and lack of connection between charges and facts would most certainly affect Cheung's preparation for defense, potentially causing Cheung to second guess the prosecution at his peril—which of the charges was legally valid (legal appropriateness, factual sufficiency) and what facts were evidentially adequate (materiality, relevancy, persuasiveness) in convicting him. Without knowing the prosecution's charges and corresponding facts, Cheung would not be informed about the prosecution's theory of the case, and could not come up with his own theory, in rebuttal.

It also forecloses successful appeal against the judgment, e.g., challenging the adequacy proof of facts as to each and every element of the crimes charged.[59]

It is best to compare the PRC criminal charge practice with that of the United States. In the United States, as a fundamental due process requirement, the U.S. Constitution provides that the defendant must be put on timely and adequate notice about the criminal charge against a defendant so that he can defend himself. Rule 3 of the Federal Rules of Criminal Procedure provides that "The complaint is a written statement of the essential facts constituting the offense charged. . . ." Rule 7 (1) provides that "The court for cause may direct the filling of a bill of particulars . . ."

### 3. The appropriateness of charges

With regard to the smuggling of weapons and ammunitions, Cheung could have been charged under the new Article 151 of the PRC Criminal Law (1997), which provides in pertinent part:

> Whoever smuggles weapons, ammunition, nuclear materials or counterfeit currency shall be sentenced to fixed-term imprisonment of not less than seven years and shall also be fined or sentenced to confiscation of property; if circumstances are minor, he shall be sentenced to fixed term imprisonment of not less than three years but not more than seven years and shall also be fined. . . . Whoever commits the crime as mentioned in the first and second paragraph, if the circumstances are specially serious, shall be sentenced to life imprisonment or death and also the confiscation of property.

However, since Cheung committed the offense of smuggling weapons and ammunitions on May 12, 1996, and before the new PRC Criminal Law (1997) (Article 151) came into effect, he was properly charged under Article 1 of "Supplemental Regulations Regarding Severe Punishment of Smuggling Offenses." The said "Supplemental Regulations" was the relevant and appropriate legal provision governing the smuggling of weapons and ammunitions then in effect. The "Supplemental Regulations" was made applicable in accordance with

Article 12 of PRC Criminal Law (1997), which gives the PRC Criminal Law only prospective effect. Since the "Supplemental Regulations" did not provide for the punishment of smuggling of explosives, he was not charged.

The more interesting legal question is how the smuggling of explosives is punished under the old and new PRC Criminal Laws.

Examining the old law, Article 116 of the PRC Criminal Law (1979) provided for the punishment of smuggling, generally. Smuggling of explosives was punished like any other smuggling offense, i.e., fixed term of three years, public surveillance, and also confiscation of property, not withstanding its dangerousness. The other related provision, Article 112, provided punishment for illegal manufacturing, trading, and transportation of arms and ammunition, not explosives. Article 1 of "Supplemental Regulations Regarding Severe Punishment of Smuggling Offenses" again outlawed the smuggling of weapons and ammunition, but not explosives. The only applicable provision against explosives was found in Article 1(4) of "NPC Standing Committee Decision Regarding the Severe Punishing of Criminals Seriously Endangering Public Security", which provided for death penalty for the manufacturing, trading, transportation, and stealing of arms, ammunition, and explosives.

Turning to the new law, as observed, Article 151 of PRC Criminal Law (1997) does not provide for the punishment for smuggling of explosives (though ironically smuggling of nuclear materials is punishable). Smuggling of explosives is made punishable under Article 125 as trading, mailing, transporting, and storing of explosives; all conduct likely to be implicated in smuggling. These were the charges of which Cheung was found guilty and was sentenced to death. There is an official interpretation that "ammunition" under Article 151 actually includes some kinds of explosives: "'Ammunition' refers to all kinds of weaponry related bullets and explosives." However, this still does not include legal explosives, e.g., commercial explosives.[60] Ultimately, the question of why the "smuggling" of explosives is not provided for in the PRC Criminal Law (1997) needs to be resolved.

Article 125 of the PRC Criminal Law provides in pertinent part: "Whoever illegally manufactures, trades in, transports, mails or stores any guns, ammunition or explosives shall be sentenced to fixed term imprisonment of not less than three years but not more than 10 years; if the circumstances are serious, he shall be sentenced to fixed term imprisonment of not less than 10 years, life imprisonment or death."

With regard to the "ammunition and explosives" charge, Article 125 revised Article 112 of the original PRC Criminal Law (1979) in the following respects: (1) Article 125 penalized the "illegally . . . mails or stores . . . explosives" while Article 112 did not deal with explosives at all. (2) Article 125 enhanced the penalty by providing for a minimum of not less than three years and not more than ten years for a regular offense and ten years to life or death penalty for serious offense. Article 112 only provided for a maximum of seven years for a regular offense and seven years to life for a serious offense. There is no minimum penalty for a less than serious offense.

The facts of the case show that during 1995–1996, Cheung paid Yip Kai-fun to purchase arms and ammunition in China. Yip purchased two AK47 rifles, one automatic assault rifle, five guns, nine packages of explosives, four bulletproof vests, and an assortment of ammunitions (Bill of Prosecution, 11). In the Bill of Prosecution, the Procurator-ate office alleged that Cheung had smuggled "arms and ammunition" (20, Line 1), but he was nevertheless charged with violating Article 1 of "Supplemental Regulations Regarding Severe Punishment of Smuggling Offenses" for smuggling of "weapons and ammunition." (20, Line 4). According to official interpretation, "weapons" refer to heavy, not small arms.[61]

Two legal issues are raised here: (1) Since AK47 and assault automatic rifles are considered to be quite lethal, why did the Bill of Prosecution conclude that they are only (less lethal, small) "arms"? (2) If, in fact, the Bill of Prosecution alleged that Cheung only smuggled in arms, why was he charged under Article 1 of "Supplemental Regulations Regarding Severe Punishment of Smuggling Offenses" for smuggling of "weapons and ammunition"?

The questions raised here are not only those of hairsplitting on words, but also pose the larger issue of fidelity to law. In this case, given the factual context (AK47), the legal difference may be small or even not discernible to law enforcement officials who intent on trying to put a dangerous criminal behind bar. However, a sound system of "rule of law" (instead of rule by law) requires that the law be applied with exactitude and consistency. The admonition that "tough case made bad law" still rings true.

### 4. What law was applied?

Before revision, "NPC Standing Committee Decision Regarding the Severe Punishing of Criminals Seriously Endangering Public

Security" (*Quanguo Renmin Daibiao Dahui Changwu Weiyuanhui Guangyu Yancheng Yanzhong Weihai Shehui Zhian de Fanzui Fenzi de Jueding*) (approved on September 2, 1983) provided death penalty for the manufacturing, trading, transportation, and stealing of arms, ammunition, and explosives. ("1. With respect to the following kinds of criminals seriously endangering public security, it is possible to add more sentence to the highest sentence to the those provided in the criminal law, including capital punishment. . . . Four, illegal manufacturing, trading, transportation or stealing of arms, ammunition, and explosives, where circumstances are particularly serious, or where consequences are serious . . .")

A judicial interpretation has been supplied by the Supreme People's Court "Responding to Certain Questions (3) Regarding Applicable Law in People's Courts Adjudication of Serious Criminal Cases" (*Zuigao Renmin Fayuan "Guanyu Renmin Fayuan Shenpan Yanzhong Xingshi Fanzuian Zhong Juti Yingyong Falu de Rugan Wenti de Dafu"*) (issued on August 21, 1985).

The Supreme People's Court above was asked to provide answer to Question no. 29 raised by Sichuan, Liaoning Province, namely to resolve the ambiguity between "NPC Standing Committee Decision Regarding the Severe Punishing of Criminals Seriously Endangering Public Security." Article 1(4) provides for the enhancement of punishment, up to and including death, for stealing of explosives and Article 112 which does not provide for the crime of stealing of explosives and for dealing with criminals who have stolen explosives under nonserious circumstances and without serious consequences.

The Supreme People's Court was of the opinion that, in effect, Article 112 should be construed as if it had incorporated the provision under "NPC Standing Committee Decision Regarding the Severe Punishing of Criminals Seriously Endangering Public Security" Article 1(4).[62]

### 5. The meaning of special serious circumstances

Cheung was charged with the smuggling of weapons and ammunition under specially serious circumstances. What constituted serious circumstances was not defined in the PRC Criminal Procedure Law or in the "Supplemental Regulations Regarding Severe Punishment of Smuggling Offenses" on which the charge is based.

In the past, official Chinese legal authorities have interpreted "minor circumstances" with respect to Article 151 as those that are of less magnitude, relatively less dangerous, and not causing serious consequences. By natural implication and logical extension, the degree of "serious circumstances" can be ascertained by looking at the number of weapons, the lethality of the weapons, and any intended use made of the weapon.[63]

More generally, "*qingjie yanzhong*" ("serious circumstances") allows for rigorous punishment for the primary offense. Article 125 of the PRC Criminal Law allows for "imprisonment of not less than 10 years, life imprisonment or death" for "serious circumstances" in illegal trading of explosives. Article 112 also provided for such aggravating circumstances. Judging from practical experience, "serious circumstances," when applied to Article 112, included: (1) being a principal or soliciting criminal to criminal gangs, reformed labor escapees, and re-offending criminals; (2) illegally manufacturing, trading, and stealing arms, ammunition, and explosives in large volume; (3) robbing arms and ammunition from armories, explosives storage, vital departments, and armed guards; (4) illegally trading, stealing, and robbing arms, ammunition, and explosives for the purpose of committing robbery, murder, or serious crimes; and (5) whether the manner of the crime was particularly heinous.[64]

"Especially serious circumstances," when applied to Article 112, included: (1) illegally manufacturing, trading, and stealing arms, ammunition, and explosives for the purpose of hijacking planes, boats, cars, causing harm to transportation facilities, robbing banks and gold depositories, and armed smuggling of drugs, thereby causing serious consequences; (2) the use of violence and coercion to obtain arms, ammunition, and explosives or kidnapping, harming, or killing of arm guards or arms possessors, thereby causing serious injuries or death; and (3) stealing and robbing of arms to be used as criminals from place to place or resisting arrest, thereby causing grave consequences.

### *Facts of the Case*[65]

The "facts of the case" were extracted from the final verdict in the case: "*Guangdong Sheng Guangzhou Shi, Zhongji Renmin Fayuan, Xingshi Panshu (1998) Wei Zhong Fa Xing Chu Di 468.*" (Guangdong Province, Guangzhou Municipality, Intermediary People's Court, Criminal Verdict (1998) Guangzhou, Intermediary, Legal, Criminal, Initial, No. 468).[66]

The PRC Criminal case judgment of the hearing of the first instance (*yishen xingshi panjue shu*), i.e., the trial court criminal judgment, should provide the following kinds of data as required by law:

1. *Initial part*: Background information: (a) case title; (b) case number; (c) litigating parties, including legal representatives; and (d) a brief summary of the legal proceedings in the case.
2. *Factual part*: Relevant facts to be included: (a) a summary account of facts from the prosecution and defense; (b) the findings of facts of the court, including what facts are substantiated or unfound; and (c) the discussion of key factual issues in dispute.
3. *Reasoning part*: Determination of criminal responsibility (guilty of what crime) and the extent of culpability (deserving of how much punishment) of the accused and the reasons thereof, having considered the applicable law and policy, finding of facts, and relevant criminal law and criminology theory.
4. *Judgment part*: Whether the accused is found guilty or innocent. If guilty, what is the crime and what is the punishment to be imposed.
5. *Concluding part*: Declaring the defendant's right to and the time period for appeal. Judgment to be signed and sealed by the court.

On the charge of organizing and directing the trading and transportation of explosives:

The case is clearly established after hearing and investigation (*jing shenli chaming*). In October of 1997, the defendant Cheung Tse-keung proposed to Qian Han-shou to purchase explosives. He further directed Lau Ding-fun to coordinate with Qian Han-shou. Lau paid Qian HK$150,000 for the purchase of explosives. In November the same year, Qian Han-shou returned to his place of origin at Guang-zhou province, Shan Wei municipality, and found defendant Jiang Chaigu to purchase illegal explosives. Jiang Chaigu introduced Qian Han-shou to his brother Jiang Ronchang. Jiang Ronchang collected HK$10,000 from Qian Han-shou and illegally purchased 818.43 kg of explosives, 2000 detonators and 750 meters of fuse line. He helped Jiang Chaigu to transport the purchased illegal explosives to Qian's home. Qian Han-shou placed the explosives in 40 foam boxes, disguising them as seafood. On January 1, 1998, Qian instructed defendant Wang Wenxiong to transport them to Ding Ling Yang near Zhu Hai municipality, to be further transported to Hong Kong on an pre-arranged fish boat belonging to Qian Han-ye: "Zhu Dan 5144." The next morning Qian Han-shou allowed the aforementioned explosives to be transported by Qian Han-ye's vehicle and his staff. Lau Ding-fun further directed Lau Kwok-wah to transport the ex-plosives to Liu Shui Xiang, Da Wo village No. 95. Cheung Tse-keung and ... (other offenders handled separately in another case) ... together removed the explosives inside the house. At noon the same day, Cheung Tse-keung together with Lau Ding-fun and others removed the explosives to Ma Cao village. On 17th of the same month, the explosives were uncovered.

On charge of organizing, directing, and financing the kidnapping of Li XX in China:

> From the end of 1995 to the beginning of 1996, defendants Cheung Tse-keung ... (and others) ... made multiple visits to Shenzhen, staying in Ming Du Hotel, Ri Sun Hostel ... secretly plotted to kidnap Li XX[67] and divided the work ... later persuaded ... (other defendants) ... to join in the criminal activities. Cheung Tse-keung put up HK$1.4 millions for the purchase of equipment and renting of premises for the locking up of the hostage ... (other defendants) ... were responsible for purchasing a vehicle, fake license plate and walkie-talkies ...

On charge of smuggling of arms (weapons), ammunition, and explosives:

> Yi Kai-fun used the money supplied by Cheung Tse-keung to purchase two AK47 automatic rifles, one miniature machine gun, six pistols, nine packages of explosives (weighting 1.887 Kg) and bullets from mainland. Cheung Tse-keung made arrangements and provided for facilitation ... (with a number of defendants) ... On May 12, 1996 ... (with other defendants, Cheung) ... smuggled the weapons to Hong Kong when Yip was arrested immediately upon landing in Hong Kong by the HKP with the weapons confiscated ...

On charge of kidnapping of Li XX in Hong Kong:

> At 6 p.m. on May 23, 1996 ... (after being informed of Li XX's whereabouts) ... Cheung ... (and other defendants) ... kidnapped Li XX and his driver near No. 80 Hong Kong Deep Bay Road. After Cheung ... went to Li's home and collected a ransom of HK$1.3 billion, the victim was released. Cheung Tse-keung received HK$.362 billion ... (with other defendants dividing the rest) ...

On charge of organizing, directing, and financing the kidnapping of Kwok XX in China:

> In April of 1997, defendant Cheung Tse-keung decided to kidnap Kwok XX, a Hong Kong resident. He grouped together ... (a number of defendants) ... in Guangzhou, Shenzhen, Dongguan to secretly

plan and divide the work. Cheung and Wu . . . put up HK$2.2 millions as expenses. . . .

On charge of the kidnapping of Kwok XX in Hong Kong:

> At 6 p.m. on December 29, 1977. . . . (after being informed of Kwok's whereabouts) . . . Cheung . . . (and other defendants) . . . kidnapped Kwok XX near Hong Kong Beach Road and transported him to No. 200 Hong Kong Ma On Kong . . . After Cheung Tse-keung asked and obtained HK$0.6 billion from the Kwok's family, the victim was released. After the crime, Cheung Tse-keung got HK$.3 billion. . . .

### *The Defense*[68]

The defendants in China are entitled to right of defense by law. In order to defend himself effectively, the accused has a right to be represented by a lawyer (Article 32(1) of the PRC Criminal Procedure Law), to consult and extract information from the case file (Article 36), to testify (Article 155), to present statements in court (Article 155), to gather evidence (Article 37), to summon witness (Article 37), to confront witness (Article 46), to request new witness, evidence, or expert evaluation (Article 159), and finally to have his guilt adjudicated by a court (Article 12).

Specifically, Article 35 of the PRC Criminal Procedure Law provides:

> The responsibility of a defender shall be to present, according to the facts and law, materials and opinions proving the innocence of the criminal suspect or defendant, the pettiness of his crime and the need for a mitigated punishment or exemption from criminal responsibility, thus safeguarding the lawful rights and interests of the criminal suspect or the defendant.

> Defendant Cheung Tse-keung confessed to the crime of kidnapping with no reservation, but in his defense he said he did not know about the origin of the explosives, denied that he paid for the purchase of the explosives, and raised the issue of alternate jurisdiction.[69] His defense agent is of the opinion that Cheung Tse-keung should not be responsible for the illegal trading and transportation of explosives in the mainland; also the charge of smuggling of weapons and am-munition was not appropriate; the evidences in support of the two kidnapping charges were not sufficient . . .

The legal basis and defense strategy of Cheung's defenses appeared to be as follows:

## Confession

First, by being forthcoming with his criminality in confessing to kidnapping without reservation, Cheung hoped to be afforded leniency for showing remorse and repentance. The longstanding PRC criminal justice principle being: "leniency to those who confess their crimes and severity to those who refuse to cooperate" ("*tan bai cong huan, kang ju cong yan*").[70]

In order for the principle of "*tan bai cong huan, kang ju cong yan*" to apply, Cheung must be considered by the public security to have shown sufficient contrition. This, in turn, raised two questions: one factual and the other judgmental. First, what was Cheung's true motivation behind confessing to the police? Did he confess to the police out of (external) fear or (internal) remorse? Second, did Cheung demonstrate sufficient remorsefulness by confessing to some (kidnapping) and not all offenses (trading in explosives within China)?

This "*tan bai cong huan, kang ju cong yan*" principle poses a dilemma for any criminal caught in a PRC criminal justice system. If "*tan bai*" (confession) is considered by the police as an outward manifestation of repentance, any real or perceived lack of "*tan bai*" reflects a lack of sincerity in owing up to one's responsibilities. This necessarily inhibits, if not totally precludes, the criminal from asserting any defense he might be legally entitled to. This means that there is no right to remain silent in China as any assertion of a defense, even legitimate, might be conceived of as an obstruction to the search for truth and justice. Worse yet, the criminal might be compelled to tell the police what they want to hear, even if untrue, in trying to earn credit for being "tan bai."

The ultimate issue seems to be, as a matter of criminal law and justice policy, whether the application and availability of "*tan bai cong huan, kang ju cong yan*" as a mitigating principle is based on confession to criminal act per se, i.e., the more the confession the less the punishment, or whether the confession and surrender are used as a manifestation and evidence of a change of heart deserving special consideration; thus only total, complete, and voluntary cooperation with the police demonstrates a change of heart.[71] The Supreme People's Court in conjunction with the Supreme People's Procuracy and the MPS had issued an opinion on how to apply the principle:

> "Tan bai cong huan" refers to the situation whereby after the relevant judicial organs are suspicious and decide to question, summon, or

otherwise adopt coercive measures with respect to the criminal element, the criminal element voluntarily confesses to his crime. If the criminal is actually able to voluntary confess, depending on the degree of honest confession and in accordance with Article 57 (of PRC Criminal Law),[72] he should be treated lightly.[73]

The principle is now codified in Article 67 of the PRC Criminal Law, which provides in pertinent part:

> Voluntary surrender refers to the act of voluntarily delivering oneself up to justice and truthfully confessing one's crime after one has committed the crime. Any criminal who voluntarily surrenders may be given a lighter or mitigated punishment. The ones whose crimes are relatively minor may be exempted. If a criminal suspect or a defendant under compulsory measures or a criminal serving a sentence truthfully confesses his other crimes that the judicial organ does not know, his act shall be regarded as voluntary surrender.

In light of Article 67, there was a factual–legal issue whether Cheung qualified for such an affirmative defense. While Cheung confessed to the police, he did not surrender voluntarily. While Cheung did confess to kidnapping, the crime might have already been known to the police all along.[74] There was also a legal issue of whether Cheung would still be treated with leniency under the broad principle of "*tan bai cong huan, kang ju cong yan*," notwithstanding the fact that he did not qualify under Article 67, i.e., by being cooperative and forthcoming with one's criminality.

Cooperation with investigation, while not being the same as contrition that is total and unconditional owing up to one's harm to the victim and society, nevertheless saves the police and society much time and resource from lengthy investigation and trial. As yet, there is no definitive answer to this legal issue on the book. But, in practice, a cooperative criminal, whatever his real motive, is more likely than not to stop things from getting worse, i.e., having the book thrown at him. In essence, in China as elsewhere, cooperation with investigation buys goodwill from the criminal justice system and most certainly better treatment in the hands of the operatives of justice. For example, detectives are taught in Hong Kong to induce cooperation by providing the criminals with favorites (e.g., coffee) and sometimes extra-legal treatment (financial support to family, reduced charge for loved ones).[75]

The more interesting question in this case is whether Cheung could claim leniency by virtue of Article 67, i.e., having confessed to crimes not known to the police (assuming that to be so), for crimes without the criminal "jurisdiction" of the PRC but nevertheless happened within the "territory" of China, i.e., crime happened in Hong Kong. The answer to the question should turn on whether as a matter of statutory interpretation or justice policy, leniency provided under Article 67 or afforded by *"tan bai cong huan, kang ju cong yan"* is based on cooperative acts of confession or reformation of character. If it is the latter, it does not matter whether the confession to crime happens within PRC criminal jurisdiction if it can be shown that the confession is sufficient to demonstrate the true remorse of a reformed person. If it is the former, an intriguing legal question is now raised, i.e., whether the confession of a criminal act, otherwise sufficing for the reduction of punishment under Article 67, is nevertheless denied because it is not the kind of criminal act contemplated under Article 67, i.e., not actionable crime within PRC criminal jurisdiction.[76] Simply put, Article 67 asks for the confession of a "prosecutable" criminal act, not the one which is without the criminal jurisdiction of the police.

Thus far, the proscription under the "one country, two systems" formula is that criminal conduct in Hong Kong could not be reached by the PRC Criminal Law. There is, however, a broader question of under what circumstances, if at all, criminal conduct as material facts and circumstances to a criminal case can ever be used in a PRC court.[77] For example, can facts and circumstances in Hong Kong be used to support a prosecution in PRC courts, either "directly" as material elements of crime, e.g., double-marriages, or "indirectly" as circumstantial evidence to support a prosecution in China? In the present context, whether the Basic Law precludes the positive or benevolent use of legal act in HKSAR to offset criminal punishment in the PRC, or negative or punitive use of criminal act, e.g., criminal record in Hong Kong as basis of determining habitual criminality in China.[78]

With regard to our discussion on *"tan bai cong huan,"* did the rule equally apply to Cheung's criminal exploits in Hong Kong? What of a situation whereby Cheung was forthcoming with criminal activities in China, but refused to confess to (or less forthcoming with) his Hong Kong deeds. Arguably, if *"tan bai cong huan"* is based on moral consideration, i.e., a criminal must show contrition (remorse) and repentance (cease and decease) in order to redeem himself and begin the journey of reform and repatriation, then any failure to owe up to one's criminal acts wherever committed would indicate that he is not sincere, or at least not wholehearted in his contrition and repentance.

However, if the "*tan bai cong huan*" is a utility principle, then whether Cheung confessed to Hong Kong crimes hardly matters, provided that he cooperates with the PRC police in settling all outstanding criminal cases on the China side. Again, this is a novel question never confronted and not explored in the literature. Still, one can make an educated guess based on one's understanding of human nature. Thus, in practice, it is likely that "*tan bai cong huan*," while justified on moral grounds, would be implemented practically, i.e., PRC police were only interested in clearing cases within China border.

One last observation on applying "*tan bai cong huan*" in the context of "one country, two systems" follows. Inasmuch as "one country, two systems" exists to shelter Hong Kong legal and justice administration from undue Chinese influence in whatever form, any attempt to breach the constitutional divide could raise an issue of meddling in the affairs of Hong Kong by China. If we were to take "one country, two systems" seriously, Cheung should be able to claim "immunity" from confessing to crimes committed in Hong Kong, and still be afforded "*tan bai cong huan*" treatment. Again, this issue was not explored in Cheung's case, nor has it been studied since then.

## Deny Paying for the Explosives

By denying paying for the explosives, Cheung tried to distance himself from the "trading of explosives" charge. If it was proven that Cheung paid for the explosives, this made him ipso facto an accomplice if not even a principal offender. This gave PRC courts the jurisdiction over the case and this allowed the court to impose capital punishment as "trading of explosives" was one of the most serious offenses Cheung was charged with. In effect, Cheung was denying that he played a leadership role or otherwise was an accomplice to the crime of "trading of explosives." The strategy here is clear: to salvage Cheung's life, not to gain him freedom. In this regard, Cheung was a pragmatist and survivor; if he could cheat death, he was confident that he could continue his criminal career.

## Lack of Knowledge

Cheung insisted that he "did not know about the origin of the explosives" because his co-defendants carried out the purchase, transport, and smuggling of the explosives from China. In so doing, Cheung refused to accept criminal responsibility for the "trading of explosives," which happened in China. His defense was based on law, i.e., he lacked *mens rea* as he lacked knowledge for the crime of "trading of explosives" in China. Article 14 of the PRC Criminal Law provides that:

> An intentional crime refers to an act committed by a person who clearly knows that his act will entail harmful consequences to society but who wishes or allows such consequences to occur, thus constituting a crime. Criminal responsibility shall be borne for intentional crimes.

The strategy of the defense was to deny "knowingly" purchasing explosives in China, which was the most serious charge Cheung faced. In so doing, he was hoping to distance himself from other Mainland criminals and defeat the jurisdiction of the PRC Criminal Law.

**Insufficiency of Evidence**

Cheung's lawyer challenged the sufficiency of evidence to support the kidnapping charge because the victims did not testify in the case.[79] The problem encountered by Cheung's defense was that the legal standard of proof or "proof requirement" is not clearly articulated in PRC Criminal Law and PRC Criminal Procedure Law.

The standard of proof[80] describes the quality (credibility) and quantity (sufficiency) of evidence required to persuade the trier of fact to convict in a criminal case. In the PRC, this issue is called "*zhengming yaoqiu*" (proof requirement) and is not settled. For the determination of guilt or innocence, Article 162 of the PRC Criminal Procedure Law provides that in order to find a defendant guilty, a PRC court must find that "the facts of a case are clear, the evidence is reliable and adequate" (*anjian shishi qingchu, keshi, chongfen*). Whereas "*keshi*" (reliable) deals with the quality of evidence, "*chongfen*" deals with the quantity of evidence needed to convict (Article 162). However, *how much* evidence is deemed adequate, i.e., *the degree* of standard of proof, is not clearly stated. In layman's term, how convinced or persuaded must the judicial official sitting in judgment be before a conviction is warranted? Absolute certainty or various degrees of probability?[81]

According to one leading PRC author, "*keshi*" and "*chongfen*" evidence means: (1) evidence verified to be objectively true; (2) there is a logical relationship between evidence and facts of the case; (3) there is no contradictions between evidence versus evidence and evidence versus case circumstances; (4) the facts and circumstances of the case that are supported by evidence lead to conclusion in the case;

(5) the evidence viewed as an integrated and comprehensive whole is not assailable; and (6) the facts and evidence in the case point to inevitable conclusion or there is no other plausible explanation given the facts and evidence on hand.[82] More generally, the "proof requirement" is interspersed within various PRC Criminal Procedure Laws. For example:

1. Article 61 of the PRC Criminal Procedure Law provides for investigative detention: "Public security organs may initially detain an active criminal or a major suspect under any of the following conditions: (1) if he is preparing to commit a crime, is in the process of committing a crime, or is discovered immediately after committing a crime; (2) if he is identified as having committed a crime by a victim or an eyewitness; (3) if criminal evidence is found on his body or at his residence . . . (7) if he is *strongly suspected* of committing crimes from place to place" (See also Article 63 for grounds allowing for immediate seizure of criminals by citizens.)

2. Article 68 of the Criminal Procedure Law provides for arrest pending trial: "After a People's Procuratorate has examined a case with respect to which a public security organ has submitted a request for approval of arrest, it shall decide *according to the circumstances* of the case either to approve the arrest or disapprove of the arrest."

3. Article 86 of the Criminal Procedure Law provides that for the opening of a criminal case file by the public security: "If it *believes* that there are facts of a crime and criminal responsibility should be investigated . . ."

4. Article 90 of the PRC Criminal Procedure Law provides for the starting of a preliminary inquiry into a case: "After investigation, the public security organ shall start preliminary inquiry into a case for which *there is evidence that supports* the facts of the crime, in order to verify the evidence which has been collected and obtained."

5. Article 129 of the PRC Criminal Procedure Law provides for a recommendation for public prosecution: "After a public security organ has concluded its investigation of a case, *the facts should be clear and the evidence reliable and sufficient* and, in addition, it shall make a written recommendation for prosecution."

6. Article 137 of the PRC Procedure Law provides for a Procuratorate to examine a case for a prosecution: "In examining a case, a People's Procuratorate shall ascertain: (1) whether the *facts and circumstances of the crime are clear; whether the evidence is reliable and sufficient* . . ."

7. Article 141 of the PRC Criminal Procedure Law provides for a public prosecution: "After a People's Procuratorate considers that the facts of a criminal suspect's crime has been ascertained, that the *evidence is reliable and sufficient* and that criminal responsibility should be investigated according to law, it shall make a decision to initiate a

prosecution and shall, in accordance with the provisions for trial jurisdiction, initiate a public prosecution in a People's Court."

8.  Article 162 of the PRC Criminal Procedure Law provides for the determination of guilty: "If the facts of a case are clear, *the evidence is reliable and sufficient* . . . he shall be pronounced guilty accordingly." (*anjian shishi qingchu, keshi, chongfen.*)

9.  Article 46 of the PRC Criminal Law provides for evidentiary proof: "In the decision of all cases, stress shall be laid on evidence . . . the defendant may be found guilty and sentenced to a criminal punishment if *evidence is sufficient and reliable,* even without his statement."

10.  Article 61 of the Criminal Law provides for sentencing: "When sentencing a criminal, a punishment shall be meted out on the *basis of facts,* nature and circumstances of the crime, the degree of harm done to society and the relevant provision of the Law."

11.  Article 204 of the Criminal Procedure Law provides for the retrial of a case on petition: "If a petition presented by a party or his legal representative or his near relative conforms to any of the following on conditions . . . (2) The evidence upon which the condemnation was made and the punishment meted out is *unreliable and insufficient . . .*"

A comprehensive review and in-depth analysis of evidentiary requirements in the PRC criminal process above reveal that: (1) facts and circumstances are critical in every stage of the criminal justice process, with law and legal requirements playing a less important role, e.g., there is a lack of identification and particularization of the quantity or quality of proof required for certain legal discretion to be exercised. For example, Article 69 provides for the People's Procuratorate to approve of an arrest by the public security: the Procuratorate "shall decide according to circumstances of the case." However, what are those circumstances justifying an arrest is not detailed in the said provision; (2) the "proof requirement" has a large range; from near certainty (e.g., caught red-handed) or "strongly suspected" (Article 61) to some "believe" (Article 86) to some "evidence" (Article 90) to "reliable and sufficient" evidence (Article 137, Article 147, Article 162, Article 204) depending on the kind of process involved, e.g., for investigative detention it is "strongly suspected" and in cases of conviction it is "reliable and sufficient" evidence[83]; and (3) the PRC legal framework governing the exercise of police, prosecution, and court discretion allows for subjective, case by case, ad hoc decision-making with few effective legislative regulation, administrative oversight, or appellate review. For example, Article 61(5) of the PRC Criminal Procedure Law allows the police to detain an "active criminal" or a "major suspect" "if there is likelihood of his destroying or falsifying evidence or tallying confessions." How convinced the public security officials have to be (proof requirement) or how likely must the risk of destroying evidence needs to be (legal requirement) before the police can act is an open question for the police to decide.[84]

The "proof requirement" in the PRC Civil Procedure Law and process is equally unclear. The overall approach is that the objective facts speak for truth. Evidence must be: (1) objectively true (*keguan*); (2) related to facts of the case (*lianxi*); (3) not contradictory between evidence versus evidence and evidence versus facts of the case (*paxue moudun*); and (4) no other plausible explanation or explanation (*paxue qita jieshi*).[85]

*The Verdict*

**The Process**

Article 162 of the Criminal Procedure Law provides: "After a defendant makes his final statement, the presiding judge shall . . . render one of the following judgments: (a) If the facts of a case are clear, the evidence is reliable, and the defendant is found guilty in accordance with law, he shall be pronounced guilty accordingly . . ." Article 163 of PRC Criminal procedure Law further provides that: "In all cases, judgments shall be pronounced publicly."

The responsibility of the People's Court of first instance in the first hearing includes determining: (1) whether it has jurisdiction to hear the case; (2) whether the facts and circumstances of the case are clearly established: crime date, place, means, motive and purpose of the crime, the harm involved, and the consequence of the crime; (3) whether facts and circumstances are supported by sufficient and adequate evidence; (4) whether the nature of crime committed corresponds to the charge; (5) whether there is any criminal conduct or responsibility not properly listed in the Bill of Prosecution; (6) whether there is any civil proceeding to be attached; (7) whether there are any instances whereby the defendant should not be held criminally responsible; and (8) whether the legal proceeding or documentation in the Bill of Prosecution is complete.[86] The above (alleged) facts were proven by the statements of victims (*chenxu*), testimony of witnesses (*zheng yan*), the recovery of stolen money (*zhuan huan*), stolen goods (*zhuan wu*), and the instrumentality of crime such as evidence, the public security organ, forensic examination reports, search and seizure property listed as evidence, and the confessions of all defendants in file.[87] Finally, the court has to decide whether the evidence is reliable and sufficient to support the case.[88]

## The Verdict

Guilty of illegal trading in explosives as a principal to a joint crime:

> It is the opinion of this court: defendant Cheung Tse-keung . . . (and other defendants) . . . illegally purchased explosives. Their conduct constituted illegal trading in explosives. The circumstances were serious. In terms of joint criminality, Cheung Tse-keung performed organization and planning functions . . . (was one of the) . . . principal criminals and should be punished for all the crimes (that he) organized, directed, and participated in. . . .

Guilty of smuggling of arms and ammunition a principal to joint crime:

> Defendants Cheung Tse-keung . . . (and other defendants). . . . avoided custom control, transported and carried arms and ammunition across the border. Those acts constituted the smuggling of arms and ammunitions. The facts and circumstances of the case were particularly serious. Amongst the joint criminals, Cheung Tse-keung . . . (and one other) . . . assumed organization and command functions. All the principal criminals should be punished for all crimes associated with the joint crime.

Proof of illegal trading and transportation of explosives:

> Regarding the crimes of illegal trading and transportation of explosives, after investigating defendant Cheung Tse-keung's . . . (and other defendants) . . . defense and their defense lawyers' viewpoints: it is found that Cheung Tse-keung financed the illegal purchase of explosives in the mainland. There were testimonies from Qian Han-shou regarding his conspiracy with Cheung, and Lau Ding-fun, who, after having received $150,000 from Cheung by way of Lau, went to purchase explosives in the mainland illegally and transported them back to Hong Kong. Lau Ding-fun also testified that he was instructed by Cheung to pay Qian Han-shou HK$150,000 to purchase explosives. During the court hearing Cheung did not deny directing Qian Han-shou to purchase explosives and received the shipment of explosives afterward. Therefore, Cheung Tse-keung should be held fully responsible for organizing, planning, and directing the trading of explosives.

Proof of kidnapping:

> Regarding the crimes of kidnapping, after investigating defendant Cheung Tse-keung's . . . (and other defendants') . . . defense and their defense agents' views: it is found that the two kidnaps were supported by oral testimonies from respective defendants[89] . . . (and also) handwritten testimonies, signed bank drafts and checks issued by the victims' families for ransom, defendants' signed identification of victims' photographs, each other's photographs and confessions, defendants' signed identification of photographs of kidnapping conspiracy sites, kidnapping sites, hostage custody sites, obtaining ransom sites and photographs of some of the instrumentality of crime and confessions . . . As a result, the above defendants' and defense agents' defenses are considered not substantiated and not accepted.

Proof of smuggling of arms and ammunition:

> Regarding the crime of smuggling of arms and ammunition. . . . Defendant Cheung Tse-keung's . . . (and other defendants') . . . defense agents' defenses have been investigated: it is concluded that Cheung Tse-keung . . . (and others have) . . . engaged in the smuggling of arms and ammunition . . . the above defendants have confessed to knowingly smuggled arms and ammunition, portion of the arms and ammunition were uncovered as evidence . . . Respective defendants are guilty of intentionally smuggling arms and ammunition, their conduct cannot be subsumed under other crimes and should be punished independently. As a result, the defendants' defenses are not substantiated and not accepted.

*The Punishment*

**The Legal Process**

Punishments are governed by Chapter III of the PRC Criminal Law. Article 32 provides that punishments are divided into two broad types, i.e., principal punishments and supplementary punishments. Article 33 provides that: "The principal punishments are as follows: (1) public surveillance; (2) criminal detention; (3) fixed term imprisonment; (4) life imprisonment; and . . . (5) the death penalty." Article 34 provides that: "The supplementary punishments are as follows: (1) fine; (2) deprivation of political rights; and (3) confiscation of property. Supplementary punishments may be imposed independently." How much punishment to be imposed is governed by Article 61: "When sentencing a criminal, a punishment shall be meted out on the basis of facts, nature and circumstances of the crime, the degree of harm done to society and the relevant provision of the Law."

The sentence:

> Defendant Cheung Tse-keung is guilty of illegal trading of explosives and is sentenced to death; is guilty of kidnappings and is sentenced to imprisonment for life, deprivation of political rights for life and confiscation of RMB 662,000,000; is guilty of smuggling of arms and ammunition and is sentenced to imprisonment for life, deprivation of political rights for life and confiscation of RMB 100,000. It is the decision (of this court) to impose capital punishment, deprivation of political rights for life and confiscation of RMB 662,100,000.

## *The Appeal*

### The Legal Process

Article 180 of the PRC Criminal Procedure Law provides that: "If the defendant . . . or their legal representatives refuse to accept a judgment or order of the first instance made by a local People's Court at any level, they shall have a right to appeal in writing or orally to the People's Court at the next higher level . . ." Article 183 further provides: "The time limit for an appeal or a protest against a judgment shall be 10 days . . . the time limit shall be counted from the day after the written judgment or order is received."

Article 189 of the PRC Criminal Procedure Law provides:

> After hearing a case of appeal or protest against a judgment of first instance, the People's Court of second instance shall handle it in one of the following manners in light of the different situations: (1) if the original judgment was correct in the determination of facts and the application of law and appropriate in the meting out of punishment, the People's Court shall order rejection of the appeal or protest and affirm the original judgment . . .

### Grounds of Appeal

Cheung Tse-keung's lawyer (Mainland lawyer Tong Jianhuan) appealed on a number of grounds, including: (1) the case should have been tried in Hong Kong courts, which had proper jurisdiction; (2) Cheung Tse-keung was not the principal defendant in the trading of explosives; (3) there were not enough evidence to support the kidnapping charges; and (4) Cheung has rendered meritorious services

**Table 3.3**
**A Summary of Grounds for Appeal and Higher People's
Court's Judgment[90]**

| Grounds for Appeal | Higher People's Court's Judgment |
| --- | --- |
| Hong Kong courts should have jurisdiction | Higher People's Court of the Guangdong Province again confirmed: Cheung Tse-keung and other defendants committed crimes of illegal trading of explosives, smuggling of arms and ammunition, and part of robbery inside the Mainland. |
| Cheung Tse-keung was not the principal offender in the illegal trading of explosives | Appellant Cheung Tse-keung was the owner of the illegally purchased explosives and the planner and leader of the crime. He furnished the money and asked appellant Qian Han-shou to purchase the explosives, directed defendant Lau Ding-fun as the point of contact in the purchase of explosives, transported the illegally purchased explosives, and shipped to Hong Kong. |
| Insufficient evidence to support kidnapping charges | Appellant Cheung Tse-keung suggested the idea for the kidnapping and provided funds for the purchase of weapons for the crime, performed organizing and directing functions in the entire crime, shared in large amount of ransom money, and was the principal offender. |
| Reporting and supplying evidence on others' criminality on appeal | Although appellant Cheung Tse-keung has provided evidence leading to the prosecution of Hong Kong residents' crime committed in Hong Kong. During the proceeding of the appeal, the Guangzhou Public Security Bureau confirmed that such evidentiary leads could not be substantiated through independent investigation and thus were not to be considered as meritorious service (*ligong*). |

in the appeal by reporting other people's offenses and providing for supporting evidence. (See Table 3.3, *infra*.)

*The Appellate Judgment*[91]

This morning, the Higher People's Court of the Guangdong Province reached a final verdict on the appeals of Cheung Tse-keung and thirty-six other defendants with respect to their cases of illegal trading and transportation of explosives; illegal trading and transportation of arms and ammunition; concealment of arms and ammunition; smuggling of weapons and ammunition; and kidnapping, robbery, and concealment of loots. The defendants' appeals are hereby rejected. With the authority vested in the Higher People's Court, (this Court found that) the sentence of death to Cheung Tse-keung, Chan Chi-ho, Ma Shan-chung, Liang Fei, and Qian Han-shou and the deprivation of political rights for life were in accordance with the law; to be executed immediately after the announcement of this verdict.[92] Below, I am going to announce to the press the relevant circumstances about the appeal (see Table 3.3):

*1. The circumstances of the defendant's appeal and defense's viewpoints*

On November 12 [1998], Guangzhou Intermediary People's Court rendered a hearing of a first-instance judgment in a criminal case against Cheung Tse-keung and other defendants. Cheung Tse-keung and twenty-nine defendants appealed to the Higher People's Court of Guangdong Province. Twenty-nine of the appellants appointed forty-four lawyers for their defense. The appellants and their defense agents submitted their written defense viewpoints to the appellate court. Those who had not appointed defense agents also submitted their written defense viewpoints to the appeal's court.

The major reasons and defense viewpoints raised by respective appellants and defense agents were: (1) a different opinion about the jurisdiction in this case; (2) the first trial judgment confirmed that certain facts were not clear and there were not enough evidence; (3) the first trial judgment confirmed that there was a lack of distinction drawn between the relationship between the principal (offender) and followers; (4) the determination of the first trial was not accurate; (5) the penalty imposed by the first trial was too severe; and (6) the first trial overlooked the defendants' surrendering and rendering of meritorious services. Respective appellants and defense agents asked the appellate court to reduce their sentences and treat them with leniency. (Table 3.3, *supra*.)

*2. Regarding the appeal process:*

After the defendants submitted their appeals, the Guangzhou Intermediary People's Court moved the case to this court in accordance with Article 184 of the "PRC Criminal Procedure Code."[93] This court formed a collegial bench (*he yi ting*) to hear the case in accordance with Article 187 of "PRC Criminal Procedure Code," with the No. 1 Criminal Court, Court President Yang Rencai as the chief judge (*shenpan zhang*), Zhao Jun as the deputy judge, Xie Wenlian and Huang Fu-zhao as judges, and Chen Xiao-fei as an acting judge.[94]

Article 186 of our country's "Criminal Procedure Code" provides: "A People's Court of second instance shall conduct a complete review of the facts determined and the application of law in the judgment of first instance and shall not be limited by the scope of appeal or protest. If an appeal is filed by only some of the defendants in a case of joint crime, the case shall still be reviewed and handled as a whole." In this case, some of the defendants appealed and some of the defendants did not appeal; the collegial court heard the whole case in accordance with the law. The collegial court read all the case materials and questioned the seventy-nine appellants and Zhu Yu-cheng and the seven other [nonappealing] original defendants individually; listening to their reasons and viewpoints. The lawyers read the materials and submitted to the collegial court their defense briefs. The collegial court, based on the defense viewpoints of the appellants and the original trial defendants and their lawyers, conducted a comprehensive review of the case. After confirming the facts and applicable law in the first trial, the court found the facts to be clear and decided not to (re)try this case in open court in accordance with Article 187 of the "Criminal Procedure Code."[95] Building on the foundation of a full review of the confirmed facts and circumstances in the case, the court issued the appellate decision after the collegial court having appraised and discussed (*pingyi*) the case and the court's judicial committee having discussed and passed on the judgment. Three days before this appellate court announced the judgment, it placed public notices within this court and judgment pronouncement activities bureau (*xuan pan huodong suo*), with the lawyers and relatives of the appellants being notified accordingly. During the whole appeal, the court has conducted itself strictly in accordance with the relevant provisions of the "Criminal procedure Code" and has protected the criminal procedure rights of the appellants and the original trial defendants.

*3. Regarding the review and affirmation of the criminal facts of the
appellants and original trial defendants:*

The Higher People's Court of the Guangdong Province adjudicated
the case without further trial (*bu kai ting shenli*). After carefully listening to the defense viewpoints of respective appellants, original
trial defendants and their lawyers, and having completely verified
and confirmed the material evidence, documentary evidence, witness
testimonies, and forensic evidence of the trial of the first instance, the
court affirmed the verdict of the court of the first instance that defendant Cheung Tse-keung and the other twenty-nine appellants, and Zhu
Yu-cheng and the other seven original trial defendants' criminal facts
were apparent and supported by valid and sufficient evidence.

Regarding the issue of court jurisdiction:

Cheung Tse-keung had submitted in the appeal that this case should be
within the jurisdiction of the Hong Kong courts, and the Mainland courts
had no jurisdictional authority over the case. On appeal, the Higher
People's Court in the Guangdong Province again confirmed: Cheung
Tse-keung and other defendants committed crimes of illegal trading
of explosives, smuggling of arms and ammunition, and part of robbery
inside the Mainland. Though they happened in Hong Kong, the crimes of
kidnapping and robbery of gold jewelry shops were conspired, planned,
and prepared in the Mainland, that is to say the preparatory conducts to
crimes committed in Hong Kong happened in the Mainland. According
to Article 6(1) of the "Criminal Code," "This Law shall be applicable to
anyone who commits a crime within the territory and territorial waters
and space of the PRC, except as otherwise specifically provided by law" and
according to Article 24 of the "Criminal procedure Code": "A criminal case
shall be under the jurisdiction of the people's Court in the place where the
crime was committed," the Mainland courts should have jurisdiction
over the case. The Hong Kong courts also have jurisdiction. With this
kind of cases where different regional courts (*bu tung diqu fayuan*)
have concurrent jurisdictions, it should be dealt with by the first trial
court in accordance with Article 25 of the "Criminal Procedure Law."
After committing their crimes, Cheung Tse-keung and others were
arrested by Mainland public security organs and a large amount of
witness testimony and material evidences were obtained and located
within the Mainland. Under this kind of circumstances and according
to the above cited legal provisions, Mainland judicial organs possessed
jurisdiction. This is very obvious, definite, and is grounded in law.

Regarding the crime of illegal trading and transportation of explosives:

Appellant Cheung Tse-keung was the owner of the illegally purchased explosives and the planner and leader of the crime. He furnished the money and asked appellant Qian Han-shou to purchase the explosives, directed defendant Lau Ding-fun as the point of contact in the purchase of explosives, transported the illegally purchased explosives, and shipped them to Hong Kong from 95 Da Huo Kuo village at Liu Shui Xiang in Hong Kong to Ma Cao village in collusion with Lau Ding-fun and others: Qian Han-shou, Lau Ding-fun, Liu Guo-hua, Qian Han-ye, Jiang Ron-chang, Jiang Cai-gu, Yu Chuan, Huang Wen-xiong, Luo Yue-ying, and Chen Hui-guang participated in the illegal trading or transportation of explosives; all were supported by valid and sufficient evidence. Cheung Tse-keung illegally traded in large amount of explosives, seriously affecting public safety. The circumstances were serious and he was the principal offender and should be punished by law as organizing and directing the whole crime. Appellant Cheung Tse-keung and his defense agent were of the opinion that Cheung Tse-keung being held responsible for the entire crime did not have any factual support. During the process of illegal trading and transportation of explosives, Qian Han-shou participated in the conspiracy and was responsible for the purchase and transportation; he performed a key role in the crime, the criminal circumstances were serious, the appellant and his defense agents were of the opinion that Qian Han-shou's criminal circumstances were lighter and were not supported by facts.

Regarding the crime of kidnapping: Appellant Cheung Tse-keung suggested the idea for the kidnapping and provided the funds for the purchase of weapons for the crime, performed organizing and directing functions in the entire crime, shared-in large amount of ransom money, is the principal offender, there were confessions and identifications of conspiracy sites, photos of kidnapping sites, instrumentality of crime, victims' cashier's check and power of attorney by (Cheung) himself and others involved in the crime, the evidences were valid and sufficient. Appellant Cheung Tse-keung's appeal based on insufficient evidence was not established.

Regarding the smuggling of arms and ammunition:

Appellant Cheung Tse-keung colluded with others to smuggle arms and ammunition to Hong Kong from the Mainland, seriously endangering public safety. The circumstances were serious and according to law, he was found guilty of smuggling arms and ammunition. Appellant Cheung Tse-keung and his defense agent suggested that the smuggling of arms and ammunition charges merged with the kidnapping crime, should not be punished separately, was not based on law and is not accepted.

Regarding illegal trading and concealment of arms and ammunition crimes and concealment of loots:

The first trail judgment confirmed that the facts were clear. Evidence was valid, adequate, and fully established. The appellants' viewpoints were not accepted.

Also, the appellant Cheung Tse-keung's defense lawyer petitioned the court for new evidence regarding the kidnapping, smuggling of arms and ammunition; the appellate collegial court after review is of the opinion that Cheung Tse-keung committed kidnapping and smuggling of arms and ammunition crimes, were supported by adequate evidence, should be affirmed, and his petition is rejected. Although appellant Cheung Tse-keung has provided evidentiary leads to prosecute Hong Kong residents' crime committed in Hong Kong during the appeal proceeding, the Guangzhou Public Security Bureau confirmed that such evidentiary leads could not be confirmed through investigation and thus not be considered as meritorious service (*ligong*).

### 4. Regarding the basis of law for the appellate court decision:

Guangdong Province's Higher People's Court, having heard the case, made appellate decision in accordance with "Criminal Procedure Law, Article 189 (1) and (2): . . . In accordance with regulations in "Notice regarding the Supreme People's Court authorizing Intermediary People's Court to check and approve certain death punishment cases," ratifies the death sentences of five defendants Cheung Tse-keung, Chan Chi-ho, Ma Shan-chung, Liang Fei, and Qian Han-shou. This judgment fully realized the principle of conviction and punishment according to law, crime, and punishment proportionality principle.

Guangdong Province's Higher People's Court's decision in the case with respect to Cheung Tse-keung and other thirty-six defendants, whether it is with regard to hearing procedures or with substantive decision, has been conducted strictly in accordance with the law, has actualized (the principles of) following the law when existed, enforcing the law with due diligence, holding accountable for law violations, and protecting the dignity of the law.

## Conclusion

The "Big Spender" is a test case of law (PRC Constitution, Hong Kong Basic Law, and "one country, two systems") as well as a showcase of trial process ("PRC Criminal Law and Criminal Procedural Law").

The "Big Spender" case is a test case for the Hong Kong and global communities, especially that of Taiwan who lacks confidence in re-uniting with China for fear of being compromising her national sovereignty, political autonomy, and way of life.[96] The issue is one of law, i.e., what does "one country, two systems" mean when applied to Hong Kong residents who have committed crimes in both jurisdictions?[97] It is also about politics, i.e., in a conflict of jurisdiction criminal case, as in here, how far and how much the PRC authorities are willing to accommodate Hong Kong peoples' legitimate interests and real concerns, as in the need to punish and protect one of its own, as Hong Kong people deem fit.[98]

The "Big Spender" case is a show trial[99] for the Chinese authority.[100] Its purpose is to show the international community that China respects the rule of law. Chinese play by the rules is the message. Hong Kong people have nothing to fear from their motherland. Chinese political leaders have Hong Kong's best interest at heart in protecting them from gangsters like Cheung. Finally, criminals, like the "Big Spender" gang, should not commit a crime in China, Mainland, or Hong Kong. "One country, two systems" does not mean that criminals can use Hong Kong as a safe haven to commit crimes in China, such as subversive activities, organized criminality, cross-border crime, and Internet offence.[101]

China also wants to use the "Big Spender" case to educate the Hong Kong people as to how her criminal justice system works in practice, in order to debunk myths, promote understanding, and enlist support. The message here is that the Chinese legal system has come of age. It has moved away from the Cultural Revolution days under Mao (radicalization of justice) and strike-hard campaign moments by Deng (instrumentalization of law) into an orderly rule-bound process (rationalization of criminal justice process). To this end, the Chinese political leaders and justice officials spared no effort in showcasing their commitment to the Constitution ("one country, two systems"), criminal law ("have law to follow, law will be follow, violation of law will be pursued"[102]), and process (guilt by evidence[103]).

What then have we (outsiders), especially Hong Kong people, learned about the Chinese criminal justice system, process, and operations ("system") that we do not already know with the "Big Spender" trial? Not much. Even with the meticulous literally blow by blow documentation of the trial, we have not learned much about how the system really functions in day-to-day operations, such as how investigative decisions are made or what *"tan bai cong huan"* means in routine cases. All we have learned is perhaps how the system should function, by the book. Given the staged and showcased quality of the trial,[104] everyone was typecasted and each step was scripted. No one should expect any surprise, and there was none. If one wants to learn about the system as designed one is better off reading standard PRC Criminal Law and PRC Criminal Procedural Law treatises. The most valuable function of the trial is perhaps in concretizing the proceedings and putting things in a particularized context.

Ultimately, good intention aside, the question is whether the "Big Spender" trial has achieved its intended objective of allaying fear and boosting confidence in "one country, two systems"? The answer appears to be no. In spite of a perfectly orchestrated show trial, the Hong Kong people were more skeptical than ever. This was so because of two reasons. First, substantively, it seems that the more Hong Kong people know about how the PRC system (should) operate, the more they "feel" uncomfortable about how it really functions, as compared to the one in Hong Kong that they have been used to. Second, procedurally, the "Big Spender" case shows clearly that the "one country, two systems" formula was not effective in keeping the Chinese authorities at bay in interfering with Hong Kong criminal justice system from its proper functioning. Indeed, the "Big Spender" show trial had the opposite effect of sanitizing the Hong Kong people to the real possibility of Chinese officials' willingness and ability to override the "one country, two systems" formula for the "welfare" of Hong Kong.[105]

## Appendix

### Public Statement of Higher People's Court of Guangdong Province

*Director of Court (Ting Zhang)Lu Botao*

This morning, the Higher People's Court of the Guangdong Province reached a final verdict on the appeals of Cheung Tse-keung and thirty-six other defendants with respect to their cases of illegal trading and transportation of explosives; illegal trading and transportation of arms and ammunition; concealment of arms and ammunition; smuggling of weapons and ammunition; and kidnapping, robbery, and concealment of loots. The defendants' appeals are hereby rejected. With the authority vested in the Higher People's Court, the sentence of death to Cheung Tse-keung, Chan Chi-ho, Ma Shan-chung, Liang Fei, and Qian Han-shou and the deprivation of their political rights for life were in accordance with the law; to be executed immediately after the announcement of this verdict. Below, I am going to announce to the press the relevant circumstances about the appeal:

*1. The circumstances of the defendant's appeal and the defense's viewpoint*

On November 12 [1998], Guangzhou Intermediary People's Court rendered a first trial judgment in criminal cases against Cheung

Tse-keung and other defendants. Cheung Tse-keung and twenty-nine defendants appealed to the Higher People's Court of Guangdong Province. Twenty-nine of the appellants appointed forty-four lawyers for their defense. The appellants and their defense agents submitted their written defense viewpoints to the appellate court. Those who had not appointed defense agents also submitted their written defense viewpoints to the appellate court.

The major reasons and defense viewpoints raised by respective appellants and defense agents are: (1) a different opinion about the jurisdiction in this case; (2) the first trial judgment confirmed that certain facts were not clear and there were not enough evidence; (3) the first trial judgment confirmed that there was a lack of distinction drawn between the relationship between the principal (offender) and followers; (4) the determination of the first trial was not accurate; (5) the penalty imposed by the first trial was too severe; and (6) the first trial overlooked the defendants' surrendering and rendering of meritorious services. Respective appellants and defense agents asked the appellate court to reduce their sentences and treat them with leniency.

*2. Regarding the appeal process*

After the defendants submitted their appeals, the Guangzhou Intermediary People's Court moved the case to this court in accordance with Article 184 of the "PRC Criminal Procedure Code." This court formed a collegial bench (*he yi ting*) to hear the case in accordance with Article 187 of "PRC Criminal Procedure Code," with the No. 1 Criminal Court,

Court President Yang Rencai as the chief judge (*shenpan zhang*), Zhao Jun as the deputy judge, Xie Wenlian and Huang Fu-zhao as judges, and Chen Xiao-fei as an acting judge.

Article 186 of our country's "Criminal Procedure Code" provides: "The people's court of appeal should conduct comprehensive review of the findings of facts and application of law of the original trial court, not to be restricted by the appellant or scope of appeal. In cases of co-conspirators, if only some of the defendants appeal, the case should be reviewed as a whole, hearing it altogether." In this case, some of the defendants appealed and some of the defendants did not; the collegial court heard the whole case in accordance with the law. The collegial court read all the case materials and questioned the seventy-nine appellants and Zhu Yu-cheng and the seven other [nonappealing] original defendants individually; listening to their reasons and viewpoints. The lawyers read the materials and submitted to the collegial court their defense briefs. The collegial court, based on the defense viewpoints of the appellants and the original trial defendants and their lawyers, conducted a comprehensive review of the case. After confirming the facts and applicable law in the first trial, the court found the facts to be clear and decided not to (re)try this case in open court in accordance with Article 187 of the "Criminal Procedure Code." Building on the foundation of a full review of the confirmed facts and circumstances in the case, the court issued the appellate decision after the collegial court having appraised and discussed (*pingyi*) the case and the court's judicial committee having discussed and passed on the judgment. Three days before this appellate court announced the judgment, it placed public notices within this court and judgment pronouncement activities bureau (*xuan pan huodong suo*), with the lawyers and relatives of the appellants being notified accordingly. During the whole appeal, the court has conducted itself strictly in accordance with the relevant provisions of the "Criminal procedure Code" and has protected the criminal procedure rights of the appellants and original trial defendants.

### 3. Regarding the review and affirmation of the criminal facts of the appellants and original trial defendants

The Higher People's Court of the Guangdong Province adjudicated the case without further trial (*bu kai ting shenli*). After carefully listening to the defense viewpoints of respective appellants, original trial defendants and their lawyers, and having completely verified and confirmed the material evidence, documentary evidence, witness testimonies, and forensic evidence of the trial of the first instance, the court affirmed the verdict of the court of the first instance that defendant Cheung Tse-keung and the other twenty-nine appellants, and Zhu Yu-cheng and the other seven original trial defendants' criminal facts were apparent and supported by valid and sufficient evidence.

Regarding the issue of court jurisdiction:

Cheung Tse-keung had submitted in the appeal that this case should be within the jurisdiction of the Hong Kong courts, and the Mainland courts have no jurisdictional authority over the case. On appeal, the Higher People's Court in the Guangdong Province again confirmed: Cheung Tse-keung and other defendants committed crimes of illegal trading of explosives, smuggling of arms and ammunition, and part of robbery inside the Mainland. The crimes of kidnapping and robbery of gold jewelry shops, though happened in Hong Kong, were conspired, planned, and prepared in the Mainland, that is to say the preparatory conducts to crimes committed in Hong Kong happened in the Mainland. According to Article 6(1) of the "Criminal Code," "This Law shall be applicable to anyone who commits a crime within the territory and territorial waters and space of the PRC, except as otherwise specifically provided by law" and according to Article 24 of the "Criminal procedure Code": "A criminal case shall be under the jurisdiction of the people's Court in the place where the crime was committed," the Mainland courts should have jurisdiction over the case. The Hong Kong courts also have jurisdiction. With this kind of cases where different regional courts (*bu tung diqu fayuan*) have concurrent jurisdictions, it should be dealt with by the first trial court in accordance with Article 25 of the "Criminal procedure Code." After committing their crimes, Cheung Tse-keung and others were arrested by Mainland public security organs and a large amount of witness testimony and material evidences were obtained and located within the Mainland. Under this kind of circumstances and according to the above cited legal provisions, Mainland judicial organs possessed jurisdiction. This is very obvious, definite, and is grounded in law.

Regarding the crime of illegal trading and transportation of explosives:

Appellant Cheung Tse-keung was the owner of the illegally purchased explosives and the planner and leader of the crime. He furnished the money and asked appellant Qian Han-shou to purchase the explosives, directed defendant Lau Ding-fun as the point of contact in the purchase of explosives, transported the illegally purchased explosives and shipped them to Hong Kong from 95 Da Huo Kuo village at Liu Shui Xiang in Hong Kong to Ma Cao village in collusion with Lau Ding-fun and others: Qian Han-shou, Lau Ding-fun, Liu Guo-hua, Qian Han-ye, Jiang Ron-chang, Jiang Cai-gu, Yu Chuan, Huang Wen-xiong, Luo Yue-ying, and Chen Hui-guang participated in the illegal trading or transportation of explosives; all were supported by valid and sufficient evidence. Cheung Tse-keung illegally traded in large amount of explosives, seriously affecting public safety, circumstances were serious. He was the principal offender and should be punished by law for organizing and directing the whole crime, appellant Cheung Tse-keung and his defense agent were of the opinion that Cheung Tse-keung being held responsible for the entire crime did not have any factual support. During the process of illegal trading and transportation of explosives, Qian Han-shou participated in the conspiracy and was responsible for the purchase and transportation, he performed a key role in the crime, the criminal circumstances were serious, but the appellant and his defense agents were of the opinion that Qian Han-shou's criminal circumstances were lighter and were not supported by facts.

Regarding the crime of robbery. . . .

Regarding the crime of kidnapping:

Appellant Cheung Tse-keung suggested the idea for the kidnapping and provided the funds for the purchase of instrumentality of crime, performed organizing and directing functions in the entire crime, shared in large amount of ransom money, is the principal offender, there were confessions and identifications of conspiracy sites, photos of kidnapping sites, instrumentality of crime, victims' cashier's check and power of attorney by (Cheung) himself and others involved in the crime, the evidences were valid and sufficient. Appellant Cheung Tse-keung's appeal based on insufficient evidence was not established.

With regard to appellant Chen Shu-han . . .

Regarding the smuggling of arms and ammunition:

Appellant Cheung Tse-keung colluded with others to smuggle arms and ammunition to Hong Kong from the Mainland, seriously endangering public safety. The circumstances were serious and according to law, he was found guilty of smuggling arms and ammunition. Appellant Cheung Tse-keung and his defense agent suggested that the smuggling of arms and ammunition charges merged with the kidnapping crime, should not be punished separately, were not based on law and were not accepted.

Regarding illegal trading and concealment of arms and ammunition crimes and concealment of loots:

The first trail judgment confirmed that the facts were clear. Evidence was valid, adequate, and fully established. The appellants' viewpoints were not accepted.

Also, the appellant Cheung Tse-keung's defense lawyer petitioned the court for new evidence regarding the kidnapping and smuggling of arms and ammunition; the appellate collegial court after review is of the opinion that Cheung Tse-keung committed kidnapping and smuggling of arms and ammunition and the crimes were supported by adequate evidence, should be affirmed, and his petition is rejected. Although appellant Cheung Tse-keung has provided evidentiary leads to prosecute Hong Kong residents' crime committed in Hong Kong during the appeal proceeding, the Guangzhou Public Security Bureau confirmed that such evidentiary leads could not be confirmed through investigation and thus not be considered as meritorious service (*ligong*).

Appellants Chen Zhihou, Liang Fei, Qian Han-shou . . . (confession not considered as meritorious service ) . . .

Also . . . Qian Han-shou used . . . fish boat for the commission of crime . . . decision not correct . . . corrected.

### 4. Regarding the basis of law for the appellate court decision:

Guangdong Province's Higher People's Court, having heard the case, made appellate decision in accordance with "Criminal Procedure Law, Article 189 (1) and (2): . . . In accordance with regulations in "Notice regarding the Supreme People's Court authorizing Intermediary People's Court to check and approve certain death punishment cases," ratify the death sentences of five defendants Cheung Tse-keung, Chan Chi-ho, Ma Shan-chung, Liang Fei, and Qian Han-shou. This judgment fully realized the principle of conviction and punishment according to the law, crime, and punishment proportionality principle.

Guangdong Province's Higher People's Court's decision in the case with respect to Cheung Tse-keung and other thirty-six defendants: whether it is with regard to hearing procedures or with substantive decision, has been conducted strictly in accordance with the law, has actualized (the principles of) following the law when existed, enforcing the law with due diligence, holding accountable for law violations, and protecting the dignity of the law.

Thank you very much.

## Notes

1.  The "Big Spender" case provides us with a rare glimpse into how the PRC criminal justice system works in its ideal, though may not be in its typical form. The importance of the case to the political–legal leaders in the PRC—from setting a good example of PRC's commitment to the rule of law to clarifying the principle of "one country, two systems"—assured that everyone involved in the case will be conducting themselves by the book and in the best of form. It is in this limited sense that we can say that the case provides an opportunity to see how the PRC criminal justice works.

2.  Guangdong Province, Guangzhou Municipality People's Procuracy: Indictment — Guangzhou Procuracy First Prosecution—No. 888. (Guangdong Sheng, Guangzhou Renmin Jiancha Yuan: Qixushu—Su Jian Qi Yi Xu—888 hao). ("The Bill of Prosecution") Only those parts pertinent to Cheung Tsekeung were translated in full. (On file at Chinese Law Program, Chinese University of Hong Kong.)

3.  "*Guangdong Sheng Guangzhou Shi, Zhongji Renmin Fayuan, Xingshi Panshu (1998) Wei Zhong Fa Xing Chu Di 468.*" (Guangdong Province, Guangzhou Municipality, Intermediary People's Court, Criminal Verdict [1998] Guangzhou, Intermediary, Legal, Criminal, Initial, No. 468). ("Criminal Judgment"). Published in full in *Ta Kung Pao*, November 13, 1998. The facts revealed by the investigative report of *Next Magazine*, "'Big Spender' Road to Thiefdom" (November 6, 1998, 38–70), agreed with the findings of facts by the PRC Guangzhou Intermediate People's Court in material details.

4.  "*Guangdong Sheng Gaoji Renmin Fayuan, Xingshi Panjue Shu (1998) Yue Gao Fa Xing Zhong Zi Di 1139 Hao. Yuan Gaoxu Jiuan Guangdong Sheng Guanzhou Shi Renmin Jiangcha Yuan.*" (The Higher People's Court of Guangdong Province, Criminal Judgement (1998) Guangzhou High Law (Court) Final No. 1139. Original Public Prosecution Organ Guangdong Municipality People's Procuracy of the Guanzhou Province). ("Appellate Decision"). Reprinted in full in *Wen Hui Bao*, A4, A6.

5.  Unless otherwise specified, all references to PRC laws and regulations were those that were in effect at the time of the trial.

6.  The public security organs do not have the exclusive responsibility to investigate crime. The people's Procuracy and the people's court are also charged with the responsibility to investigate crimes, e.g., economic crimes and official wrongdoings.

7.  Historically and especially during Mao's era, the Communists believed that a crime is only a crime if the "mass" think so. *Selected Works of Mao Tse-Tung*, vol. 1 (Beijing: Foreign Languages Press, 1977), 28. ("The peasants are clear sighted. Who is bad and who is not quite vicious, who deserves severe punishment and who deserves to be let off lightly. The peasants keep clear accounts and very seldom has the punishment exceeded the

crime.") More recently, the PRC police subscribed to the view that criminals cannot long evade the watchful eyes of the community. In the uncovering of crime, the police play only a supplementary role. "*Renmin Jingcha he Zhian Baoweiyuan Ying Jubi de Wuge Tedian*" ["Five Characteristics Possessed by People's Police and Security Committee Member"] (April 6–14, 1956). National meeting to recognize representative models of people's police and security committee members (April 14, 1956); Luo Ruixing, *Lun Renmin Gongan Gongzuo* [Treatise on Public Security Work] (Beijing: Mass Press, 2003), 288–97 esp. 292.

8. Literally speaking, "*li*" is to establish, and "*an*" is a case. "*Lian*" is thus to have a case established.

9. Article 89 of the PRC Criminal Procedure Law.

10. Literally speaking, "*yu*" is to make preparation for and "*sheng*" is to adjudicate.

11. It is interesting to note that the "attitude" of the defendant is of key importance in the investigation, prosecution, adjudication, and correction process. In the Chinese criminal justice system, as reflecting the general culture, one's "attitude" toward one's wrongdoing is important. For example, depending on an offender's attitude (remorse versus defiant, obstructive versus cooperative) he might receive more or less punishment. Such is the case with "*Tan bai cong huan, kang ju cong yan*" (Leniency to those who confess to their crimes and severity to those who refuse to cooperate) is the accepted maxim for criminal investigation, adjudication, and punishment. Guo Xiang, "Comparative Studies of Criminal Policy 'Leniency to Those Who Confess Their Crimes' and Plea Bargain System," *Journal of Hubei University of Police* 6 (2009).

12. Zhen Yuegan and Guan Shuguang, *Gongan Neiqin Gongzuo Shouce* [Public Security Internal Working Manual] (Jingguan Jiaoyu Chubanshe, 1994), 216–22. See "Qixu yijianshu," 218.

13. Literally, "*qi*" is to begin and "*xu*" is to prosecute.

14. Yuegan and Shuguang, *Gongan Neiqin Gongzuo Shouce*, 216–22. See "Qixu yijianshu," 218.

15. "'Big Spender' Road to Thiefdom," 38–70.

16. "TNT Trio Ran Risk of Accidental Detonation," *SCMP*, February 12, 1999, 3.

17. "'Big Spender' Road to Thiefdom," 38–70. See a copy of the "Confidential" memo in *Shida Chao*, no. 15, 1988, 37. (Cheung was forced to be on the run after the HKP issued the memo for his arrest. The article did not reveal when the memo was issued.)

18. Ibid., 54.

19. Lao Tang, *Cheung Tse-keung Zhuan* [Biography of Cheung Tse-keung] (Guangzhou: Huaren Wenhua Chubanshe, 1998), 259. (The news story about Li Kar-shing complaining to Jiang came from Singapore. According to the story, reliable sources in Beijing informed that Li had complained to Jiang about the kidnapping. As a result, Li's case was discussed in the Communist Party Central Politbureau. The story cannot be verified.)

20. I say "fashioned after" because Hong Kong has never been given the right to enjoy full democracy even now. However, first under the British colonial

rule and now with the SAR government, Hong Kong people enjoy a high degree of personal freedom and the right to participate in government affairs.

21. Hong Kong Criminal Procedural Ordinance (Cap. 221) s89.

22. In order not to make work for themselves, police officers everywhere are taught by their training officers or seniors to talk people down; from serious crime to minor incursion or no crime at all. For example, citizens' complaints for pickpockets could easily become lost property and domestic abuses turned into family discords.

23. For a summary specification of charges, see *Ta Kung Pao*, A9. See also "Big Spender Case: The Rest of the Gang," *SCMP*, November 13, 1998.

24. "In the mainland, how many Hong Kong people were convicted?" *Jiusinianda*, July 1987.

25. S. C. Grenville Cross (Director of Public Prosecution), "Letter: Criticism over the Big Spender Case Unfair," *SCMP*, November 4, 1998. (It is a matter of regret that there has been no formal rendition agreement between Hong Kong and the Mainland over the transfer of fugitives or criminal cases.)

26. Article 51 of the Criminal Procedural Law. For a theoretical treatment, see "V. Community Prosecution and Sanction," 253–372. David R. Karp, ed., *Community Justice* (New York: Rowman & Littlefield Publishers, 1998), 3–31.

27. M. R. Dutton, *Policing and Punishment in China* (Cambridge: Cambridge University Press, 1991).

28. Victor Shaw, *Social Control in China* (Westport, CT: Praeger, 1996), 14.

29. In reality, legal limitations on investigative detention are often abused, if not totally ignored. See Kam C. Wong, *Police Reform in China* (New York: Taylor and Francis, 2011), 306 (Extended detention is the norm).

30. Criminal Procedure Law of the People's Republic of China (Adopted by the Second Session of the Fifth N.P.C. on July 1, 1979, and amended pursuant to the decision on amending the Criminal Procedure Law of the People's Republic of China adopted by the Fourth Session of the Eighth N.P.C. on March 17, 1996).

31. Liu Jihua, "Detention and Arrest System Reform and Improvement Proposal," ["拘留逮捕制度改革与完善刍议"] *People's Prosecutorial Semi monthly* 14 (2007): 12–18 (detention of a suspect is based on necessity, emergency, temporality, and proportionality principles), 13R.

32. Article 12: "No person shall be found guilty without being judged as such by a People's Court according to law."

33. Wuhan Law School is known for doing pioneer work on social justice, and more famously providing legal services to the poor. The project was assisted by and otherwise consulted with Professor Lin Li-hung, Director of The Center for Protection for the Rights of Disadvantaged Citizens of Wuhan University, and professors from Hubei Police Officers College and Heinan Public Security College. Zhang Cao, "Investigation Report on Criminal Detention Term Enforced by the Police" ["公安机关实施刑事拘留期限状况调查报告"] *Journal of China Lawyer and Jurist* 6, no. 3 (2007): 1–12.

34. Zhang., Table 10, 11 at 8.

35. It would be of interest to compare samples of detention cases/people with the nondetention ones.

36. In 2006, this author (Wong) has been consulted by Mr. So (an executive manager of a German electronic company) who was detained by public security for over two years, in order to obtain a financial settlement over a contract dispute.

37. The formal arrest of Cheung signified the end of the police investigative phase. On July 21, 1998, the official PRC news agency, the Xinhua News Agency broke the news that the "Big Spender" gang had been arrested and Cheung had confessed. *Tian Di* [Heaven-Earth], no. 48, January 1999, 90.

38. For an account of the police interrogation of Cheung, see *Tian Di*, chap., 85–90. (Cheung was arrested on January 25, 1998 and interrogated on January 26, 1998. He did not disclose his true name or address until the middle of June 1998.)

39. For a discussion of PRC investigative detention power, see Kam C. Wong, "Sheltering for Examination (Shoushen) in the People's Republic of China: Law, Policy, and Practices," *Occasional Papers/Reprints Series in Contemporary Asian Studies* (School of Law, University of Maryland), no. 3 (1997): 1–140 esp. 26–30.

40. Cheung was not a common criminal. He was the target of an investigation (secret case file coded "9810") coordinated by the Ministry of Public Security from Beijing. Cheung's identity and characteristics were known in advance to the interagency work group consisting of MPS, Ministry of State Security, and Guangdong Province Public Security Bureau. *Tian Di*, 65. More significantly, it was clear that the PRC interrogators were certain of Cheung's identity, notwithstanding his less-than-effective denial, as early as January 26, 1998. Ibid., 86.

41. At the time of the arrest, the PRC police had accumulated a substantial amount of information bearing upon Cheung and his gang's personal background and criminal activities. In fact, there was a war room dedicated to the "Big Spender" case investigation with a lady officer in charge of records and documentations of the "Big Spender" gang. There were eighty volumes of files, two meters high. Ibid., 70.

42. On April 10, 1998, one of the gang members, Cheung Chi-fung, began to confess and identified Cheung as the leader of the criminal gang. Ibid., 87.

43. See also Article 97 of PRC Criminal Procedure Law (1979). If a crime has been committed and the evidence is found to be sufficient, a public prosecution will be initiated under Article 143 of the PRC Criminal Procedure Law (1979) with a Bill of Prosecution.

44. See Editorial Committee, *Prosecutor Manual* [Jianchaguan Shouce] (Shanxi: Shanxi Renmin Chubanshe, 1995), 79–80.

45. The data is extracted and translated from the Bill of Prosecution. Only those portions related to Cheung's criminality are reported.

46. Cheung was charged with some and not for all the offenses appearing in the Bill of Prosecution. The Bill of Prosecution details *all* charges applicable to every defendant in the "Big Spender" case.

47. The Bill of Prosecution, 9.

48. Quanguo Renmin Dahui Changwu Weiyuanhui "*Guangyu Chengzhi Zousi Zui de Baochong Guiding*" (Adopted on January 21, 1998, at the 26th

Meeting of the Sixth NPC Standing Committee. Promulgated on January 21, 1998, by Order No. 62 of the President of the PRC). Article 1 of the said regulations provides in pertinent part: "Whoever smuggles in opium and drugs, weapons and ammunition, or counterfeit currency shall be punished to fixed term imprisonment of not less than seven years and shall also be fined or sentenced to confiscation of property; if circumstances are particularly serious shall be sentenced to imprisonment for life or death; if circumstances are minor, he shall be sentenced to fixed term imprisonment of not more than seven years and fined."

49.    Article 12 of PRC Criminal Law provides: "If an act committed after the founding of the People's Republic of China and before the entry into force of this law was not deemed a crime under the laws at the time, those laws shall apply . . . However, if according to this Law the act is not deemed a crime or is subject to lighter punishment, this law shall apply."

50.    Quanguo Renmin Dahui Changwu Weiyuanhui "Guangyu Yancheng Guaimai, Banjia Funu, Ertong de Fanzui Fenzi de Jueding" de Baochong Guiding" (Adopted on September 4, 1991, at the 21st Meeting of the Seventh NPC Standing Committee). Article 2(3) provides: "Whoever kidnaps others for the purpose of extorting money, shall be punished in accordance with item 1." Item 1 to Article 2 provides: "Whoever (kidnaps) for the purpose of selling . . . shall be sentenced to fixed term imprisonment of not less than 10 years to life imprisonment, and also fine of not more than $10,000 or confiscation of property; if circumstances are particularly serious shall be sentenced to death and confiscation of property."

There was no kidnapping offense in the old PRC Criminal Law (1979). The only kidnapping-related provision was that of Article 141: "Whoever abducted people for sale should be sentenced to fixed term imprisonment of not more than five years; if the circumstances were serious, should be sentenced to fixed term imprisonment of more than five years." "Decision Regarding Severe Punishment of Criminals Abducting for Purposes of Trafficking and Kidnapping of Female and Young Children" was the first time that kidnapping charge appeared and only as an incidental provision appended to a larger broader scheme. Until then, the preoccupation of the country was with the abduction of females and kids for sales. Cui Nam-san (Editor-in-Chief), *Xingshi Fanzui Anli Congshu: Guaimai Renkou zui* [Series on Criminal Cases: Regarding Abduction for Sales Crime] (Beijing: Zhongguo jiangcha chubanshe, 1991), 12 (Between 1980 and the first half of 1983 abduction for sale of people was a major concern, e.g., abduction grew 500 percent between 1984 and 1992.) Later, in the 1980s and 1990s, the preoccupation was with kidnapping one as hostage to resolve commercial disputes. See Legal Policy Research of the Supreme People's Procuracy, *Practical Interpretation to Amended Criminal Law Provisions* [Xiuding Xingfa Tiaowen Shiyong Jiesuo] (Beijing: Zhongguo Jiancha Chubanshe, 1997), 317 (Interpretative note to Article 239).

51.    Article 239 of the PRC Criminal Law provides: "Whoever kidnaps another person for the purpose of extorting money or property or kidnaps another person as a hostage shall be sentenced to fixed term imprisonment of not less than 10 years or life imprisonment and also to a fine or confiscation of property; if he causes death to the kidnapped person or kills the

kidnapped person, he shall be sentenced to death and also to confiscation of property."

52.     Article 69 of the PRC Criminal Law provides: "For a criminal who commits several crimes before a judgment is pronounced, unless he is sentenced to death or life imprisonment, his term of punishment shall be not more than the total of the terms of all the crimes but not less than the longest of the terms for the crimes, depending on the circumstances of the crimes. However, . . . the term of criminal detention may not exceed the maximum of one year, and fixed term imprisonment may not exceed the maximum of 20 years . . ." Article 69 is identical to Article 64 of the PRC Criminal Law (1979).

53.     Article 25 of the PRC Criminal Law provides: "A joint crime refers to an intentional crime committed by two or more persons jointly." There are three elements to the offense: (1) Subject (*zhuti*) must be committed by two or more persons with criminal responsibility (Article 17—age, Article 18—mental capacity); (2) Subjective intent (*zhuguan*)—knowingly and purposively (Article 12); (3) Objective conditions (*keguan*)—joint offenders working separately but toward an agreed-upon common goal. See Legal Policy Research of the Supreme People's Procuracy, *Practical Interpretation to Amended Criminal Law Provisions*, 198 (Interpretative note to Article 151), 30. See also exposition on Editorial Committee, *Judges Manual* [Faguan Shouce] (Shanxi: Shanxi Renmin Chubanshe, 1995) (Judicial officials must determine whether evidence bears a logical relationship with alleged facts in the case), 63.

54.     Article 26 (para. 1) of the PRC Criminal Law provides: "A principal criminal refers to any person who organizes and leads a criminal group in carrying out criminal activities or plays a principal role in a joint crime." Historically, PRC justice officials have looked upon "principal offender" with grave concern. For a policy statement over the treatment of a principal criminal, see Supreme People's Court, Supreme People's Procuracy, MPS: "Clarification on actual legal application issues regarding the current handling of criminal gang cases" (Zui Gao Renmin Fayuan, Zui Gao Renmin Jianchayuan, Gongan Bao, "Guanyu danqian chuli jituan fanzui anjian zhong de juti yingyong falu de rugan wenti de jieda") (June 15, 1984). (Question 4: In dealing with criminal gangs in major case and joint offenders to major crimes, how to implement party policy and provide for differential treatment? "In handling the above two kinds of cases, should handle them differently, based on the status of the criminal in the criminal activities, his role and degree of harm, and in accordance with party policy, criminal law, and related NPC Standing Committee's rules and decisions. Ringleader to criminal gang and principal offender to regular joint serious crime should be severely punished according to law. In cases of special seriousness, they should be executed to pacify the public emotion.") See Editorial Committee, *Compendium of PRC Public Security Law* (Jinlin: Jilin Renmin Chubanshe, 1995), 712.

55.     Article 26 (para. 4) of the PRC Criminal Law provides: "Any principal criminal not included in Paragraph 3 (ringleader of permanent criminal group) shall be punished on the basis of all the crimes that he participates in or that he organizes or directs."

56. The PRC has repeatedly claimed that how she had treated her nationals, including Hong Kong residents, is a domestic and internal affair. However, this does not obviate the fact that the Joint Declaration is an international treaty, the breach of which attracts international condemnation if not even sanction. See, for example, the "right of abode" case. Simon Macklin, "Britain Defend Right to Comment," *SCMP*, February 13, 1999. (A spokesman for British Prime Minister Tony Blair has hit back at a statement from the Chinese Foreign Ministry that suggested Britain had no right to comment on the Court of Final Appeal ruling in this case. Prime Minister Blair insisted that Britain has not only a right, but also an obligation to comment on legal developments in China affecting Hong Kong residents because Britain is a party to the Joint Declaration.)

57. Shenzhen is the city across the northern border of Hong Kong.

58. See Editorial Committee, *Prosecutor Manual*, 79.

59. Cui Min and Zhang Wen-qing, *The Theory and Practice of Criminal Evidence* [Xingshi Zhengju de Lilun yu Shijian] (Beijing: Zhongguo renmin gongan daxue chubanshe, 1992), 42. (Evidence establishing the defendant's guilt must bear a necessary relationship with alleged criminal facts in the case.) See Editorial Committee, *Judges Manual*, 244.

60. See Legal Policy Research of the Supreme People's Procuracy, *Practical Interpretation*, 198 (Interpretative note to Article 151), 182.

61. Ibid., 181. (Interpretative note to Article 151; "Weapon" means various kinds of guns and cannons with great destructive powers.)

62. Ju Yong-chun (Editor-in-Chief), *Xingshi Fanzui Anli Congshu: Youguan Qiangzhi, Tanyao, Baozhawu de Fanzui* [Series on Criminal Cases: Regarding Crimes of Arms, Ammunition, Explosives) (Beijing: Zhongguo jiangcha chubanshe, 1992), 1–2.

63. See Legal Policy Research of the Supreme People's Procuracy, *Practical Interpretation*, 193 (Interpretative note to Article 151).

64. Ju Yong-chun (Editor-in-Chief), *Xingshi Fanzui Anli Congshu: Youguan Qiangzhi, Tanyao, Baozhawu de Fanzui*, 25.

65. See Criminal Judgment.

66. Published in full in *Ta Kung Pao*. The facts revealed by the investigative report of *Next Magazine* "'Big Spender' Road to Thiefdom," 38–70 agreed with the findings of facts by the PRC Guangzhou Intermediate People's Court in material and substantial details. It is most likely that the *Next Magazine* extracted such facts from the opinion and/or obtained firsthand information from paid (official) informants.

67. The Procuratorate officials are allowed to avoid registering the victim's name in the record if it is going to harm the victim's reputation. See Editorial Committee, *Prosecutor Manual*, 82.

68. See "Defense in Criminal Litigation" (*Xingshi xusong zhong de bianhu*) in Editorial Committee, *Judges Manual* (The accused and his defender are allowed to present material and viewpoint to show that the accused is innocent or deserves to be punished less. Particularly, he has a right to: (1) participate in court investigation and hearing, including confronting witness; (2) participate in court argument; and (3) appeal the case), 243.

69. The defense challenged the Guangzhou Intermediary People's Court's jurisdiction under Article 6 of the PRC Criminal Law: "This Law shall be

applicable to anyone who commits a crime within the territory . . . of the People's Republic of China, except as otherwise specially provided by law . . . If a criminal act or its consequence takes place within the territory . . . of the People's Republic of China, the crime shall be deemed to have been committed within the territory . . . of the People's Republic of China." The defense argued that Article 18 of the Basic Law precluded PRC Criminal Law from being applied to HKSAR, i.e., reaching Cheung's criminal acts in Hong Kong.

70. Jerome Alan Cohen, *The Criminal Process in the PRC 1949–1968* (Harvard University Press, 1968), 30. For a practical application of such a principle, see Bao Ruo-Wang and Rudolph Chelminski, *Prisoner of Mao* (New York: Coward, McCann & Geoghegan, 1973), 33. In every police *yushen* interrogation room, the sign *"tan bai cong huan, kang ju cong yan"* is prominently displayed. See Margret Ng, "Endangered by Lack of Action on Suspect Law," *SCMP*, November 20, 1998 (Xinhua photo interrogation room).

71. Ruo-Wang and Chelminski, *Prisoner of Mao*, 73. In the PRC context, the attitude of the offender is closely observed and meticulously recorded. Yuegan and Shuguang, *Gongan Neiqin Gongzuo Shouce*, 218 (During the preliminary examination, the officer should pay attention and record the offender's confession attitude (*yingzui biaoxian*). Attitude of an offender has always made a difference on how an aggrieved victim or a harmed society reacts to a transgression. A regretful and apologetic offender is viewed differently than a nonremorseful and resentful one. The former is a repentant offender, ready to be reintegrated. A repentant offender pacifies the victim (fulfilling retribution needs) and assures the society (serving deterrence functions). The latter is a defiant offender, ready to strike again. A defiant offender aggravates the victim (exciting revenge) and challenges the society (calling for defensive measures). Erving Goffman's extensive study of the interaction in the public place suggested that when expectations and norms were broken in the public place, the rule breaker and the victim were forced to confront each other in a series of negotiations over how to fix the problem for the purpose of reestablishing social control, a process which Goffman termed "remedial exchanges." See Erwin Goffman, *Relations in Public* (New York: Harpers, 1971), 108–18. There are two parts to remedial exchanges for a public wrong: accounting and apology by the offender.

72. Article 57 of the Criminal Law (1979) provides: "In determining punishment for the criminal, (the court) should consider the nature and circumstances of the crime and the degree of harm to the society in accordance with this law."

73. Zui Gao Renmin Fayuan, Zui Gao Renmin Jianchayuan, Gongan Bao, "*Guanyu danqian chuli zishou he youguan wenti juti yingyong falu jieshi*" (April 16, 1984). Interpretation of related issues regarding current treatment of surrendering (Question 5: How to apply "Leniency to those Who Confess?"). See Editorial Committee, *Compendium of PRC Public Security Law*, 71.

74. Zui Gao Renmin Fayuan, Zui Gao Renmin Jianchayuan, Gongan Bao, "*Guanyu danqian chuli zishou he youguan wenti juti yingyong falu jieshi*" (April 16, 1984). Interpretation of related issues regarding current

treatment of surrendering (Question 1: What is surrendering? It must be voluntary. He must confess to all his crimes. He must inform upon the codefendants.) See Editorial Committee, *Compendium of PRC Public Security Law*, 71.

75. The author served with the HKP in the late 1960s and early 1970s. He has taught many serving officers, including CIDs.

76. This is separate from the evidentiary question of whether the act of confession, especially to a nonactionable crime, is probative of voluntariness and thus reform-mindedness. There is some indication that only certain acts qualified under Article 67, for example, a new crime not known to the police, suffice under Article 67.

77. In their haste to assert HKSAR's judicial autonomy, the defenders of Hong Kong's legal and criminal justice system failed to address this most critical issue and insisted that all criminal activities in Hong Kong are within the exclusive jurisdiction of the Hong Kong courts. Likewise, in the rush to demonstrate the reliability of the "one country, two systems" framework, the PRC judicial authority has been quick to give off the impression that nothing that happened in Hong Kong is ever of interest to the PRC. Both sides neglect that crime as a social activity has little respect for state boundary, either in its causation and/or effect.

78. The issue turns out to be how to construe "autonomy" and "interference." Does "autonomy" preclude benevolent assistance? Is benevolent assistance, interference? This recalls the debate about punishment in the United States, namely, is paternalistic rehabilitation of prisoners a kind of punishment? Ultimately from whose perspective are we to understand the term "interference"? See discussion of "Introduction" to Part III "The Socialized Juvenile Court" in Frederic L. Faust and Paul J. Brantingham, *Juvenile Justice Philosophy*, 2nd ed. (St. Paul, MN: West Publishing, 1979), 139–46. (Socialization of juvenile court deprived the juveniles of their constitutional rights).

79. Personal conversation with Ivan Tang, October 27, 1998, Radio Television Hong Kong.

80. "The burden of proof required in a particular type of case, as in a criminal case where the prosecution has the standard (i.e., burden) of proof beyond a reasonable double . . ." Henry Campbell Black, *Black's Law Dictionary* (St. Paul, MN: West Publishing, 1983), 30R.

81. In the United States, reasonable suspicion (*Terry v. Ohio* [1967] stop and frisk), probable cause (Fourth Amendment), preponderance of evidence (civil litigation), and beyond a reasonable double (criminal trial).

82. Cui Min and Wen-qing, *Theory and Practice of Criminal Evidence*, 90.

83. Ibid., 86 (Evidentiary requirement is made depending on stages of criminal justice process as reflecting the incremental accumulation of evidence and correspondently increases the certainty of guilt. In terms of evidence, proof, and guilt, the point to note here is that unlike in the common law system where a person is considered innocent until proven guilty, during trial, China adopts no innocent-until-proven guilty proposition, but rather believes in "cumulative guilt," literally as one moves along the conveyor belt of justice, a person is more guilty from one day to the next, until at the day of the trial his guilt is all but determined. The trial is really

a "degradation" ceremony, to confirm more so than to dispute a finding of guilt.)

84.  Min and Wen-qing, *Theory and Practice of Criminal Evidence*, 85. (The degree of "proof requirement" is elastic and depends on the kinds of case and circumstances.)

85.  See PRC Criminal Procedure Law, chap. 6, esp. Article 55. See also Wang Fa-rong and others, *Chinese Civil Litigation Study* [Zhongguo Minshi Shenpan Xue] (Beijing: Falu Chubanshe, 1991), chap. 15; "Burden of Proof in People's Courts" (*Renmin Fayuan de zhengming zeren*), 182ff.

86.  See "Hearing on Public Prosecution Case," Editorial Committee, *Judges Manual*, 258–59.

87.  Article 42 of PRC Criminal Procedure Law provides: "All facts that prove the true circumstances of a case shall be evidence. There shall be the following seven categories of evidence: (1) material evidence and documentary evidence; (2) testimony of witnesses; (3) statements of victims; (4) statements and exculpation of criminal suspects or defendants; (5) expert conclusion; (6) records of inquests and examination; and (7) audio visual materials. . . ." Evidence to be admissible must be objective (*keguan*), i.e., corresponding to objective reality, relevant (*guanlian*), i.e., evidence bearing some relationship with the facts of the case, and legal (*hefa*), i.e., evidence must be obtained by legal process. Min and Wen-qing, *Theory and Practice of Criminal Evidence*, 36–67.

88.  There is no specific burden of proof ("[Latin. *Onus probandi*] In the law of evidence, the necessity or duty of affirmatively proving a fact or facts in dispute on an issue . . ." Black, *Black's Law Dictionary*, 102R.) Provisions in the PRC Criminal Procedure Law. Article 43 of the PRC Criminal Procedure Law provides: "Judges, procurators and investigator must, in accordance with the legally prescribed process, collect various kinds of evidence that can prove the criminal suspect's or defendant's guilt or innocence and the gravity of his crime . . ." This is identical to Article 32 of the PRC Criminal Procedure Law (1979).

The burden of proof in PRC courts follows Article 20 of the Soviet Criminal Procedure Code. Specifically: (1) The prosecution has the burden of proof (*zhengming zheren*) to establish the facts pointing to guilt; more appropriately to establish the *truth* of the matter. (2) The public security, Procuratorate, and judicial officials have an affirmative duty to collect evidence both for and against the defendant's innocence, i.e., uncovering the *whole* truth. (3) The defense has no burden of proof as to his innocence. (4) The defense has a right to assert and prove his innocence or entitlement to lesser punishment. Min and Wen-qing, *Theory and Practice of Criminal Evidence*, 15, 95–96. See Harold J. Berman, *Justice in the U.S.S.R.* (New York: Random House, 1963), 366. (Soviet court process was paternalistic in nature and designed to protect the citizens. Pretrial and trial procedures were designed to uncover the whole history of the situation.)

More generally, the defense has a duty to cooperate with a criminal investigation, including the volunteering of information, production of evidence, answering of pertinent questions, submitting to examination, and ultimately admitting to guilt and accepting responsibility. In this regard, Article 48 of the PRC Criminal Procedure Law provides in pertinent part: "All those who have information about a case shall have the duty to testify . . ." The command to cooperate with investigation of a crime does not draw a distinction between criminal defendants or regular citizens. PRC judicial authorities consider it more important to seek the truth than protecting the rights of defendants. Article 6 of the PRC Criminal Procedure Law provides that: "In concluding criminal proceedings, the People's Courts, the People's Procuratorates and the public security . . . base themselves on facts and take law as the criteria . . ." The PRC judicial authorities further believe that facts are paramount in reflecting the truth. Simply put, it is a basic principle in criminal investigation to "*shishi quishi*" ("seek truth from facts"). Ibid., 8. Given this mentality, it is odd to allow anyone with information to crime, including the defendant, to withhold such information in obstructing the search for truth and justice. Article 45 of the Criminal Procedure Law thus provides in pertinent part: "The People's Courts, the People's Procuratorates and the public security organs shall have the authority to collect or obtain evidence from the units or individuals concerned. The units or individuals concerned shall provide truthful evidence. . . ." Conversely, there is no right to remain silent for a criminal defendant, as in the United States. U.S. Constitution, Amendment V: "No person . . . shall be compelled in any criminal case to be a witness against himself." See "Self-Incrimination" in John Kaplan, Jerome H. Skolnick, and Malcolm M. Feeley, *Criminal Justice* (New York: The Foundation Press, 1991), 217–55. (The privilege against self-incrimination in American law dates from the Massachusetts Body of Liberties of 1641 and the Connecticut Code of 1650). Article 93 of the PRC Criminal Procedure Law provides that in pertinent part: "The criminal suspect shall answer the investigators' questions truthfully, but he shall have the right to refuse to answer any questions that are irrelevant to the case." Nor, is there a right to refuse answering questions based on fear of self-incrimination. Ibid., 34.

89. Article 46 of the PRC Criminal Procedure Law provides that: "In the decision of all cases, stress shall be laid on evidence, investigation and study; credence shall not be readily given to oral statements. A defendant cannot be found guilty and sentenced to a criminal punishment if there is only his statement but no evidence . . ."

90. Guangdong Province, Higher People's Court reached a final verdict and was reprinted in full in *Wen Hui Bao*, A4, A6. "*Guangdong Sheng Gaoji Renmin Fayuan, Xingshi Panjue Shu (1998) Yue Gao Fa Xing Zhong Zi Di 1139 Hao. Yuan Gaoxu Jiuan Guangdong Sheng Guanshou Shi Remin Jiancha Yuan.*" (The Higher People's Court of Guangdong Province, Criminal Judgment (1998) Guangzhou High Law (Court) Final No. 1139. Original Public Prosecution Organ Guangdong Municipality People's Procuracy of the Guangdong Province).

91. See "Public Statement of Higher People's Court of Guangdong Province" by the Director of Court (*Ting Zhang*) Lu Botao, reprinted in full *Wen Hui Bao*, November 13, 1998, A4.

92. Article 199 of the PRC Criminal Procedure Law provides: "Death sentences shall be subject to approval by the Supreme People's Court." The PRC Supreme People's Court has approved of the death sentence. Ibid.

93. Article 184 of the PRC Criminal Law provides: "If a defendant . . . files an appeal through the People's Court, which originally tried the case, the people's Court shall within three days transfer the petition of appeal together with the case file and the evidence to the People's Court at the next level . . ."

94. Article 187 of the PRC Criminal Procedure Law provides: "A People's Court of second instance shall form a collegial panel . . ."

95. Article 187 of the Criminal Procedure Law provides: "A People's Court of second instance shall form a collegial panel and open a court session to hear a case of appeal. However, if after consulting the case file, interrogating the defendant and heeding the opinions of the other parties, defenders and agent ad litem, the collegial panel thinks the criminal facts are clear, it may open no court session."

    Procedurally, there are three ways the People's Court of the second instance can conduct the hearing on appeal: (1) review on record (*shumian shenli*); (2) questioning the defendant (*tishen bigao ren*); and (3) hearing in open court (*kaiting shenli*). Cheung's case was disposed of in the second way, which is also the most popular one. "Criminal case hearing of the second instance procedure" (*xingshi dier shen chengxu*). Editorial Committee, *Judges Manual*.

96. Guiguo Wang and Priscilla M. F. Leung, "One Country, Two Systems: Theory into Practice," *Pacific Rim Law & Policy Journal* 7 (1998): 279.

97. H. L. Fu, "Battle of Criminal Jurisdictions," *Hong Kong Law Journal* 28 (1998): 273.

98. Ann D. Jordon, "Lost in the Translation: Two Legal Cultures, the Common Law Judiciary and the Basic Law of the Hong Kong Special Administrative Region," *Cornell International Law Journal* 30 (1997): 335.

99. Mark Findlay, "*Show Trials in China*: After Tiananmen Square," Law and Society 16, no. 3 (1989): 352 (Criminal justice process used to legitimize military suppression); "Opinion: Show Trial in Chins," New York Times, December 12, 1995. ("China's leaders want to make an example of Mr. Wei, who has already suffered more than 14 years' imprisonment for advocating political freedom. Their goal is to intimidate the intellectuals who began speaking out again on human rights issues earlier this year.")

    David Rennie, "Corruption Thrives in China Despite the Show Trials," *Telegraph*, December 2000. ("Cheng Kejie, the most senior official to die for corruption in communist Chinese history, was convicted of taking more than £3 million in bribes," in a highly publicized trial to set an example for others.)

100. Doctrinally, Communist China is a propaganda state, meaning it used propaganda to control as well as to educate people. Franz Schurmann, *Ideology and Organization in Communist China* (Berkeley: University of California Press, 1966); David Shambaugh, "China's Propaganda System: Institutions, Processes and Efficacy," *The China Journal* 57 (2007): 25–58.

101. Anthony Spaeth, "The State v. Big Spender," *Time*, November 9, 1998. ("If Hong Kongers start getting prosecuted in China for crimes committed in their own territory, the two systems become indistinguishable. . . . Even more troubling is suspicion that Cheung is being prosecuted in China precisely because of its swifter courts and tougher justice.") (Hong Kong

does not have the death penalty, for example; China does.) The kidnapped victims' families, who have good connections in Beijing, have been conspicuously uncooperative with HKP. http://www.time.com/time/world/article/0,8599,2053882,00.html#ixzz1SYftZHON

102. *"You fa ke yi, you fa bi yi, wei fa bi gou."*

103. Not the same as "innocence until proven guilty" but "incremental guilt," or as the Chinese put it "seeking truth from facts." See Timothy A. Gelatt, "The People's Republic of China and the Presumption of Innocence," *The Journal of Criminal Law and Criminology* 73, no. 1 (1982): 259–316.

104. The "Big Spender" case recalled another showcase trial of the century, that of the "Gang of Four" trial of 1980. David Bonavia, *VERDICT IN PEKING: The Trial of the Gang of Four* (New York: Putnam's Sons/Don Mills (Ontario): General Publishing, 1984). (The testimonies and verdicts are preprogrammed.) While the CCP still maintained, decades later that the "Gang of Trial" marked a turning point in Communist China justice administration wherein legality was placed before politics and rule by (or of) law above rule of man, many people within and without China, were quick to point out nothing much have changed with the core mission and operational style of the Chinese justice system. To outsiders and especially to foreign observers, the "Gang of Four" was a political trial, from the beginning to the end. For a classical rendition of CCP's position, see Li Hai-wen (Division Three, Central Party History Research Office) "The Trials of the LIN Biao Clique and the Gang of Four and Their Historical Lessons," *Contemporary China History Studies* 5 (2001) 10. As "show trials" the only difference between the "Gang of Four" and "Big Spender" is perhaps the fact that in the "Gang of Four" trial, the CCP was not able to script the role and control the conduct of the defendants, allowing the defendants to use the widely publicized forum to challenge the legitimacy of the CCP and legality of the proceeding, in persecuting them, notwithstanding the legal proceedings. For example, Jiang Qing's defiant outbursts and Zhang Chunqiao's deadly silence revealed to the public much more than the "show trial" was willing to expose.

105. Danny Gittings, "Changing Expectations: How the Rule of Law Fared in the First Decade of the Hong Kong SAR," *Hong Kong Law Journal* 3 (2007).

# 4

# One Country, Two Systems

### The "Big Spender" as a Test Case

As observed, the "Big Spender" case is the first legal case in China to test the limits of "one country, two systems." More particularly, it is the first time a Hong Kong legal resident was arrested, prosecuted, tried, and convicted in China under the PRC Criminal Law for criminal acts largely perpetrated in Hong Kong.

Before the "Big Spender Case," there were press reports of Hong Kong residents being tried and convicted in China for committing crimes inside China.[1] For example, Shenzhen government data showed that from 1981 to September 1983 the Shenzhen People's Armed Police handled 60 cases involving foreigners and arrested 105 Hong Kong residents. Between January 1983 and November 1983, Shenzhen public security and judicial officials uncovered 4,000 odd cases of smuggling offenses involving Hong Kong residents with 70 Hong Kong residents being arrested and prosecuted. The most famous political cases were the arrests of Wu Zhongren in March of 1981 for counter-revolutionary activities and Liu Qing-shan in December 1981 for sympathizing with dissidents. None of these involve crimes committed in Hong Kong, but prosecuted in China.

There were also official reports of Hong Kong resident fugitives being returned to Hong Kong for prosecution and trial.[2] Finally, there were anecdotal accounts of Mainland fugitives being expatriated as illegal immigrants.[3] This is, however, never reported in the news or documented officially.

There is much difficulty in ascertaining whether the "Big Spender Case" is the first of its kind in which a Hong Kong resident was punished in a PRC court for crimes committed in Hong Kong. Obtaining official information on how cross-border crimes have been handled by the HKSAR government turned out to be more difficult than expected. Initially, the HKP promised cooperation. In the course of research,

101

HKP was nevertheless reluctant to provide this researcher with needed data—rules and practices dealing with cross-border crime and the statistics and facts of PRC–SAR police cooperation cases on grounds of confidentiality (Official's Secret Law)[4] and privacy (Data Privacy Act.)[5] Later, after rounds of discussion on the phone and with a letter of "Request of Information for Academic Research," the police supplied data on PRC–HK official requests for assistance.[6] The HKP still declined to supply data regarding police regulations and procedures because "they are operationally related . . . not made available to the public."[7]

The secretary for security was more forthcoming with the requested information. Letter on "Request of Information for Academic Research" to Senior Assistant Solicitor General asking for information relating to police cooperation and judicial assistance in Mainland/HKSAR cross-border crimes was referred to Mrs. C. Willis, secretary for security office, for further action. On December 28, 1998, the secretary for security provided the following information in English and in Chinese: "LegCo Panel on Security: Arrangements with Mainland on Surrender of Fugitive Offenders" (December 3, 1998); "LegCo Panel on Security, LegCo Panel on Constitutional Affairs, LegCo Panel on Administration of Justice and Legal Services: Cross-Border Co-operation in Criminal Matters" (June 4, 1996); "LegCo Panel on Security, LegCo Panel on Administration of Justice and Legal Services: Cross-Border Co-operation on Legal and Judicial Matters" (January 29, 1996); "LegCo Panel on Security, LegCo Panel on Administration of Justice and Legal Services: Cross-Border Co-operation in Legal and Judicial Matters" (January 29, 1996); "Information Paper on: Legal and Procedural Co-operation in the Civil and Commercial Field between Hong Kong and Mainland China" (May 1996). The secretary for security, however, did not see it fit to release any information that is not already on public record.

There is anecdotal evidence suggesting that some Hong Kong residents were returned to China to stand trial for crimes committed outside Mainland China, e.g., in Macau. One Chinese newspaper confirmed that:

> Over time, we have arrested 60 suspected criminals, including [those engaging in] smuggling, financial offence, corruption and bribery, illegal immigration, murder, robbery and kidnapping, from 30 odd countries, including United States, Canada, Russia and Hong Kong-Macau-Taiwan regions.[8]

If this PRC press report is to be believed, there were indeed some Hong Kong residents being prosecuted in China for crimes committed outside of China, e.g., Taiwan–Macau–Hong Kong. For example, in October of 1980, seven armed robbers robbed an armored car of Nan Tung Bank in Macau for HK$1.416 million, Macau$170,000, and nine checks totaling HK$1.8 million. The robbers killed a bank officer in the process. The principal offenders, Zhou Tie-sheng and Jiang Timei, both Hong Kong residents, escaped to Guangzhou and were arrested there. In August 1983, the Guangzhou Intermediary People's Court sentenced Zhou to death and Jiang to fifteen years of imprisonment. They appealed against their sentences unsuccessfully. On October 19, 1983, Zhou was executed in Zhuhai.[9] This case raised similar cross-border crime legal issues as those of the "Big Spender Case," i.e., the extraterritorial reach of PRC Criminal Law. The case is, however, distinguishable from the Cheung Tse-keung's case in one major respect, i.e., Zhou Tie-sheng and Jiang Timei did not commit a crime in Hong Kong. At this point of time, Macau was still a colony of Portugal. Hong Kong residents were thus not protected by the Basic Law of Hong Kong. However, the critical observation here is that the PRC has tried and convicted Hong Kong residents in PRC courts for crimes committed outside China.[10]

## Test Case Explained

Before we move on, we need to determine what a "test case" is. To say that the "Big Spender" is a test case is to say that it is a case chosen to test the limits (applicability) or clarify the meaning (interpretation) of an established legal principle or rule of law, e.g., the meaning of "a high degree of autonomy." According to U.S. Legal Definitions:

> A test case is a lawsuit that is brought to test the legality of a law or legal principle. It is usually chosen as representative of a similar factual situation that exists in other pending cases involving the same issues. Test cases are limited by the case or controversy doctrine which prohibits parties from bringing collusive suits before the court.
>
> The purpose of a test case is to set a legal precedent. Under the legal practice of following precedents, the outcome of the case will be a model for determining other cases that apply the law or legal principle at issue to a similar set of facts.[11]

According to Child Poverty Action Group (CPAG), test cases are mounted to:

1. Deter unlawful administrative practice and lead to improvements in this area.
2. Lead to improvement in standards of adjudication.
3. Highlight the improved standards of adjudication.
4. Generate publicity for CPAG and promote the aims of the organization.
5. Promote an interpretation of the law that maximizes benefits to claimants.
6. Highlight injustices and help build pressure to remedy these, even if the case is not actually won.[12]

The "Big Spender" case is technically not a "test case" since it is not mounted by interested parties to challenge the law proactively and deliberately as a policy "where the outcome will have significance not only for the person bringing it but for others too. It seeks a ruling on an untested point of law or seeks to overturn or confirm a prevailing judicial interpretation." Nevertheless, it has all the attributes of a test case and can be treated as such.

## Taking Issues with Test Cases

The qualities that make for a good test case—publicity, sensationalism, controversy—also detract from critical analysis, studied reflection, rational debate, and informed discussion of important and complicated social or political problems.[13] Such has been Hong Kong's experience with the "Big Spender" debate. The "Big Spender" debate was carried on with very little information on the factual circumstances of the case. Long before all the facts were known, pro-Hong Kong advocates were arguing that the PRC has no right to try the case. Without a full investigation and comprehensive understanding of PRC and HKSAR police, and cooperative and judicial assistance in cross-border crime, the same advocates were arguing that the PRC had intended on interfering with HKSAR's autonomy.

There is also the question whether the "Big Spender Case" was a good test case to test the outer limits of "one country, two systems." More often than not, controversial test cases presented themselves not as a matter of choice; they entered into the public discourse by force of circumstances. The sensational nature of the "Big Spender Case" aroused people's passion reaching into their guarded consciousness. However, public awareness of a case is only a necessary but not sufficient condition for a test case to be successful in changing public attitude, and in time government law and policy. Public debate and legislative advocacy are also required.

As public interest advocates, public intellectuals and political elites can do much to set the direction, define the issues, provide the framework for analysis, and influence the outcome of a test case. First, as moderators of public debate, they can do much to shape public-discourse. Second, as gatekeepers, they can pick the right case to present the issues and advance their political agenda. Third, as advocates, they can set the tone, text, and emotion of the public discourse.

The problem with using the Cheung Tse-keung as a test case over "one country, two systems" is that what made for a good test case in the first place, i.e., sensationalism, also "stacked the deck" in favor of the PRC; the public wanted substantive justice done, i.e., speedy trial and severe punishment for Cheung in China, not procedural justice preserved, i.e., maintaining the jurisdictional integrity of Hong Kong courts. In this regard, Cheung Tse-keung though charismatic and like-able was not easy to be sympathized and identified with. Some have even said that Cheung resembled a modern-day Robin Hood who robbed the rich (which is appealing to most) without giving to the poor (which is objectionable to many). One must ask, in "picking"[14] the "Big Spender Case" to advocate for the legal autonomy of Hong Kong, was the decision ill-advised?

## News Coverage

### Hong Kong

All major newspapers in Hong Kong made the "Big Spender Verdict" *the* major news event for the day. On November 12, 1998, *Ming Bao Daily News* devoted nearly all its domestic sections to the reporting of the verdict. Particularly, page A1 was for advertisement, page A2 was on Cheung's verdict, page A3 was on Cheung's family background, page A4 was on the legality of the trial, page A5 was on reactions of Cheung's family, page A11 was on an expert's opinion on Cheung's criminality, page A12 was on the course of execution, and page A13 was over Cheung and other defendants' attempt to escape punishment. Likewise, *Apple Daily* devoted the first four pages to the verdict—page A1 reported upon the verdict, page A2 was for advertisement, page A3 reported upon the missing ammunition, and page A4 reported on the legal and political controversy surrounding the trial. *Ta Kung Pao* devoted three pages to the event, i.e., pages A9, A10, and A12.

It reprinted the Guangzhou Intermediate People's Court's opinion in full, i.e., on A10 and A11. *South China Morning Post* provided an exclusive for the verdict entitled "Big Spender Verdict."[15] *Hong Kong Economic Journal* devoted half of their back-front page (8) and its editorial—"Plug judicial cooperation loophole, prevent criminals from using the gaps" (2)—to the event.

*China*

The "Big Spender Case" received a fair share of publicity in China, particularly in the local (Guangzhou) newspapers. However, it neither captured as much attention nor provoked as big a controversy as in Hong Kong. For example, the fact that Cheung was going on trial in Guangzhou triggered a barrage of news coverage in Hong Kong. It received a passing notice in Guangzhou. For example, on October 21, 1998, the day Cheung went on trial, *Guangzhou Daily* devoted only a 4 by 3.75 inch column, left of the middle, coverage on the front page. The story was sandwiched within other local news. The headline for the day was not the "Big Spender Case," but "Guangzhou private bosses have high education and young in age." News items occupying about the same space as those occupied by the "Big Spender" story were: annual statistics on fires in Guangdong [one died each other day from fire] and a fire ran out of control [has to be fought with urine]. The "Big Spender" final verdict received more prominent coverage than other stories, but still much less than what was reported in Hong Kong. Three of the most prominent Guangzhou newspapers—*Guangzhou Daily*, *Yangcheng Wanbao*, and *Nanfang Daily*—reported upon the final disposition of the case. On November 13, 1998, the day after the verdict, *Nanfang Daily* reported the case on the second page: "Cheung Tse-keung sentenced to death in the first trial" with a brief summary of the case. The *Guangzhou Daily* reported the case as one of the most important, though not exclusive, news event of the day. The paper reported the case on A1–A2 with the caption "'Big Spender' Cheung Tse-keung sentenced to death." The report provided an abbreviated summary of the verdict of Guangzhou Intermediary People's Court. It was also accompanied by a commentary on "Why sentence Cheung Tse-keung to death penalty" on page A1, which was extracted from the Guangzhou Intermediary People's Court's press release explaining why Cheung was tried in China, why he was convicted, and why he was sentenced to death. The *Yangcheng Wanbao* devoted substantial, though still not exclusive, coverage to the case on pages A1 and A2 on November 12, 1998, the evening the verdict was rendered. The lead story on the first page (A1)—'Big Spender' Cheung Tse-keung sentenced to death"—was a brief summary of the facts and a tabulation of the charges of the defendants. The other story on the inside page (A2) "Stringent application of the law in the open trial of Cheung Tse-keung's case, Guangzhou Intermediary Middle Court explained the trial circumstances" reported that Guangzhou court had the jurisdiction to try the case, made decision based on law and as supported by facts, and had accurate and adequate evidence to convict and sentence Cheung.

Overall, as reported in China, the case was also much less controversial. In fact, the case was reported in a factual manner. The focus was on how law was being strictly followed and how justice was done. The amount of coverage and the manner of reporting in the case were indicative of the PRC's overall interests and attitude in the case. The case was used mainly as a legal education tool. Whatever the reasons, the fact that the case was considered as much less important and controversial in the PRC than Hong Kong should help put the Hong Kong people on notice that there is more than one perspective in approaching the case. The Hong Kong people should not only consider the impact of the "Big Spender Case" locally but should also look at the significance of the "Big Spender Case" in a broader, especially "national" perspective. At a minimum, the settlement of cross-border crime issues in general, and the "Big Spender Case" in particular, must take into account China's national interests, e.g., eventual re-integration of Hong Kong after 1950s, and local concerns, e.g., maintaining law and order in Guangdong Province of which Hong Kong is an integral part. This adds a new dimension to the debate that has so far escaped attention.

## Public Opinions

### Martin Lee, Democratic Party Chairman

Martin Lee wanted people who have committed crime in Hong Kong to be tried in Hong Kong. In the case of Cheung Tse-keung, he should have been tried in Hong Kong for kidnapping charges. Hong Kong justice officials should be more solicitous of Hong Kong people's rights, interests, and welfare. The justice officials should have asked for the rendition of Cheung Tse-keung to stand trial in Hong Kong, notwithstanding the lack of a rendition agreement. In this regard, he felt that Hong Kong justice officials were inexplicably "nervous" and too submissive to the Chinese authority.[16] He was of the opinion that "one country, two systems" would not function properly without some sort of rendition agreement. He called for negotiations with the PRC over details of such an agreement. "This is not an isolated case . . . Until there is an acceptable arrangement governing the rendition for offenders between Hong Kong and Mainland China, the one country, two systems cannot be administered."[17]

### Margret Ng, LegCo Member (Law)

Margret Ng is one of the staunchest supporters of SAR's judicial autonomy. She was more concerned that the rights of Hong Kong citizens were not being protected while in China. She believes that PRC law does not apply to Hong Kong.[18] She was also critical of the SAR government officials for failing to protect Hong Kong people's right under the Basic Law. Particularly, she failed to understand why the secretary for justice gave up the "Big Spender Case" without a fight or why the secretary for security refused to follow through the investigation of the case for lack of victim's report.[19]

### James To Kun-sun, Democrat Legislator

James To Kun-sun wanted the government to be more open to the public in explaining their decision not to prosecute "Big Spender" in Hong Kong and otherwise seek his return.[20] He also felt that China should be able to try crimes happened in China, e.g., conspiracy to kidnap, with Hong Kong trying crimes happened in Hong Kong, e.g., illegal import of weapons.[21]

### Gladys Li, S. C., ex-President, Hong Kong Bar Association

Gladys Li objected to HKSAR officials—secretary for justice and secretary for security—for failing to protect Hong Kong people's rights even though it is their duty to do so.[22]

### Amnesty International

Amnesty International was concerned that the "Big Spender" trial was not made public.[23] It was also concerned with the possible death sentence for the defendants after an unfair and closed trial. It wanted the public to appeal to the chief executive of the SAR.[24]

### Apple Newsgroup

Consistent with its liberal stance, the Apple Newsgroup has been very outspoken about the conduct of the "Big Spender Case." Apple was most concerned with possible political interference by the PRC central government, at the behest of Li Kar-shing and with the acquiescence of the Hong Kong legal/security officials, in the defense of Hong Kong judicial independence and political autonomy.[25] Apple was in fear that the line dividing "one country, two systems" would be eroded.[26]

### South China Morning Post

*South China Morning Post* feared that the case would set a precedent for the gradual erosion of Hong Kong's legal independence and political autonomy.[27]

### Police

The police were frustrated over the lack of prosecution in the case as a result of lack of cooperation from the victims.[28]

### Hong Kong Bar Association

The Hong Kong Bar Association was concerned that instead of having a "one country, two systems" formula which separates Hong Kong and China as co-equals, the impression one gets from the "Big Spender Case" is that Hong Kong's legal system is subordinate to that of the Chinese.[29]

## Public Surveys

It is interesting to note that notwithstanding worldwide legal experts' concern and Hong Kong politicians' outcry, the public did not seem to feel the urgency of the "one country, two systems" crisis. There were a number of sources of information buttressing this observation.

First, a reader's call in poll (based on a self-selected sample) reported that a little more than half (56 percent) of the respondents were concerned about the PRC interfering with Hong Kong's legal system.[30]

Second, a scientific random phone survey conducted after the conviction by *Ming Bao Daily News* on November 12, 1998, showed that only 13 percent of those surveyed believed the verdict to be unfair.[31] Another scientific random phone survey of 302 on December 6, 2008, by *Apple Daily* revealed that 48 percent agreed that Cheung obtained a fair trial with only 24 percent saying he did not (20 percent had no opinion).[32] Third, on November 18–19, 1998, the Hong Kong Policy Research Centre conducted a random stratified telephone survey of Hong Kong population of 947 people between the ages of eighteen and sixty-four to measure the confidence of Hong Kong people in their legal and judicial system.[33] The survey showed that while the Hong Kong people were losing confidence in Hong Kong legal and judicial system by a wide margin, i.e., 88 (11/98) versus 100 (10/98), they were gaining confidence in "one country, two systems," i.e., 157 (11/98) versus 100 (10/98).

The loss of confidence in the legal system was traceable to the mishandling of the "Big Spender Case."[34] The best interpretation of this return is that the people of Hong Kong were unhappy with the performance of the justice officials in protecting Hong Kong from China, but were not unduly concerned with interference of the HKSAR legal system from the PRC to do justice in the "Big Spender Case." In essence, the public was conflicted—condemning Hong Kong officials in not defending the "one country, two systems" principle in general, but approving of Chinese courts in convicting Cheung in particular. This interpretation was supported by a phoned-in survey with a self-selected sample in response to solicitation by a Hong Kong investigative report magazine, the *Next Magazine*.[35] The readers were asked to call in to register their opinions on the statement: "If Leung Oi See's appointment is not terminated, the future of re-establishing the authority and respect of the justice administration is bleak."[36] Seventy-three percent agreed that the secretary for justice should be terminated in order to re-establish the integrity and authority of, and respect for the Hong Kong criminal justice system.[37]

Third, convenient sample interviews of citizens in Hong Kong after the conviction of Cheung showed (by and large) that the people supported the decision of the court with little concern about the jurisdictional problem. The overall reaction was that justice had been done. "It's better to execute him in China . . ." "He deserves the death penalty . . ." "The system in Hong Kong is too lenient . . ." "I think he really should die for his crimes . . . Big Spender would at most get a life sentence here."[38] Same reactions were registered after the confirmation of execution of Cheung on appeal in the Chinese press on December 6, 1998[39]:

> Ms. Lee, a retired person, observed: "He has done a lot of bad things and sentenced to death. No one would help (pity) him."
>
> Ms. Chung, a travel agent, said: "He has done wrong and should be responsible. . . ."
>
> Mr. Yip, a taxi driver, responded: "Regarding the trying of Cheung Tse-keung, I have no right to interfere . . ."

There were to be many detractors:

> An English press found the reaction to be mixed.[40] "Some said Cheung should be returned to Hong Kong to face trial while others said he deserved the death sentence for what he had done."
>
> Ms. Kan Lam, a university graduate, lamented: "He did not kill one single person. He should not have been executed."
>
> Ms. Biance Hung, a financial industry worker, suggested: "Under the principle of one country, two systems, the mainland government should have returned Cheung to the SAR Government for trial."
>
> Ms. Wu, a teacher, commented: "I think Hong Kong officials had not done enough to ask for a rendition."[41]

Fourth, Clarence Yang, Head of Public Affairs (Projects) at Radio Television Hong Kong (RTHK) and program director of "Headline," observed that the public clearly wanted Cheung Tse-keung to be arrested, prosecuted, and executed wherever he could be found, even in China. He noted that his repeated calls for more calm and reflective judgment from his audience were in vain: "You (public) should not condemn Cheung before he is legally tried and convicted." He attributed this to Hong Kong people's pragmatism and lack of principle, in wanting substantive justice over procedural justice and immediate retribution for Cheung instead of long-term political authority under the "one country, two systems" principle.[42]

Professor Davis from the Chinese University of Hong Kong, however, was more critical of the Hong Kong public's approval of executing Cheung in China. He suggested that the Hong Kong people might not be as pragmatic as much as they were being conservative. In this regard, the lack of open-mindedness is less a trait of the Hong Kong people per se as much as it is a characteristic of uniformed individuals, such as rural people from Minnesota.[43] The suggestion that Hong Kong people's choice was conservative at best and uninformed at worse, if true, spelled trouble for "one country, two systems" advocates.[44] Hong Kong people's preference for and commitment to "one country, two systems" is skin deep, and made contingent on the nature of a case (serious versus nonserious), identity of criminals (occasional violators versus habitual criminals), and intent of China (usurping jurisdiction versus seeking justice).

## Conclusion

It is clear from the above discussion that Hong Kong people are behind the execution of Cheung Tse-keung—in China (or wherever he could be found). It is also clear that Hong Kong people do not have faith in the Chinese legal system. For example, a random interactive phone survey was conducted in China[45] with the following questions: "With regard to the 'Big Spender' Cheung Tse-keung execution. Do you think it is too severe? [If it is too severe, turn to question 2]" "What do you think is an appropriate sentence?" "The court has not published the video or photo of the execution. Will you be suspicious that "Big Spender" is still alive?" "You feel that the court has no duty to publish the 'Big Spender' execution video or picture to prove that he was executed?" Four hundred and eight persons responded.[46] Seventy-one percent of the respondents agreed that the punishment was appropriate. Only 10 percent were of the opinion that the punishment was too heavy, i.e., four. Most of the respondents felt that the court should have released the execution video or pictures.[47]

Finally, it is clear that there was a wide gap between Hong Kong people (surveys and interviews) and the political elites (Davis—scholar, Martin Lee—democrats, Gladys Li—lawyer, Hong Kong Bar Association) as to the importance of "one country, two systems" in securing judicial independence of Hong Kong and the need to deliver (substantive) justice in the "Big Spender Case." Particularly, the strong and pervasive public attitude in favor of trying and executing Cheung in China raises the question of whether the "Big Spender" debate was not an engineered debate by the experts, professionals, and politicians for self-serving reasons, i.e., to validate liberal political stance or consolidate Hong Kong democratic base. If that should be the case, is this public confidence crisis over "one country, two systems" much to do about nothing?

In this regard, three observations need to be made, which bear upon the true nature and proper discourse over the meaning of "one country, two systems."

First, recalling Professor Davis' observation that the people in Hong Kong were conservative because they were uniformed about the import and impact of "one country, two systems" in securing legally vulnerable Hong Kong from menacing Chinese political influence. In suggesting that the Hong Kong people were necessarily uninformed (without information) and ill-informed (distorted information) when they have taken a more "conservative" stance against "one country, two systems" (than one would prefer) is more certainly offensive to Hong Kong people's identity and hurtful to their feelings, besides attracting legitimate, but yet unsubstantiated and imputed, claims of cultural insensitivity and/or elite arrogance. The validity of the charge and the countercharge of public ignorance (uneducated Hong Kong people) and elite arrogance (learned intellectuals from the West) aside in the heated "one country, two systems" debate, the characterization and finger-pointing from both sides pointed to a larger truth, i.e., there existed a wide and widening cultural gap between Chinese common people on the street and Western and Western-trained elites as to what law, order, and justice mean in post-1997 Hong Kong. It is this cultural gap that should be investigated and debated, and not (at least less) the integrity of "one country, two systems" or the constitutionality or legality of Cheung's verdict.[48]

Second, the perceived differences between the people and the elite toward the utility of "one country, two systems" in general, and the necessity of disposition of the "Big Spender Case" in China, in particular, pointed to difference between Chinese versus Western idea-thinking (communist political system is bankrupted at its core) and ideal-feeling (rule of law should override community security) to justice administration. Specifically, Hong Kong people on the street are more concerned with substantive justice than the professional elites who are more interested in procedural justice. It has also been pointed out that Hong Kong (Chinese) people are more pragmatic; some stay conservative in justice administration (individual and situated justice) than the rule-bound and system-oriented legal professionals or liberal political elites (who are trained in the West).

Third, in the final analysis, the disparity of views toward legal protection—one for procedural justice (professionals) and the other for substantive justice (the public)—makes for a good study of legal culture in Hong Kong.[49] Such a discourse over legal culture between professional/elite (with Western orientation) versus common people (from Chinese culture) must start with a discussion of people's "thinking" versus "feeling" toward legal culture.

It is observed here that people, as individuals (attitude) and collective (culture), have strong emotions toward things, and appreciation (feelings) for good, justice, and beauty come to mind. "Thinking" (rationality) and "feeling" (emotion) are integrated mental–body activities and interdependent objective–subjective experiences that together drive action, give meaning to life, and ultimately define our identity—existence as persons, community, people, and nation.

In the words of Damasio who reflected and expounded on the relationship between feeling and thinking as functions of mind versus body: "Nature appears to have built the apparatus of rationality not just on top of the apparatus of biological regulation, but also *from* it and *with* it" (128; emphasis in original).[50] In so doing, Damasio rejected Descartes' bold assertion that "I think therefore I am" in arguing for the prominence of mind over matter. Instead, Damasio astutely observed and later scientifically demonstrated[51] that: "in the beginning it was being, and only later was it thinking ... We are, and then we think, and we think only inasmuch as we are, since thinking is indeed caused by the structures and operations of being" (248).

Damasio postulated that in order for people to see and do justice, one must first picture and feel justice. This he calls the "somatic marker hypothesis"[52]:

> [S]omatic marker hypothesis, which I believe is relevant to the understanding of processes of human reasoning and decision making. The ventromedial sector of the prefrontal cortices is critical to the operations postulated here, but the hypothesis does not necessarily apply to prefrontal cortex as a whole and should not be seen as an attempt to unify frontal lobe functions under a single mechanism. The key idea in the hypothesis is that 'marker' signals influence the processes of response to stimuli, at multiple levels of operation, some of which occur overtly (consciously, 'in mind') and some of which occur covertly (non-consciously, in a non-minded manner). The marker signals arise in bioregulatory processes, including those which express themselves in emotions and feelings, but are not necessarily confined to those alone. This is the reason why the markers are termed somatic: they relate to body-state structure and regulation even when they do not arise in the body proper but rather in the brain's representation of the body. Examples of the covert action of 'marker' signals are the undeliberated inhibition of a response learned previously; the introduction of a bias in the selection of an aversive or appetitive mode of behaviour, or in the otherwise deliberate evaluation of varied option-outcome scenarios. Examples of overt action include the conscious 'qualifying' of certain option-outcome scenarios as dangerous or advantageous. The hypothesis rejects attempts to limit human reasoning and decision making to mechanisms relying, in an exclusive and unrelated manner, on either conditioning alone or cognition alone.[53]

Oriental thinkers, with Confucius in the lead, have long postulated the holistic and integrated nature of body, soul, and mind, in decision-making. As such, Chinese (common people in Hong Kong) are situational feelers–thinkers, who think in contextual, concrete, and above all intuitive (emotive) way, as distinguished from Westerners (by extension Western-trained professionals), being dispositional (and disproportionate[54]) rationalistic thinkers, think individually, generally, abstractly, and most significantly for our purpose, logically. The observation here is that who we are as a people and how we think and feel as individuals affect the process, content, and outcome of decision-making, more generally life choices. As observed by Nibsett:

> Each of these orientations—the Western and the Eastern—is a self-reinforcing, homeostatic system. The social practices promote the worldviews: the worldviews dictate the appropriate thought processes; and the thought processes both justify the world views and support the social practices. Understanding these homeostatic systems has implications for grasping the fundamental nature of the mind, for beliefs about how we ought ideally to reason, and for appropriate education strategies for different peoples.[55]

Such an understanding of the Chinese (Hong Kong people) feeling–thinking process and style influenced Chinese jurisprudential thoughts in material and discernable ways. In traditional China, "emotions" and "feelings" matter in justice administration.[56] Doctrinally, "*qing*" and "*li*" were found to be as important if not more important than law in settling disputes. Eugenia Lean, after an in-depth review of a court case in imperial (Qing) China, concluded that "the moral authenticity of emotions has been a powerful motivating force" (212) in justice administration.[57]

In the critique of Hong Kong people's choice of substantive justice for Cheung Tse-keung over procedural security of "one country, two systems," Western-trained elites in Hong Kong have a tendency to substitute Western style of learned "thinking" for Chinese natural-born "feeling"[58] over crime, social control, and justice.

There are a number of reasons for the West (or those westernized) to prefer "thinking" about China than having a "feeling" for Chinese:

First, philosophically, Western thinkers from Plato to René Descartes have successfully and artificially separated the mind from the body as two distinctive and independent domains. The mind thinks, and is thus viewed as autonomous in defining the objective reality. The body only feels and acts, hence it is considered as an extension of and an instrument to the mind. Descartes famously declared "I think therefore I am" ("Cogito, ergo sum"), insisting that mind (or "soul") motivated (literally "caused to move") and ruled the machine of the body.

Second, pragmatically[59], Western civilization, since the eighteenth century and with the arrival of Industrial Revolution, promotes the idea of rationalism as the sole engine of industrial progress and bulkhead against arbitrary governance. During the Enlightenment era, rationality was established as a de facto state ideology, with legitimacy and authority to match. Rationality is useful, and should be harnessed. Emotion is dysfunctional, and must be constrained.

Third, intellectually, academic disciplines—law, economic, and political science, as understood, practiced, and promoted in the West— are all exclusively devoted to rationality as a process of discovery and enterprises of learning. Intellectuals prefer reasoning over intuition as a process, and are more comfortable with and attune to logic than sentiments as analytical-understanding tools.

Fourth, "rationality" (or how to reason) can be taught and "sentimentality" (or what one feels) must be lived. The former is transferable as ideas. The latter is inaccessible as feelings. Empathy in seeking to transfer (export–import–implant) something that is not transferable, i.e., imagination, replication, approximation of sentiments with no shared experience (conditions), or common roots (history), makes things worse. While one's empathetic feelings for others, imported through standing in the shoes of others and exported by following the "golden rule,"[60] is sincere and real to the empathizer. There is no assurance that the nature (sad versus mad), degree (like versus love), scope (focused versus diffused), depth (superficial versus embedded), and duration (fleeing versus lasting) more generally impact (psychological versus physiological) and reaction (resignation versus revolution) of empathetic feelings projected onto empathy corresponds to that which was experienced. More often than not, people, blinded by lofty goals to help, are tempted to act on such empathy-generated chivalrous feelings, without due regard to whether such feelings and in turn actions are warranted; thus paternalism prevails.

Denial of "feelings" has dire consequences and lasting impact on the people who have their "feelings" denied or replaced.

First, feelings, emotions, and sentiments are powerful cultural markers. They define one's way of thinking, acting and, most important, of being. The denial of "feelings" is the denial of the autonomy, centrality, and importance of self in its totality, resulting in alienation, drift, and in acute form anomie, in time escape or rebellion.

Second, denial of feelings subjugates individual will and uproots national spirit. It speaks of colonization (at least overseeing) of a people, surrendering (at least contamination) of a culture, and transformation (at least sublimation) of one's national identity. In this regard, denial of feelings to a people is similar to the deprivation of freedom to a wild tiger. The colonization of a people as with the domestication of a tiger destroys the very essence and spirit of being that the animal–people once possessed and exemplified, in order to cater to the utility of the captor and expectations of the observers, aloft and afar.

Third, denial of feelings together with legitimizing of reason generates typical cognitive dissonance syndrome[61] in the afflicted person that requires reconciling of natural feelings (e.g., substantive justice is China) with positive thinking (e.g., procedural justice is United States), with anxiety, anger, and frustration, to match.

Finally, denial of feeling privileged intellectuals who "know" the world through cognition and discriminate against the public who "experience" life through sensations. Zhou Guangquan, a member of the Legal Committee of the National People's Congress and Tsinghua University professor, has this to say about elitist, antidemocratic and countermajoritarian, tendency of thinking versus feeling:

> There will always be a gap between popular thinking [lit., "intuition"] and the judgment of legislators when it comes to capital punishment—this is true throughout the world. In some European countries where the death penalty has been abolished, opinion polls show that nearly 80 percent of people oppose abolition. Legislative choices cannot entirely follow popular thinking; in the end, some decisions must be made that go against popular thinking.[62]

Evidence of "clash of culture"[63] in thinking (elites) versus feelings (common people) is evident everywhere between and within civilizations. In the case of Hong Kong, it is manifested in the fight over utility of "one country, two systems" versus the necessity of punishment for Cheung Tse-keung.

## Notes

1. "In the Mainland, How Many Hong Kong People were Convicted?" *Jiusinianda*, July 1989, 45–47. Wang Changyin (Editor-in-Chief), *Analysis of Criminal Cases Involving Foreigners and Hong Kong and Macau in the Shenzhen Special Economic Zone* (Shenzhen Jingji Tequ She-wai She-Kang- Aou Xingshi Anli Pingxi) (Beijing: Renmin fayuan chubanshe, 1990), Chapter 1, esp. 1–5.
2. Danny Gittings, "Thin Line Diving Standards of Justice," *SCMP*, October 28, 1998. (the PRC sent back 128 criminal suspects to Hong Kong since 1992 [sic]. The SAR did not send back any PRC criminals.) For detailed

official figures from HKSAR, see "Mrs. Ip Is Not Concerned about Similar Incidences Like Cheung Tse-keung's Case Before an Agreement," *Hong Kong Economic Journal*, December 12, 1998. The PRC press has reported another figure, 150 plus suspects returned since 1990. "Did Not Interfere with Hong Kong Judicial Jurisdiction," *Guangzhou Daily*, November 13, 1998, A. 7. (Since 1990, 150 criminals have been returned to Hong Kong.)

3. Personal interview with HKP informants.

4. Phone interview with SSP Albert Cheuk, Security Branch, November 20, 1998; SSP Hunt, Support Branch, November 23, 1998.

5. Letter dated November 30, 1998, and January 19, 1999, by CSP J. H. H. Bicknell.

6. Letter dated December 23, 1998, by SSP (now CSP) Paul Hung, HKP, HQ.

7. Letter dated January 19, 1999, by CSP J. H. H. Bicknell.

8. "Chinese Criminal Police (INTERPOL) Spread All Over the World," *Guangzhou Daily*, November 9, 1998, A1, A3.

9. "Special Topic: Hong Kong People under the Legal Net of Dictatorship," *Jiuxi Nian Dai Monthly*, July 1986, 42–56.

10. Basic Law of the Hong Kong Special Administrative Region of the People's Republic of China (April 1990) (Basic Law). (Adopted on April 4, 1990, by the Seventh National People's Congress of the People's Republic of China at its Third Session.) (Hereinafter, Basic Law.)

11. Test Case Law & Legal Definition, http://definitions.uslegal.com/t/test-case/ (accessed December 22, 2011).

12. CPAG Test Case Strategy unpublished.

13. Roger Smith, "Experience in England and Wales: Test Case Strategies, Public Interest Litigation, the Human Rights Act and legal NGOs," Justice, U.K. (2003), http://www.justice.org.uk/images/pdfs/testcase.pdf (accessed December 22, 2011).

In the United States, test cases are used as a law reform tool. The test case litigators, e.g., legal aid lawyers in the 1970s, stirred up community agitation through partisan advocacy and (over-)zealous representation. They justified the use of such strategy and tactics by arguing for the empowerment of the disfranchised. This is one of the few ways, if not the only way, that the existing political structure, government bureaucracy, and legal establishment could be successfully penetrated to entertain the views of the powerless—minority, poor, dissidents, etc. Test cases also force the conservative establishment to come to terms with new, emerging, and unsettling ideas. This is especially the case when entrenched interests preclude any meaningful reform from without and established institutions made impossible any effective changes from within. Observations by the author who for years (1979–1982) served as a trainer for Legal Service Corporation in the subject matter. The author was the Managing Attorney of Calhoun County, Battle Creek, Michigan, responsible for test case litigation.

14. The "Big Spender Case" was not "picked" as much as it was "dropped" on the lap of the political pundits, left and right, in making their respective case for the safety and security (Democratic Alliance) versus independency and autonomy (Democratic Party).

15. According to one informed SCMP reporter, it has been planning for the news event for weeks.
16. Interview with Michelle Han, "Cheung Tse-keung's Case" 9:45–10:00 p.m., December 9, 1998, CNN, Hong Kong.
17. "Basic Law Fears in Big Spender Case," *SCMP*, November 2, 1998.
18. Margret Ng, "Right to Autonomous Law," *SCMP*, November 6, 1998. ("Article 18 provides that PRC law shall not apply in Hong Kong unless included in Annex III. Article 19 provides that Hong Kong courts have jurisdiction over all cases in Hong Kong. Article 22 precludes mainland authorities from interfering with matters which the SAR has power to deal with on its own.")
19. "Cheung Tse-keung Should Have a Fair Trial," *Ming Bao Daily News*, October 28, 1998, A5. True or not, such labeling of Hong Kong people's choice, without empirical evidence, is also disturbing.
20. Chris Yeung, "Criticism Damages Faith in Legal System," November 4, 1998. (People are very worried about the case, the government should explain more.)
21. Jimmy Cheung, "Grey Areas over First Legal Move," *SCMP*, November 9, 1998. (At the City Forum on November 8, James To asked why an accomplice of Cheung was being tried by Mainland for carrying firearms in Hong Kong.)
22. Letter: "Alarmed by Top Officials' Lame Excuse," *SCMP*, October 28, 1998. While the secretary for security statement was literally correct, i.e., no crime report–no investigation–no prosecution–no extradition, it is not legally so. The statement did not reflect HK people's common understanding, mutual expectation, and general experience with the police, i.e., Hong Kong law requires the police to enforce the law, protect public safety, investigate crimes, and apprehend criminals. It certainly is not the law of Hong Kong not to take action against a known kidnapping. The Police Force Ordinance Chapter 235, Vol. 15, Laws of Hong Kong. "Section 10: The Duties of the police force shall be to take lawful measures for (1) preserving the public peace; (2) preventing and detecting crimes and offences; (3) preventing injury to life and property; (4) apprehending all persons whom it is lawful to apprehend and for whose apprehensive sufficient grounds exists." When a crime is committed (law violated) the police have a legal duty to investigate and prosecute, if sufficient evidence can be found. This is the case notwithstanding the lack of direct evidence due to noncooperation of (consensual) victims or reluctant witnesses. In actual fact, the victim as a material witness can be forced to give evidence under HK law. Criminal Procedure Ordinances, Chapter 221, Section 91, provides penalty for misprision of a crime. The clear example is victimless crime, e.g., use of illegal drugs or assisted suicide. The sole issue for Secretary for Security Mrs. Ip in this case was whether a crime (kidnapping, possession of explosives and firearms) has been committed in Hong Kong, and whether there were sufficient evidence to support the arrest of Cheung.
23. Chris Williams, "Secret Trials Rights Covenant, Claims Amnesty," *SCMP*, October 20, 1998. (Secret trial was against the UN International Covenant on Civil and Political Rights.)

24. Audrey Parwani, "Secret Hearing below Standard, Says Amnesty," *SCMP*, October 20, 1998. (The death penalty violates Art. 3 of the Universal Declaration on Human Rights.)

25. Editorial: "The Case of Cheung Tse-keung: Central (government) Interferes and Damages One Country Two Systems," *Next Magazine*, October 30, 1998. (Notwithstanding the fact that there was no extradition agreement in the past, 128 criminals have been returned to Hong Kong. It is hard to believe that none of these violated PRC criminal laws, thereby foreclosing their eventual return. In this case, Cheung was not returned because the leadership in the highest level instructed that he should not be returned.)

26. Editorial—Lo Feng, "Much to do after the Verdict," *Apple's Daily*, November 13, 1998. ("One country, two systems" must not be a guaranteed on paper but also in practice. This requires removing the ambiguity over the dividing line between the two systems.)

27. Editorial: "Slippery Slope," *SCMP*, November 11, 1998. ("Even more than the Big Spender case, the decision to try Li in Shantou represents the start of a slippery slope that could erode Hong Kong's legal autonomy.")

28. Audrey Parwani, "Police Morale 'Hit by Lack of SAR Hearing," *SCMP*, November 9, 1998. ("Of course we are angry. We have been following this guy for ages and gathered so much evidence.")

29. Christ Yeung, "The Case That Threatens Our Autonomy," *SCMP*, November 14, 1998. ("A clear demarcation was seen as crucial to the viability of the 'one country, two systems' experiment . . .")

30. *Next Magazine*, November 6, 1998, Editorial—bottom, 1. (Methodology: The readers were asked to call in to register their opinions to the statement: "Central government indirectly interfered with the Cheung Tse-keung's case." The responses were solicited on *Next Magazine*, October 30, 1998. There were a total of 1,012 people responses: 682 from overseas and 330 from Hong Kong.) Of note is the fact that the solicitation was placed immediately under the *Next Magazine* editorial, itself a liberal magazine with antigovernment readership, entitled: "Cheung Tse-keung case: Central government interference destroyed the 'one country, two systems.'"

31. *Ming Bao Daily News* on November 12, 1998.

32. The question asked was: "Did Cheung Tse-keung obtain a fair trial?" See "Apple Survey: Near 70% Agreed with the Death Sentence," *Apple Daily*, December 6, 1998, A4. (Another survey of 315 Hong Kong people on the question: "Whether 'Big Spender' Cheung Tse-keung's crime should be punished with death?" showed that 70 percent agreed that he should be executed.)

33. The Hong Kong Policy Research Centre established the "Hong Kong judicial and legal system index" in October of 1998 with a base line measure of 100.

34. Reported in *Hong Kong Economic Journal*, November 21, 1998, 5.

35. *Next Magazine*, November 20, 1998, Editorial—bottom, 1.

36. *Next Magazine*, November 13, 1998.

37. *Next Magazine*, November 20, 1998, Editorial—bottom, 1. (A total of 1,092 people responded, worldwide by November 17, 1998, at 9 p.m. Six hundred forty-eight were from overseas. Four hundred forty-four were from Hong Kong.)

38. For Hong Kong public's opinion after Cheung was convicted, see "The Public: 'He Should Be Executed as Soon as Possible,'" *SCMP*, November 13, 1998, 3.
39. For Hong Kong public's opinion after Cheung was executed, see "Apple Survey," A4.
40. See "News of Death Sparks Mixed Reactions in HK," *Hong Kong Standard*, 3. The only exception in this English paper was Ms. Amy Chiu, a housewife, who affirmed: "He broke the law. He was arrested on the Mainland, so he should be tried there . . . Hong Kong and the Mainland should be considered as one . . ."
41. A word of caution about the validity, reliability, and utility of these surveys and interviews. These survey responses should be used most carefully, with other more reliable evidence, e.g., scientific (sampled) survey versus self-selected opinions, before any firm conclusion can be drawn. These interviews and survey results are at best suggestive, not conclusive. The major problem with these surveys and interviews are familiar to researchers—too small a sample, too selected a group, too suggestive question(s), interactive effect, interviewers not objective, interviewers looking for support than answers, etc.
42. Personal discussion with Clarence Yang on November 30, 1998, at RTHK. ("Hong Kong people are pragmatic in the sense that they are more interested in solving problems than sticking to principles.")
43. Professor Michael Davis at the Department of Government and Public Administration, Chinese University of Hong Kong. I thank Professor Davis for his insight. (Discussion on November 21, 1998.) I note his comment to show how certain social facts (here opinion of Hong Kong) can be variously construed.
44. True or not, such labeling of Hong Kong people's choice, without articulated empirical evidence in support, is also disturbing.
45. *Shidai Chao*, issue 15, special ed., 11.
46. There was no indication of response rate.
47. *Shidai Chao*, issue 15, special ed., 11.
48. Kam C. Wong, "Chinese Jurisprudence and Hong Kong Law," *China Report* 45, no. 3 (2009): 213–39. (A high degree of autonomy for Hong Kong to decide and design its own legal system should include consideration of indigenous Chinese jurisprudential thoughts, such as "Qing-Li-Fa.")
49. See Berry Shu, *The Common Law in Chinese Context* (Hong Kong: Hong Kong University Press, 1995). (Nearly half of the Chinese sample [45 percent] expressed negative value toward the doctrine of *nullum crimen sine lege*. Some 34.37 percent believed that: "Sometimes secret torture by the police is essential to extract evidence." This is to be compared with 29 percent and 13.43 percent, respectively, within an English population.) Ibid., Table 6.5, 71, Table 6.6, 72. See also Hsin-chi Huan, "Support for Rule of Law in Hong Kong," *HKLJ* 27, no. 2 (1997): 187ff. (About 79.2 percent of Hong Kong residents agreed that "A suspect should be presumed innocent before proven guilty." But only 16.1 percent agreed that "A conduct not explicitly prohibited by law is not a crime.")
50. Antonio Damasio, *Descartes' Error: Emotion, Reason and the Human Brain* (New York: Harper Perennia, 1995), 128. "Descartes' Error: Emotion, Reason

and the Human Brain," *Canadian Journal of Experimental Psychology*, September 1996. Review by Corinne Zimmerman.

51. See Chapter 1 to Damasio. Ibid.

52. Antonio Damasio, "The Somatic Marker Hypothesis and the Possible Functions of the Prefrontal Cortex," *Philosophical Transactions of the Royal Society London B: Biological Science* 351, no. 1346 (1996):1413–20.

53. Ibid., Abstract.

54. Disproportionate in two senses: (1) Westerners are more inclined to use their brain (cognition) than their heart (sentiments) in processing information and making decision; and (2) Westerners prefer certain value over others, categorically and absolutely.

55. Richard Nisbett, *The Geography of Thought: How Asians and Westerners Think Differently...and Why* (Free Press, 2003).

56. Michael Slott, "Comments on Bryan Van Norden's Virtue Ethics and Consequentialism in Early Chinese Philosophy," *Dao* (2009); Michael Slott, "The Mandate of Empathy," *Dao* 9, no. 3 (2010): 303–7.

57. Eugenia Lean, *Public Passions. The Trial of Shi Jianqiao and the Rise of Popular Sympathy in Republican China* (Berkeley and Los Angeles: University of California Press, 2008).

58. Jeffrey Kinkley, *Chinese Justice, the Fiction: Law and Literature in Modern China* (Stanford, CA: Stanford University Press, 2000), 212.

59. The earmarks of pragmatism are rationalism, instrumentalism, utility, and economics.

60. Alternatively, the categorical imperative: "Act only according to that maxim whereby you can at the same time will that it should become a universal law." Kant, Immanuel, translated by James W. Ellington, *Grounding for the Metaphysics of Morals*, 3rd ed. (Indianapolis, IN: Hackett, 1785/1993), 30.

61. Leon Festinger (1954) describes it as: "the feeling of psychological discomfort produced by the combined presence of two thoughts that do not follow from one another." Leon Festinger and James M. Carlsmith, "Cognitive Consequences of Forced Compliance," *Journal of Abnormal and Social Psychology* 58 (1959): 203–10.

62. "Translation and Commentary: Greater Steps Can be Taken to Reduce the Capital Punishment," *Dui Hua Human Rights Journal*, September 1, 2010. ("Interview with Zhou Guangquan, member of the Legal Committee of the National People's Congress and Tsinghua University professor, *Southern Weekend*, August 26, 2010.)

63. Samuel P. Huntington, "The Clash of Civilizations?" *Foreign Affairs* 72, no. 3 (1993): 22–49.

# 5

# Cross-Border Cooperation: HK versus the PRC

### Past Practices, Cases, and Negotiation Over Cross-Border Crime

In order to inform the present, it is beneficial to look at the past.[1] Looking back provides us with a more balanced perspective in our discussion and resolution of cross-border crime jurisdiction and jurisprudential issues. In this regard, we can pose a number of questions, including: What is the prevalence and magnitude of the cross-border crime problem—for law enforcement and justice officials?[2] What has been the impact of such cross-border crimes on Hong Kong and Chinese criminal justice systems?[3] How critical and/or urgent is the cross-border problem? Is the Cheung Tse-keung's case unique as a kind of cross-border crime? Looking back also provides us with information on how such cross border cases had been dealt with before and raises yet another question: why cooperation between PRC and HKSAR governments have not been more forthcoming? In this regard, there are four avenues of investigation one can pursue. First, how were such cross-border crime cases handled legally versus extralegally, i.e., formally versus informally? Second, how were such cases handled administratively? Third, how were such cases handled customarily? Finally, how were such cases handled politically?

To put the "Big Spender Case" in a historical perspective, the "Big Spender," as a species of cross-border crimes, is neither unique nor special. The basic facts of the case—a Chinese citizen/Hong Kong resident committed a crime in China and Hong Kong—is not that unusual to deserve all the attention it attracted. Thousands of Hong Kong residents live, work, play, and commit crime in China every year. Nor were the legal issues raised by the case—concurrent criminal jurisdiction and conflicts of law—unfamiliar questions to law students and

123

legal scholars everywhere. The fact of the matter is that cross-border crime cases and disputes are common occurrences in Hong Kong[4] as in other parts of the world, in time past as well as present.

## Past Practice in Dealing with Cross-Border Crimes:
## HKP Perspective

At a formal level, there was no rendition agreement between PRC and HKP officials in dealing with the exchange of cross-border criminals. However, there were informal working arrangements. In asking for the rendition of criminals to Hong Kong, the secretary for security will make the request if the following conditions are met: (1) The fugitive committed a crime in Hong Kong; (2) the fugitive is a Hong Kong resident; and (3) the fugitive is not currently on trial in the PRC.[5]

When it comes to border crime control at the operations level, Hong Kong has a close working relationship with PRC police.[6] Hong Kong and the PRC are both members of the INTERPOL.[7] The PRC established an INTERPOL National Central Bureau in Beijing in 1984 and an INTERPOL liaison center in Guangdong in 1987 to work with Hong Kong, a branch of China INTERPOL. PRC and HKSAR police officials meet twice a year at the "China-Hong Kong INTERPOL bilateral working session."[8] The PRC and the HKSAR also established an INTERPOL liaison officer system to facilitate mutual cooperation on a daily basis: sharing criminal intelligence, assisting in criminal investigation, ascertaining the authenticity of documents and identity of accident victims, helping with the location of missing persons, procuring of evidence and witness, enforcement of confiscation and forfeiture, and attacking on drug smuggling and conducting search for suspects and criminals. In practice, the HKP routinely informs the PRC police authority[9] about the existence of dangerous or at-large Hong Kong criminals, as part of the INTERPOL network, especially when they escaped into China.[10] Hong Kong communicates and works with China mainly through the "China-Hong Kong INTERPOL bilateral working session" and "Guangdong–Hong Kong border liaison annual working meeting." Since 1987 and until 1997, Guangdong and Hong Kong exchanged 471 notes for mutual assistance. Through the years, the PRC, and especially Guangdong PSB, has provided material assistance in the investigation of robbery, smuggling of drugs, commercial crime, kidnapping, and car theft.

Theoretically, PRC police authority is free to act upon the information supplied by HKP officials. However, in practice, the PRC police usually act upon the information with due diligence. Upon finding the suspect or criminal, the PRC Police authority usually inform the HKP of when and where the criminal suspect would be "expelled" from the PRC and handed over to the HKP.[11] Between 1990 and 1995, the PRC-Guangdong PSB arrested seventy Hong Kong criminals, including the number two fugitive from Hong Kong, Ye Yusheng, and transferred them to Hong Kong.[12] In 1995 alone, there were eighteen transfers of criminals.[13] By October 1997, there were 111 altogether.[14] PRC-Guangdong PSB also helped HKSAR police in the interdiction of drugs, rescue of kidnap victims, and recovery of stolen goods and vehicles, e.g., thus far the PRC has returned 110 stolen vehicles and 9 luxury yachts to Hong Kong. In 1998 (January to November 5), there were seventeen cases of transfer of criminals.[15] (See Table 5.1.)

**Table 5.1**
**Numbers of Hong Kong Fugitives Transferred from the Mainland: 1990–1997**

| Nature of Offense | 1990–1997 | January 1998– November 11, 1999 |
|---|---|---|
| Murder, manslaughter, homicide | 15 | 1 |
| Assault, injury to person | 6 | – |
| Rape | 3 | 3 |
| Kidnapping, unlawful detention | 5 | 2 |
| Robbery | 21 | – |
| Blackmail | 4 | 1 |
| Arson | 2 | – |
| Burglary, theft, receiving stolen property | 20 | 5 |
| Fraud, forgery, coinage | 6 | 3 |
| Dangerous drugs offenses | 19 | 1 |

*continued on next page*

**Table 5.1 *(continued)***

| Nature of Offense | 1990–1997 | January 1998–<br>November 11, 1999 |
|---|---|---|
| Possession of arms and ammunition | 2 | – |
| Others | 8 | 1 |
| Total | 111 | 17 |

*Source:* Figures supplied by the secretary for security.
*Notes:* (1) Transferring of fugitives from the PRC is only based on an informal administrative arrangement. (2) In the past, the transfer of fugitives only involved transferring of fugitives from the PRC to Hong Kong. (3) Such transfers only applied to fugitives who were Hong Kong residents committing crimes in Hong Kong. (4) If the fugitive had committed crime in the Mainland and Hong Kong, he would only return to Hong Kong after the Mainland criminal proceeding was completed.[16]

Since 1987, PRC-Guangdong and HKSAR established the "Guangdong–Hong Kong border liaison annual working meeting" to facilitate mutual judicial-police assistance (*sifa xiezuo*). The "Guangdong–Hong Kong border liaison annual working meeting" is sponsored by the Guangzhou Province Foreign Affairs and Public Security Bureau and HKSAR government. The meeting is typical of the nature and level of police cooperation and mutual judicial assistance rendered between the two parties. For example, in a recent (1995) "Guangzhou–Hong Kong border working meeting," the Guangzhou party raised the following issues: management of the Shenzhen river project, transfer of Guangzhou-Hong Kong criminals,[17] compensation for dead fishes at Dingling Island outside Zhuhai municipality, and the scope and issues of Guangzhou–Hong Kong border work meeting and cross-border smuggling issues.[18]

The overall conclusion one can draw from this historical account of PRC–HKSAR cooperation over cross-border crimes is that there was at all times a healthy dialogue and reciprocal actions between PRC-Guangzhou and HKSAR police officials resulting in coordinated investigations, major arrests, and foiling of criminal enterprises. However, the record also showed that, in cases of repatriation of criminal suspects, it has always been a one-way street, from the PRC to HKSAR, until now. This picture of police cross-border cooperation was best depicted by Hong Kong Commissioner of Police in a press conference over Hong Kong public order in January of 1996:

> HKP has been cooperating with the mainland public security now
> for over ten years, the achievements are everywhere in evidence. In
> 1995 alone, with the cooperation of the mainland public security,
> there were 18 criminals repatriated to Hong Kong. With car thefts,
> in 1995 14 container tractors and 8 luxury cars were recovered and
> returned. Two other luxury yachts were also found and returned.[19]

It is thus not correct to observe, as some did, that the PRC political authority in general or the Guangzhou Public Security Bureau in
particular was intended on interfering with Hong Kong's justice
administration and legal autonomy. It appears that on contrary,
Hong Kong has been obstructing China from enforcing her domestic
law in not rendering the needed assistance due to the lack of "legal" channels.[20] It was observed by a PRC author that an "unequal"
(*bu pingdeng*) situation existed in the mutual judicial assistance
relationship between the PRC and HKSAR:

> For example, in cases of transfer (*yijiao*) of criminals, when Hong
> Kong residents who have committed crime in Hong Kong and
> escaped into China to hide, after the Guangzhou (police) received
> request for assistance to arrest, they would use their utmost effort
> to arrest the suspect and transfer him to Hong Kong. However
> when Hong Kong residents committed crimes in the mainland and
> escaped to Hong Kong or even mainland resident criminals who have
> fled to Hong Kong, HKP often received the request for assistance
> to investigation, but as a result of difference in legal system was not
> able to transfer the criminals back.[21]

The level and nature of PRC–HKP cooperation in the investigation of crime and return of criminals can best be illustrated by the
following cases. These reported cases of PRC and HKSAR police cooperation involving cross-border crimes serve to illustrate the nature
of "quiet" cooperation before the "acrimonious" debate over the "Big
Spender."[22]

*1. "King Fook" and "Po Shing" jewelry shops robbery*

On August 28, 1990, two jewelry shops—"King Fook" and "Po
Shing"—were robbed of jewelry worth $4 million by armed robbers.
The HKP arrested two Hong Kong criminals. The HKP sent two police
officers to Guangdong province, Public Security Bureau (Guangdong
PSB), to ask for assistance and supplied them with leads. Within
twelve hours, the two Mainland resident accomplices were arrested.

Inasmuch as they were also wanted criminals inside China, they were prosecuted and tried in China according to the law.

### 2. Armored car armed robbery

On July 12, 1991, an armored vehicle from Kai Tak airport was robbed at gunpoint of 169 million dollars. The Deputy Assistant of Police went to Guangzhou to seek help from the Guangzhou PSB. The Guangdong PSB notified all banks in the province of the robbery. When one of the top members of the gang (residency not clear) was spotted with the robbed US dollars, he was arrested and returned to Hong Kong.

### 3. Chow Sang Sang jewelry shop robbery

On April 23, 1992, at 6.50 p.m. the Chow Sang Sang jewelry shop on 529 Nathan Road was robbed by five persons armed with machine guns. They escaped with the booty. The next day (April 24, 1992) the five suspected robbers resisted arrest when confronted by the police. They had a firefight with the police in the open streets using AK47 rifles and grenades. Seventeen people were injured, including five police officers and twelve citizens. On April 28, 1992, the HKP requested the Guangdong PSB to assist in the arrest of the five suspected criminals—Feng Wei-han, "rat An," Pan Wei-xue, and Pan Wei-min (no indication of residency). On May 8, 1992, the police arrested Feng Wei-han (identified as a HK resident) and turned him over to the HKP.

### 4. Shui Hing mahjong shop armed robbery and murder

On the evening of May 5, 1995, Hong Kong criminal Wong Kin-wai conspired with three criminals from Mainland to rob Shui Hing mahjong shop in Kowloon. Three Hong Kong people were killed. The police fired and injured three criminals. On May 10, 1992, the Hong Kong INTERPOL requested assistance from Guangdong INTERPOL. Upon receiving the request, the Guangdong PSB formed a special task force and arrested the three Mainland criminal defendants—Cen Wei-hong, Li Ganfei, and Tang Yuzhang (all Mainland residents). The Guangdong PSB further sent police officers to Hong Kong to gather information and exchange intelligence. Defendants Cen and Li were tried and executed in China according to law. Tang was sentenced to death with execution suspended.

The overall impression one gets from these cases is that when the crimes were committed in Hong Kong by Mainland residents they would be prosecuted and punished inside China. However, when the crimes were committed in Hong Kong by Hong Kong residents they would be transferred back to Hong Kong for prosecution. If this is true, this is consistent with established international norm, i.e., a State can refuse to surrender one's own citizens, and PRC's espoused position, i.e., in cross-district cases,[23] a local resident should not be surrendered.

## Past Practice in Dealing with Cross-Border Crimes: PRC Police Perspective

The opening of China's border in 1979 brought new criminality of all kinds.[24] These included cross-district and cross-border[25] crimes.[26] Cross-district and especially cross-border crimes created enormous investigation and prosecution problems for the police, such as suspects eluding police capture by hiding in foreign countries or criminals planning a crime in foreign countries and executing the crime in China. The problem is most acute in the coastal areas, especially at the Shenzhen Special Economic Zone (SEZ).[27] The cross-border criminals escape local control and require international cooperation. One major characteristic of cross-border crimes in Shenzhen SEZ was that most of them involved foreigners, including Hong Kong and Macau residents, with the part of the criminal conduct, consequence, or effect taking place between the Shenzhen SEZ and Hong Kong or Macau. Some of the most frequent cross-border crimes were smuggling between Hong Kong and Shenzhen, illegal elements (e.g., gangs) coming to Shenzhen to commit crime (e.g., drugs trafficking), Hong Kong visitors going to Shenzhen for vice and prostitution, illegal immigrants committing crimes in Hong Kong (robberies), and organized criminals committing crimes in both Hong Kong and Shenzhen (e.g., car thefts stealing in Hong Kong and transported to China on order).

PRC–Hong Kong–Macau police cooperation arrangement was built upon the structure of INTERPOL.[28] China established an INTERPOL National Central Bureau in Beijing in 1984. In 1985, China invited the Commissioner of HKP in the capacity as INTERPOL representative to Beijing to exchange views and set forth an avenue for cooperation. The parties agreed upon five areas of cooperation:

1. Both parties agreed to establish regular and ad hoc working sessions to exchange views and discuss issues on how to improve and expand

the scope of cooperation. China agreed to set up an INTERPOL liaison center in Guangdong PSB in 1987 to facilitate liaison work with HKP.

2. Both sides agreed to exchange information on hijacking.

3. Both sides agreed to exchange intelligence and information over coinage crime. HKP agreed to provide experts in training of Guangdong PSB officers in discriminating forged money.

4. Both sides agreed to exchange intelligence and information over drugs. Both sides also agreed to exchange drug enforcement officers.

5. Both sides agreed to exchange intelligence and information on smuggling of cultural relics. HKP further agreed to stop the smuggling of Chinese cultural relics to Hong Kong and their export abroad. PRC MPS and HKP police officials were to meet twice a year in the "China–Hong Kong INTERPOL bilateral working session"[29] to be held alternatively in Hong Kong and Beijing. By 1995, there were twenty-one such meetings. According to unconfirmed data, from 1985 to 1995, over a ten-year period, the PRC assisted Hong Kong with 10,000 more cases and the HKP has assisted China through the INTERPOL in handling 500 cases.[30]

In the early part of 1986, two MPS officers were allowed to visit Hong Kong twice for the investigation of three major corruption cases that happened in Hubei, Shanghai, and Guangzhou. In 1987, HKP assisted the PRC police in gathering evidence in the investigation of corruption cases of Guangzhou, Donggang (Oriental) Hotel manger. The HKP also assisted the PRC in the repatriation of major corruption criminals to China for prosecution.

In 1992 and as a result of increase in cross-border violence and gang-instigated crimes, the PRC and HKP decided to improve their level of cooperation. At the fifteenth "China-Hong Kong INTERPOL bilateral working session," both sides agreed upon the following measures to increase communication and exchange of information: (1) The Ministry of State Security would station a permanent official in Hong Kong to facilitate the gathering and transmission of information. (2) In order to improve upon the PRC INTERPOL liaison center in Guangdong, the officer was upgraded to be headed by Guangdong Public Security Bureau head, Chen Shaoji. This allowed better coordination between Hong Kong and Guangdong Province. (3) In order to improve upon the coordination of operations and facilitation of communication between Hong Kong and Shenzhen, Shenzhen police would be directed personally by Shenzhen Public Security Department head, Liang Da. (4) To improve upon communication and exchange of intelligence and information, both sides agreed to establish a twenty-four-hour duty roster.[31]

Overall, the PRC police is rightfully concerned about the level of cooperation they receive from the HKP. Notwithstanding the rise in cross-border crimes, the HKP have been less than helpful, for legal and political reasons, to assist PRC police in their law enforcement activities. A top police official observed that once a criminal escaped into Hong Kong there was little the PRC police could do.[32] This has led the PRC to take the law into their own hands in violating Hong Kong territory in the arrest of criminals, e.g., by luring Hong Kong back to China or intruding into Hong Kong territory.[33]

In this respect and comparatively speaking, cross-border cooperation between Macau and Taiwan fares much better. For example in Macau, in the first half of 1992 alone, there were ten cases of exchange of criminals with Mainland police helping Macau in three cases and the Macau returning fugitives in seven cases. As examples, in May of 1992, a Macau murderer escaped into China. The Guangdong public security arrested and turned over the said fugitive within days on May 17. In early 1992, two Macau criminals committed murder in Zhuhai municipality and returned to Macau. Mainland police asked for the assistance of Macau. Macau police promptly investigated and returned the criminals to the Guangdong Public Security Bureau. In the case of Taiwan, the PRC and Taiwan worked with each other through two channels. One is through official INTERPOL channel. The other is through private organizations and informal arrangements. The first case of cooperation was the dispatch of a fugitive for justice from the PRC to Taiwan in August of 1988. Taiwan murderer, Yang Ming, was arrested by the PRC police and returned to Taiwan through Singapore.[34] Informally, the PRC has first worked through the Red Cross for the return of criminals to the PRC. In September of 1990, the PRC working through the Red Cross was able to enter into two agreements with Taiwan over the return of smugglers and criminal suspects and offenders—"Extradition transactions agreement" (Qianfan Zuoye Xieyi Shu) and "Jin Meng Xie Yi." The police cooperation agreement was put to good use one month later for the return of a PRC embezzler. On, February 22, 1989, Wu Daipeng, a Beijing Bank employee stole US$3.44 million and escaped to Taiwan. The PRC police posted Wu on a wanted list with INTERPOL and asked Taiwan to help. On March 17, 1990, Taiwan, Taipei district court sentenced Wu to one-year sentence for fraudulent documents. After he served his time, he was extradited to China through arrangement with the Red Cross.[35]

The multijurisdictional cross-border robbery on board of the hydrofoil "Eastern Star" best illustrates the lack of reciprocal cooperation by the HKP to PRC police request for assistance. On June 13, 1995, PRC police requested the return of the principal offender, Liang Bin who escaped and was arrested in Hong Kong as a result of incompatibility of the legal system. In November of 1995, the Chinese INTERPOL National Central Bureau Chief Zhu Yin-tao formally asked for the extradition of Liang Bin at the "Guangdong–Hong Kong border liaison annual working meeting," but to no avail. He expressed his views to the Hong Kong press, criticizing that Hong Kong should not be a safe haven for cross-border criminals.[36]

Another case illustrating the frustration confronted by PRC police authority in dealing with cross-border crime without the help of HKP is the Wah Ye watch and jewelry shop murder and robbery case. On December 28, 1989 at about 9 p.m., the Wah Ye watch and jewelry shop in Guangzhou was robbed by three robbers armed with two guns and one hammer. The robbers killed a shop keeper and a security staff and ran away with HK$100,000 jewelry. In May 1990, the Guangzhou Municipality Public Security Bureau arrested two suspects—Guo Rui and Li Ping-wei. They were prosecuted and sentenced to death. The other principal criminal—Lu Jing escaped to Hong Kong. The Guangzhou Public Security Bureau sought the help of HKP through the INTERPOL. In early December 1991, the suspect Lu Jing was arrested by the Hong Kong immigration for using a false passport to enter Hong Kong and was handed over to the police. The Guangzhou public security sought his return for being a Mainland resident and committing a murder in China. The HKP refused to hand over Lu Jing to the Guangzhou police, but prosecuted him for relevant counts of using a false passport and illegal stay. He was given a sentence of twenty-five years. The HKP promised to return Lu Jing after he served his sentence in Hong Kong.

*Prior Negotiation*

It was repeatedly claimed that the failure to ask for the return of Cheung Tse-keung to Hong Kong was due to a lack of a formal rendition agreement between the PRC and the HKSAR making possible for his return.[37] People who were familiar with the negotiation—Tam Wai-zhu, Martin Li, and James To—all acknowledged that the lack of an agreement was not a result of the failure of effort. The main obstacle in reaching a rendition agreement with the PRC was Hong Kong's lack of confidence in China's criminal justice system. Specifically, Hong Kong wanted China to promise not to use capital punishment over criminals returned to China under such an agreement.[38] Hong Kong feared that the return of criminals to China would violate Hong Kong's commitment to rule of law and international treaty commitments over human rights.[39] In this regard, the Hong Kong SAR government was bound by the Chinese Expatriation Ordinance (Cap. 235), which provided that if the crime for which a fugitive is wanted is punishable by death in the requesting country but not in Hong Kong, Hong Kong normally will not extradite or render that fugitive to the requesting country unless an undertaking is given to the effect that he would not be sentenced to death. The *Final Report on Conflicts of Laws, Extradition, and other Related Issues* by the Special Group on Law further suggested that any agreement to return criminals to China must follow international norms and practice,[40] i.e., double criminality,[41] prima facie rule,[42] political crimes are not extraditable,[43] and previous crimes not sought for extradition are not triable.[44]

During the Basic Law drafting process, there were extensive discussions over judicial assistance. At that time, Hong Kong's negotiation was guided by three principles:

1.   the rendition offense must also be a crime in Hong Kong, i.e., the double criminality rule;
2.   the punishment between the PRC and HK should not be too wide, e.g., the PRC with death penalty versus HK without any death penalty; and
3.   there must be clear criminal procedures.[45]

The PRC Hong Kong SAR Consultation Committee Report on Conflict of Laws and Extradition openly acknowledged the inevitability of conflict of laws given the coexistence of two distinctly different legal systems side by side.[46] The report confirmed that except for the PRC Constitution, no national law applies to Hong Kong. However, it also anticipated the problem of concurrent criminal jurisdiction, thus raising the issue of double jeopardy. The report recommended a "territorial" jurisdiction approach: "Should be handled by the place the criminal committed the crime . . . whether (the criminal) is a Hong Kong resident or mainland resident, if the criminal conduct is in Hong Kong, should be tried and prosecuted in Hong Kong."[47] This alleviated and provided for a solution to problems caused by the operations of the two "different" legal systems. The report suggested judicial assistance to be agreed in the future.

On November 27, 1998, the HKSAR government established the following principles in its future negotiation with China over a rendition agreement: (1) rendition agreement must conform to Basic Law, Article 95; (2) any rendition arrangement must follow Hong Kong Laws; (3) any rendition agreement must be acceptable to Hong Kong and the PRC; and (4) any agreement must take into account the principle of "one country, two systems" and the differences between the two legal systems. It should protect people's rights as well as prevent cross-border criminals from avoiding justice. The protection of a criminal's rights offered by rendition agreements China signed with other countries can be used as a source, e.g., double criminality, should not be further transferred to a third country, waiver of death sentence, and exception to political crime; (5) all rendition must comply with Article 19 of the Basic Law.[48] On December 8, 1998, the secretary for security made one critical change to the earlier given principles for negotiating a rendition agreement with the PRC, i.e., Hong Kong will not insist on waiver of death penalty as a condition of return.[49]

## Notes

1. The Hong Kong Justice Department would not release any information pertaining to past or present negotiation with China over rendition or extradition of criminals. Peter Wong, Senior Assistant Solicitor General (policy), was of the opinion that any release of such sensitive information, especially at this juncture, would intervene with any future negotiation with China over cross-border crime cooperation. (Phone interview, November 20, 1999; letter to "Request of Information for Academic Research" was not responded to.) A justice official, Linda Lam, Extradition section, Hong Kong Justice Department, was willing to confirm that there was no existing legal avenue for the rendition or extradition of criminals. No criminals from Hong Kong were ever surrendered. (Phone interview, October 28, 1998).

2. What is needed in any public policy analysis and debate, including legal ones, is a sense of proportion as informed by pertinent facts—what is the problem, how important is the problem, what are the alternatives. William N. Dunn, *Public Policy Analysis* (NJ: Prentice-Hall, 1981), 44 ("The provision of information about policy problems is the most critical task of policy analysis, since the way a problem is defined governs our ability to search out and identify appropriate solutions. Inadequate or faculty information . . . may result in a fatal error: solving the wrong formulation of a problem when instead one should have solved the right one"). The impression one gets from reading the newspaper and watching the TV is that the "Big Spender" case is one of its kind. For that reason alone, it has been suggested

that the case must be dealt with judiciously and immediately, lest a "bad" precedent will be created or worse yet, no decision made at all. Nothing could be further from the truth. While it is true that the "Big Spender" case in Hong Kong, much like the O. J. Simpson case in the United States, has the potential of defining the legal landscape—interpretation, practice, and culture—in Hong Kong as a result of its high profile, it is not the only case nor the best case to tackle sensitive and nuanced cross-border crime issues. The highly charged case distracted our attention from asking more fundamental legal–factual or political–ideological questions. It also forced us to adopt a more reactive case-by-case approach than a more reflective and comprehensive approach.

3.  Looking at the "Big Spender" case, and with the hysteria stirred up by the public opinion makers, the impression one gets is that the PRC central government could not be trusted to protect Hong Kong's legal autonomy and would take every opportunity to interfere with Hong Kong's legal authority. Nothing could be further from the truth. For example, in the past, the PRC government has been most supportive of Hong Kong law enforcement officials by sending as many as 128 offenders back with none being surrendered by Hong Kong in return. The more instructive observation is that without any formal police/judicial cooperative arrangement, the two sides have been working out solutions for cross-border crime problems one case at a time. The building up of trust between the PRC and HKSAR, leading to common expectations or mutual understanding of how to resolve conflict of criminal jurisdictions, is yet another way of customary law-making, i.e., law from the bottom-up through practice rather than from the top-down by decree.

4.  Ease of transportation and lowering of immigration control make traveling between the PRC and HKSAR effortless; cross-border crimes prosper as a matter of course. A high-ranking (retired) police officer who was familiar with cross-border liaison matters informed this author that HKP routinely dealt with cross-border criminal cases as part of cross-border duties. (Phone interview on October 28, 1998, and personal interview on November 17, 1998.)

5.  "Mrs. Ip Is Not Concerned about Similar Incidences Like Cheung Tsekeung's Case before an Agreement," *Hong Kong Economic Journal*, December 12, 1998.

6.  *Police Annual Review* (1996), 27.

7.  For INTERPOL in China generally, see chap. 7 to Xian Dang, *Police work implicating foreigners to China* [Zhongguo shewai jingwu] (Beijing: Zhongguo renmin gongan daxue chubanshe, 1997).

8.  Wu Zhiqiang, *HKP* (Guangzhou: Guangdong renmin chubanshe, 1996), 362.

9.  The HKSAR government justice officials have officially acknowledged the existence of informal and ad hoc administrative arrangements for the extradition of criminals to Hong Kong. S. C. Grenville Cross (Director of Public Prosecution), "Letter: Criticism over the Big Spender Case Unfair," *SCMP*, November 4, 1998. ("Without such an (rendition) agreement, the mainland authorities, nonetheless, have assisted Hong Kong through administrative arrangements to secure the return of suspected criminals who are Hong

Kong residents.") Information is transmitted to the other side by way of a "speaking note" (*suo tie*).

10. David McClean, *International Judicial Assistance* (New York: Clarendon Press, 1992). (INTERPOL or International Criminal Police Organization was first established in 1923 and had since grown to be a 150-member-country organization. Its headquarters is at Lyon, but works through a network of National Central Bureau. It operates a system of international notices for wanted (red) and professional (green) criminals. It has 100,000 files on international criminals and processed 350,000 messages a year.) Both the PRC and HKSAR are current members of INTERPOL sharing in criminal intelligence and mutual assistance.

11. John Bassett Moore, *Extradition*, vol 1 (Boston: The Boston Book Company, 1891), 1 (Expulsion was another way of getting rid of undesirable inhabitants in a State.)

12. Zhiqiang, *HKP*, 362.

13. Ibid., 366.

14. From the data gathered from official sources, the pattern of PRC's extradition of criminals to Hong Kong is as follows: 1990–1994 (52/48 or 1.1/month), 1994–1995 (18/12 or 1.5/month), 1995–1997 (31/24 or 1.3/month), 1997–November 5, 1998 (17 or 1.54/month). The data revealed a constant trend.

15. "Mrs. Ip is not Concerned about Similar Incidences Like Cheung Tse-keung's Case before an Agreement."

16. Ibid. (Figures provided by the secretary for security.)

17. We do not know what other issues were discussed at the meeting. Inasmuch as such of the agenda items were brought up by the Guangzhou Public Security Bureau, we can draw an inference that the PRC side was not happy with some aspects of the cross-border crime cooperation arrangement, i.e., lack of reciprocity over the surrendering of criminals from HKP to the PRC. This reading of the agenda was buttressed by a public statement of PRC MPS that China was not happy about the current "informal" arrangement with HKP. The public statement by MPS is important. Constitutionally and administratively, HKSAR government is directly under the control and supervision of the central government. Guangzhou could not work directly, but only through the central government in seeking cooperation from Hong Kong. See Article 94, Basic Law of Hong Kong, SAR.

18. The cooperation offered by PRC police in fighting crime and arresting cross-border criminals are acknowledged by the past and present Commissioner of Police, since 1991. See *Police Annual Review* (1991) (HKP cooperation with PRC police helped in foiling smuggling rings.) *Police Annual Review* (1992) (Cooperation with PRC police continued to improve with escaped criminals from Hong Kong brought back to justice.) *Police Annual Review* (1993) (As a result of PRC–HKP cooperation, cross-border gangs were destroyed and many criminals were returned to Hong Kong to be dealt with by law.) *Police Annual Review* (1994) (Because of the excellent cooperation between HKP and PRC public security, the escape of fugitives into China and cross-border crimes are under control.) *Police Annual Review* (1995) (MPS officials made clear that China would not be made a shelter for Hong Kong criminals. The PRC and HKP shared intelligence and mounted

joint operations to arrest and deport cross-border criminals. This resulted in the monthly extradition of Hong Kong fugitives from China). *Police Annual Review* (1996).

19. Zhiqiang, *HKP*, 366.

20. Liu Guoxiang, "Current Existing Problems Confronted by Mainland Public Security Organ in the Handling of Criminal Cases Implicating Hong Kong and Post-1997 Strategies" [Danqian neidi gongan jiguan banli xiegang xingshi anjian zhong cunzai de falu wenti ji 1997 nian hou de duice], *Gongan Yinjiu* [Public Security Studies] 51: 32–37. See discussion in "Past practice in dealing with cross-border crimes: PRC police perspective."

21. Ibid., 367.

22. Zhiqiang, *HKP*, 370–90.

23. Legally, HKSAR is a part of China. Any jurisdictional disputes are to be settled under the PRC Constitution and Basic Law.

24. Kam C. Wong, *Police Reform in China* (New York: Taylor and Francis, 2011), chap. 1. Feng Shuliang, *Methods of Crime Prevention in China* [Zhongguo Yuefang Fanzui Fanlue] (Beijing: Falu chubanshe, 1994), 20–39 (Between 1984 and 1993, crime rose from 510,000 reported cases to 1,618,000 cases with major crimes rising from 63,000 to 539,000. There was noted increase in the seriousness, violence, sophistication, organization, youthfulness, and variability of crimes.)

25. In China, "cross-district crime" is "*kua qu fanzui*" and "cross-border crime" is "*kua jin fanzui*." A cross-border crime occurs when the conduct (*xing wei*) or consequence (*hou guo*) of a crime overlaps two criminal jurisdictions. When a cross-border crime is committed by a foreigner, it becomes a *xie wei* case meriting different treatment. A criminal case involving Hong Kong residents (*xie kang*) is characterized by the following: (1) The criminal defendant is a Hong Kong resident. (2) The victim of the crime is a Hong Kong resident. (3) Either the conduct (*xing wei*) or consequence (*hou guo*) of a crime overlapped China–Hong Kong criminal jurisdictions. Wang Changy (Editor-in-Chief), *Analysis of Criminal Cases Involving Foreigners and Hong Kong and Macau in the Shenzhen Special Economic Zone* [Shenzhen Jingji Tequ She-wai She-Kang- Aou Xingshi Anli Pingxi] (Beijing: Renmin fayuan chubanshe, 1990), 3.

26. Shuliang, *Methods of Crime Prevention in China*, 27–28 (Cross-district crimes in 1980 were 230 percent of that of 1980).

27. Ibid., 32. (In 1991, 31,900,000 people visited Shenzhen, an increase of 11.3 percent from a year ago. In 1984, there were 184 foreign criminals.) Changyin, *Analysis of Criminal Cases*, 1. (Shenzhen SEZ was established by "Guangdong Province Special Economic Zone Regulations" ["Guangdong Sheng Jingji Tequ Tiaoli"]. The said regulations were adopted and promulgated by the NPC in August of 1980 to attract foreign investment, technology transfer, and promote trade. The SEZ attracted large numbers of outside criminals; between 1981 and 1982 the number of crimes rose by 70 percent. In 1984, they rose by another 100 percent.)

28. Dang, *Police Work Implicating Foreigners to China*, 458–61.

29. Zhiqiang, *HKP*, 362.

30. Dang, *Police Work Implicating Foreigners to China*, 459.

31. Ibid., 460.

32. Guoxiang, "Current Existing Problems," 32–37.

   (The Hong Kong government routinely rejected rendition requests from the Mainland based on spurious grounds: no crime has been committed in Hong Kong; no sufficient evidence produced by PRC police; the offense is not extraditable as a capital crime; the crime should be prosecuted in Hong Kong.) See Darren Goodsir, "Hijack Suspect to Stay in Hong Kong," *SCMP*, June 30, 1995.

33. "Hui Ki-an Acknowledged That Part of the Crime Rate Resulted from Economic Downturn," *Hong Kong Economic Journal*, January 8, 7. (The Hong Kong Commissioner of Police denied reports that PRC public security has been entering Hong Kong waters to arrest criminals.)

34. Ibid., 462.

35. Ibid., 463. More specifically, the PRC and Taiwan have negotiated informal private agreements through the PRC Hai-Xia Lian-an Guanxi Xiehui (Cross-straits two borders relations association) and Taiwan Hi-Xia Jiaoliu Jijin hui (Foundation on cross-straits exchange) to deal with extradition of hijackers. In 1995, they entered into two agreements: "Lian-an Jieji-fan deng qianfan ennti" (Business concerning cross-straits hijacking criminals). The agreement made possible the apprehension, detention, and extradition of hijackers and "*Weifan you guan guiding jinru duifang dicu renyuan de qianfan ji xiang guan wenti*" (Questions related to the extradition of persons intruding into others' area in violation of regulations. The agreement dealt with illegal immigrants and unauthorized fugitives into each other's territories.)

36. Zhiqiang, *HKP*, 368.

37. Cross, "Letter: Criticism over the Big Spender Case Unfair." (It is a matter of regret that there has been no formal rendition agreement between Hong Kong and the Mainland over the transfer of fugitives or criminal cases.)

38. "Hong Kong Government Confirmed that it will Respect Mainland's Verdict" *Tai Kung Pao*, November 13, 1998, A5. (In a press conference after the "Big Spender" verdict, the secretary for security confirmed that the Hong Kong government had exchanged ideas with PRC officials over return of criminals. The major obstacle was over death penalty; Hong Kong had no death penalty while the PRC did.)

39. United Nation has a model rendition/extradition agreement. The model agreement did not make exemption from death penalty for returned criminals mandatory. For example, England and Canada both have the discretion of no extradition in capital cases. England has on two occasions returned to Germany two capital offenders without promise of exemption of death sentence. Hong Kong has strictly abided by the rule of no capital punishment in the past. "Yip Suk-yi Said That the Death Penalty Issue Should Be Dealt with According to Situation, the Government Has Difficulty in Arriving at Judicial Assistance with the Mainland," *Hong Kong Economic Journal*, December 4, 1998.

40. The Extradition (Hong Kong) Ordinance, Cap. 236, making Extradition Act 1870 (the Act) applicable to Hong Kong.

41. First Schedule to the Act.

42. Section 10 of the Act.
43. Section 3 of the Act.
44. Section 19 of the Act.
45. "Tam Wai Chu: Hong Kong Doing Away with Death Penalty Increase Difficult for Judicial Assistance," *Ming Bao*, November 9, 1998.
46. "Conflict of Law, Extradition and Other Related Issues: Final Report" (approved by the Executive Committee, June 12, 1987), *Right of Revision to Basic Law Final Report* (approved by the Executive Committee, June 12, 1987) (PRC Hong Kong SAR Consultation Committee, central government, and SAR Relations Special Committee).
47. Ibid.
48. "SAR Discussed China–Hong Kong Rendition Arrangements, Political and Capital Offenders Will Not Be Transferred," *Hong Kong Economic Journal*, November 28, 1998, 4.
49. "Yip Suk-yi Said That the Death Penalty Issue Should Be Dealt with According to Situation." The sudden change in position outraged liberal legislators who promised a "take no prisoner" fight ahead, including internationalizing the issue. (Martin Lee, Chairman, Democratic Party, would fight until the "end of the world" including internationalizing the issue if waiver of death penalty is not made a mandatory agreement of any of the rendition agreements with China.) Martin Lee was also concerned about the secretary for security making critical concession before the negotiations started. "Martin Lee is Critical of Yip-Lau Suk-yi: On the Transfer of Fugitive Arrangement, Weakening Once Stance without Negotiation," *Ming Bao*, December 8, 1998.

# 6

# Legal Analysis

## Introduction

The literature on legal issues in Hong Kong and China cross-border crime is sparse and mostly in Chinese.[1] However, there are a few good academic papers informing upon the topic.

As early as 1986, Prof. Chen from Hong Kong University Law Faculty first raised the issue of a possible conflict of jurisdictional issues in criminal law between the PRC and HKSAR in cross-border crime cases.[2] In his article, Chen raises the much anticipated issue by citing Hong Kong people's concern about reported cases of a criminal being arrested and executed in China for a robbery and murder in Macau and a Hong Kong resident being fined for selling a boat stolen in Hong Kong and later punished again by the Hong Kong authority. He suggests amending the PRC Criminal Law to make provisions for five kinds of possible conflict of law situations, namely: (1) a person who has committed an act in Hong Kong, which is a crime in HKSAR as well as a crime in Mainland China, e.g., killing a Chinese diplomat; (2) a person who has committed an act in Hong Kong, which is a crime in HKSAR but is a not a crime in Mainland China, e.g., burning a Chinese flag; (3) a person who has committed an act in Hong Kong, which is not a crime in HKSAR but is a crime in Mainland China, e.g., Falun Gong; (4) a person who has committed a crime in Mainland China and escaped to Hong Kong; and (5) a person who has committed an act which can be deemed as happened in Hong Kong and violating Hong Kong law as well as deemed as happened in Mainland violating Mainland law, e.g., "Big Spender" case.

Professor Chen is of the opinion that the PRC Criminal Law (Art. 3 [on territorial jurisdiction], Art. 4 and 5 [on nationality jurisdiction]) should have no application in Hong Kong, except in situations where the consequence or effect of the Hong Kong criminal deeds impacted upon the PRC in material and substantial ways. He further points out that whether PRC Criminal Law Article 5, on criminal jurisdiction over overseas PRC citizens, should apply to Hong Kong must be carefully studied and judiciously provided for. With concurrent jurisdiction cases (conflict of law type 5 above), both HK and the PRC have the right to prosecute and try the case.

Professor Chen opines that Article 7 of PRC Criminal Law dealing with investigation and prosecution of a Chinese national without Chinese territory should be made to apply. Professor Chen suggests that the HKSAR should not stand in the way of the PRC assuming primary criminal jurisdiction in such cases. However, he also implores the PRC legal and judicial authorities to respect and accept the overlapping jurisdictional interests and claims of the Hong Kong courts as real and compelling, deserving of careful consideration. He did not address the issue on who should have the right to try the case first.

Professor Chen's article, albeit short and not fully argued legally, was insightful in anticipating the kinds of cross-border crime cases and concurrent jurisdictional disputes we have to deal with in the "Big Spender" case. Its major contribution is in providing a useful analytical framework for future discussion. However, regrettably, it did not go far enough in suggesting a viable solution to such an intractable problem.

Recently, Professors Mushkat[3] and Fu wrote articles[4] discussing jurisdictional issues raised in cross-border crime cases, making them pioneering authorities in this emerging field of "one country, two systems" legal scholarship.

Mushkat wrote her article in 1993 when there was no in-depth legal analysis on the jurisdictional reach of Hong Kong criminal law. One of the questions she  posed anticipated the "Big Spender" case, namely "To what extent is Hong Kong guaranteed a right to exercise jurisdiction over its territory free from interference? Could Chinese criminal jurisdiction be extended to acts committed in Hong Kong?"[5]

Professor Mushkat starts by observing that the PRC exercised criminal jurisdiction consistent with international law practice, i.e., criminal jurisdiction based on "territorial principle" (PRC Criminal Law [1979],[6] Art. 3 (1) (2))[7]; "active personality principle" (PRC Criminal Law [1979], Art. 4,[8] 5)[9]; "protective principle" (PRC Criminal Law [1979], Art. 6), and "passive personality principle" (PRC Criminal Law [1979], Art. 6); and "universality principle" (PRC Criminal Law [1979], Art. 7). Nevertheless, circumscribes and restricts the exercise of PRC jurisdiction to the narrowest territorial ambit, i.e., Chinese criminal law applies only to criminal conducts and consequences within China. She made the following observations in support of her contention.

First, Professor Mushkat fears that the PRC might allow "ideological considerations" to come into play in exercising (extraterritorial) criminal jurisdiction, thereby violating "international norms." "Specifically, an assertion of Chinese criminal jurisdiction over acts committed in Hong Kong based on such construction of the territorial principle would transgress the proscription of non-intervention . . . self-determination of national entities."[10] Professor Mushkat does not clarify what constituted "ideological considerations"[11] nor how any such "ideological considerations" might contaminate Chinese criminal jurisdiction, otherwise properly exercised. She also does not explain why issues of transgression of nonintervention were not implicated anytime any country exercised an extraterritorial jurisdiction.

A fair reading of her article suggests that Prof. Mushkat was not concerned with the "proper" excise of extraterritorial jurisdiction by the PRC, which after all is well accepted as an international norm. What she disapproved of is the legitimate legal authority (e.g., the extraterritorial reach of domestic criminal law) to achieve impermissible political ends, e.g., punishing political dissidents. If that should be Prof. Mushkat's objection, she did not address the issue of why certain ideological (liberal) use of extraterritorial criminal jurisdiction is proper, e.g., criminalizing Vietnam war protesters overseas, while others are not, e.g., punishing people overseas for assisting June 4 students.

Second, Prof. Mushkat fears that liberal (and indiscriminate) exercise of PRC criminal jurisdiction might encroach upon, and would in time destroy the "high-degree of autonomy pledged by China under the Sino-British Declaration . . . (and) . . . formal constitutional document (e.g., the Basic Law)." While Prof. Mushkat's fear and concern are real, her conclusion that the Joint Declaration and later the Basic Law "implied" or otherwise "intended" the categorical exclusion or displacement of PRC criminal jurisdiction in cases of concurrent jurisdiction is not warranted by a fair reading of the language of the Basic Law (Art. 18) as supported by a detailed analysis of the legislative history of the Basic Law. The issue of PRC criminal jurisdiction applying to Hong Kong, in particular issues with concurrent jurisdiction and conflict of law were discussed but never resolved. More pertinently, the Basic Law drafters were aware of such problems, but chose not to decide.

The detailed examination of the legislative historical account (May 1986 to December 1987)[12] leading up to the drafting of Article 18 showed that the issue of conflict over criminal jurisdiction was not discussed.[13]

The clearest statement of the PRC versus SAR criminal jurisdiction in broad terms dealing with conflict of law arising out of concurrent jurisdiction cases is to be found in the *Final Report on Conflicts of Laws, Extradition, and Other Related Issues* prepared by the Special Group on Law to the Basic Law Consultative Committee.[14] The Report proposed that, in dealing with criminal cases involving Hong Kong and China, the principle should be based on place of commission of offense.[15]

> This means when a person, whether a Hong Kong inhabitant or an inhabitant of mainland China, who has committed an offense in Hong Kong should be prosecuted and tried according to the law of Hong Kong; whereas a person, whether a Hong Kong inhabitant or an inhabitant of mainland China, who has committed an offense in China should be prosecuted and tried according to the law of mainland.[16]

A careful reading of the Consultation Report on the draft Basic Law reveals the following "Issues to be clarified"[17] under Article 18[18]:

> If a resident of the HKSAR is suspected of having committed in other parts of China, a crime which may or may not relate to defense or foreign affairs, and has returned to Hong Kong, what will the Central People's Government or the Hong Kong Government do? Will the suspect stand trial in the HKSAR, or in the place where his alleged crime was committed? If a resident of the China is suspected of having committed in the HKSAR a crime which may or may not relate to defense or foreign affairs, and has returned to his original domicile, what will the Central People's Government do? Will the suspect stand trial in his original domicile, or in Hong Kong the HKSAR?

Finally and most emphatically, the Consultation Report on the draft Basic Law Article 94 (which provided for judicial assistance over cross-border crime issues) clearly articulated the problem facing the drafters of the Basic Law in dealing with cross-border crime—there are issues searching for answers in the Basic Law:

> This article fails to address the question of cross-border crimes. If the purpose of holding consultation is to find an answer to this

question, there will be no need for the Basic Law since such a practice is against the principle of ruling cases in accordance with law.

There are no extradition arrangements between China and Hong Kong at present. Special provisions should be made in the Basic Law on how such matters will be dealt with in the year subsequent to 1997.

In all, one gets the distinct impression from reading the legislative history to the Basic Law that the drafters were keenly aware of the legal issues, especially jurisdictional ones, implicated in cross-border crimes but chose to deal with other more pressing issues, e.g., how Basic Law is to be interpreted, and allow such other issues to be dealt with on a case-by-case basis.

Eager to reach a result protective of Hong Kong's "autonomy," Professor Mushkat overstated her case.

My problem with Prof. Mushkat in this regard is that her construction of international law practice in general, and PRC's legal obligations in particular, under the Basic Law, is more informed by expressed liberal values (human rights) and unarticulated conservative fear (Communist ideology) than a balanced reading and considered judgment of the requirements of the law, in the PRC–HKSAR sociopolitical context, post-1997. In sum, Prof. Mushkat has weighted in and taken side, good intention notwithstanding.

Professor H. L. Fu provides us with a more comprehensive and balanced assessment of the "relevance of Chinese Criminal Law to Hong Kong and its Residents."[19] Professor Fu of Hong Kong University Law School is a subject matter expert on the PRC–SAR criminal (conflict of) law relationship, including cross-border crime. As a lawyer trained in the PRC and Toronto, he analyzed cross-border crime issues with a dual legal–cultural perspective. His approach to resolving Cheung's type of case is one of legal pragmatist. Fu takes the position that the PRC and HKSAR legal (criminal justice) systems, as a result of historical, economic, social, political, and cultural reasons of necessity and for utility have to interact and accommodate each other. The "one country, two systems" approach does not contemplate complete separation but anticipates strategic alliance. However, cooperation must be based on the principles of equality and respect. In the Cheung case, Fu is in favor of allowing PRC courts to assume jurisdiction over Cheung, in as much as Cheung has committed serious crimes in China. Fu recognized that in assuming criminal jurisdiction, the PRC courts might have appeared to have pre-empted and usurped Hong Kong criminal jurisdiction in prosecuting and trying Cheung for crimes committed in Hong Kong.

The Chinese (the PRC) literature on the subject—cross-border crime, concurrent criminal jurisdiction, and judicial assistance—is much more substantial, though, as can be expected, much less analytical and critical. However, there are still some discernible differences of views[20]; reflecting a lack of consensus and closure over the "one country, two systems" subject matter, e.g., what is the legal status of Hong Kong–Taiwan–Macau as an administrative division of the PRC?

The PRC scholars have long been interested in and perplexed by legal problems raised by the "one country four legal districts" problems, e.g., how PRC's legal system accommodates three kinds of distinctly different—Hong Kong, Macau, and Taiwan—if not even completely incompatible—in philosophy, purpose, organization, and practice—legal systems. All conceded that conflicts over jurisdiction are real and inevitable, and should be catered for. There is a common characterization of the problems and mutual identification of the issues involved. There is less of an agreement  on how such conflicts could be satisfactorily resolved.

Professor Zhao Bingshi of the Law Department of the People's University is an eminent PRC authority on legal issues involved in cross-border crime, particularly on issues involving the PRC–HKSAR–Taiwan–Macau. He has written a number of influential articles in Chinese as well as in English on the subject matter of crimes involved.[21] His work is representative of the PRC official viewpoints. But first one must address the HKSAR view.

### HKSAR Government's Position

The HKSAR government's legal position is more clearly stated in a public statement issued by the Government Information Centre on November 11, 1998,[22] entitled: "Government clarify court's jurisdictional authority over Cheung  Tse-keung and Li Yuk-fai." The public statement stressed the following points with respect to the Cheung Tse-keung's case: (1) According to Article 18 of the Basic Law, the only national laws applicable to Hong Kong were those specified in Annex III and "PRC Criminal Law" is not one of the national laws mentioned. (2) Although Cheung Tse-keung is a Hong Kong resident, he was suspected of perpetrating criminal acts in China referenced under Article 6 of the "PRC Criminal Law." Thus, "PRC Criminal Law" jurisdiction is applicable to Cheung's case. Article 6 provides that if any of the "conduct or consequence" of a criminal act happened within Chinese territories, the PRC will have jurisdiction over the case. (3) According to Article 19 of the Basic Law; "The courts of Hong Kong Special Administrative Region shall have jurisdiction over all cases in the Region." But Article 19 does not give HKSAR court exclusive jurisdiction over cross-border crime cases implicating the PRC as well as HKSAR jurisdictions.

The government's position summarizes the opinions more elaborately discussed in three articles by three prominent SAR government serving justice officials[23] and at a closed-door briefing to the legislators on the case. Together they raised three pertinent questions:

First, was the secretary for justice's decision not to prosecute Cheung Tse-keung in Hong Kong legally justifiable? More specifically, by PRC law, did the PRC have jurisdiction to hear the case, exclusively or concurrently?[24] This is a question of the proper exercise of criminal jurisdiction over the prosecution and adjudication of the Cheung's case, in a conflicting and competing jurisdictional context and contest. "Jurisdiction concerns the powers of the state to affect people, property and circumstances and reflects the basic principles of state sovereignty, equality of states and non-interference in domestic affairs."[25]

Second, collaterally, whether secretary for justice's decision not to seek extradition/rendition is legally justifiable?[26]

Third, as a policy mater, how should the secretary for justice have balanced the rights and expectations of Hong Kong people versus PRC people in trying the case?[27]

In response to the first question, the Acting Solicitor General and former chairman of Local Prosecutors' Association are in agreement—if part of the kidnapping case happened in China, China acquired and retained undisputed jurisdiction, Hong Kong's claim of jurisdiction notwithstanding.[28] In sum, the official position is that *both* Hong Kong and the PRC have concurrent jurisdiction over the case.[29] Their argument is based on the commonly accepted principle of "territorial" jurisdiction in international law.[30] More specifically, Article 6(3) of PRC Criminal Law provides that: "If either the commission of an offense or its effect takes place within the territory of the PRC, the offense shall be considered to be an offense committed within the territory of the PRC."

There is very little factual dispute in the Cheung's case that the act of conspiracy to commit kidnapping happened in China, i.e., in hotels in Shenzhen, and the actual kidnapping happened in Hong Kong. This gives the PRC undisputed territorial jurisdiction over the case.[31] HKSAR's legal position is best captured by the secretary for security in her closed-door briefing for the legislators on November 3, 1998:

> Mr. Cheung and his gang are being tried in the mainland for offences committed in the mainland against the mainland criminal codes . . . Article Six (of PRC Criminal Law) . . . provides that if an act or part of the crime or a consequence of the crime is committed in the mainland, mainland authorities have every right to prosecute the people concerned . . . this case, although the act of kidnapping may have occurred in Hong Kong, the mainland authorities are trying Cheung and his gang for conspiracy and the very detailed planning which took place in mainland, and the conspiracy . . . and illegal procurement of ammunitions and explosives—all of which occurred on the mainland.[32]

In response to the second question—on extraditing Cheung Tse-keung to Hong Kong to stand trial,[33] the HKSAR officials ruled out any attempt to ask for the return of Cheung Tse-keung at any time, either for prosecution on the basis of charges in Hong Kong or for serving the sentence imposed by China.[34] The position was based on three reasons: (1) there was not enough evidence for prosecution; (2) there was no rendition and no judicial assistance agreement between the PRC and Hong Kong; and (3) Hong Kong should respect PRC's legitimate exercise of criminal jurisdiction, once violations of PRC Criminal Law by Cheung were substantiated.

As to why HKSAR officials considered that there was not enough evidence to warrant prosecution, the Secretary for Security Mrs. Regina Ip made clear that since the kidnap victim did not report to the police, there was insufficient evidence to prosecute.[35] As to why there was a lack due diligence to collect evidence (from other sources through independent HKP investigation), the secretary for security did not explain.[36] On the issue of evidence, Li Shaoqiang, former chairman of Local Prosecutors' Association, made it clear that the evidentiary standard applied to criminal cases in Hong Kong courts, i.e., beyond a reasonable doubt, should not be compromised (in the Cheung case) to satisfy public needs for summary justice or retribution.[37]

However, notwithstanding the lack of evidence to arrest and prosecute Cheung Tse-keung, the HKP nevertheless assisted the PRC in the prosecution of the Cheung's case. The HKP further took decisive actions to seize all the ill-gotten gains of Cheung under the Organized and Serious Crimes Ordinance[38] on August 19, 1998, long before the case came to trial in China.[39] Ultimately, the Court of First Instance sided with the HKSAR government: "The courts have concluded that the offences specified in the affidavit have not been satisfactorily established because the victims have not provided the information."[40]

As to the request for surrendering of criminals between HKSAR and the PRC, the secretary for security made clear that any such arrangements must be based on mutuality and reciprocity as a matter of principle. HKSAR must stand ready to respect PRC's legal rights under the PRC Constitution before Hong Kong could expect her legal autonomy honored under the Basic Law. "One country, two systems" must be built upon a foundation of mutual respect and spirit of equality.[41]

> "Central to the formula (of 'one country, two systems') is mutual understanding. While the mainland authorities do not interfere with the judicial system of the SAR, so also must the SAR respect the legal processes of the mainland."[42] Particularly, in cases of concurring jurisdiction, if our justice officials were to insist on our legal autonomy, so can the PRC. If, as one of our legislator suggested, Hong Kong should demand an explanation from PRC on their rightful assumption of jurisdiction or exclusion of Hong Kong's jurisdiction in cross-border crime cases, should not the PRC authority be able to do the same? The ultimate issue is whether the PRC can hold legitimate rights and expectations over the autonomy of their own legal system. Our own confidence in Hong Kong's legal system does not provide legitimate grounds for us to interfere with the operations of the China's legal system, however much we dislike its application in Hong Kong.[43]

## China's Legal Position

In a press conference held in Guangzhou, the presiding judge in the "Big Spender" case,[44] Shi Anqi, made clear that the Guangzhou courts had jurisdiction in trying the case since all of the defendants, including Cheung Tse-keung, had either committed a crime in China, e.g., conspiracy to kidnap, or had engaged in cross-border crime, e.g., smuggling of firearms. In sum, either the conduct (*xingwei*) or the consequence (*houguo*) of crimes has taken place in China.[45] More specifically, in answer to Cheung and other defendants' jurisdiction argument, the Guangzhou Intermediary People's Court stated:

> Besides, defendants Cheung Tse-keung and Lau Ding-fun have raised objections over jurisdiction in regard to illegal trading and transportation of explosives, kidnapping and robbing of Hong Kong gold shops. After investigation, for people who were involved in the above crimes, some of the defendants are Hong Kong residents, some of the defendants are mainland residents; the kidnapping and robbing of gold shops were conducted in Hong Kong, but the conspiracy, planning, and preparatory conduct, all happened in the mainland; the explosives and instrumentality of crimes were all illegally procured in the mainland and transported to Hong Kong; defendants were all arrested in the mainland[46]; a lot of proceeds of crime, loots, and evidence were all recovered in the mainland.[47] Thus according to PRC Criminal Procedure Law, Article 24, the judicial organization in mainland possessed jurisdiction over the case.

## Legal Analysis: The Problems of Criminal Jurisdiction

The issue of criminal jurisdiction raised by "one country, two systems" was much anticipated, but never resolved. The issue was publicized in the press,[48] analyzed by scholars,[49] discussed by the Basic Law drafters,[50] and commented upon during the public consultation process.[51] For example, the Special Group on Law to the Basic Law Consultative Committee raised the question of conflicting criminal jurisdictions between the PRC and HKSAR:

> What coordinating arrangements should be made concerning the criminal jurisdictions of the courts of the HKSAR and mainland China in order to safeguard double jeopardy in cases where both Hong Kong and a mainland Chinese court might claim jurisdiction?[52]

With respect to competing PRC versus HKSAR criminal jurisdictions, the following issues were raised:

First, was there a proper exercise of jurisdiction by the PRC judicial authority? This is a legal–factual question to determine whether the judicial authority in China has acted extralegally.

Second, was the exercise of jurisdiction by the PRC, even if legal by domestic law, could be considered to be encroaching upon or usurping of other legal system's proper exercise of jurisdiction over the same case? This again is a legal–factual question to determine whether judicial authority has acted extraterritorially or extrajurisdictionally.

Third, in cases of concurrent jurisdiction or conflict of jurisdiction how should such conflicts of jurisdiction be resolved?

Article 6 of the PRC Criminal Law provides in pertinent part:

> This Law shall be applicable to anyone who commits a crime within the territory and territorial waters and space of the PRC, except as otherwise specifically provided by law ... If a criminal act or its consequence takes place within the territory or territorial waters or space of the PRC, the crime shall be deemed to have been committed within the territory and territorial waters and space of the PRC.

According to the facts of the Cheung Tse-keung's case, as found by the Guangzhou Intermediary People's Court and as independently verified by Hong Kong investigative report, Cheung Tse-keung had committed the following criminal acts in China:

1. In October 1997, the defendant Cheung Tse-keung supplied HK$150,000 and directed others to purchase 818.43 kg of explosives, 2,000 detonators, and 750 meters of fuse line from Mainland China.

2. From the end of 1995 to the beginning of 1996, Cheung Tse-keung and other defendants made multiple visits to Shenzhen, staying in Ming Du Hotel and Ri Sun Hostel, to secretly plot the kidnapping of Li XX. Cheung Tse-keung put up HK$1.4 million for the purchase of equipment, including two AK47 automatic rifles, one miniature machine gun, six pistols, and nine packages of explosives (weighing 1.887 kg), and renting of premises for locking up the hostages. Cheung also helped to smuggle the arms and ammunitions to Hong Kong.

3. At 6 p.m. on May 23, 1996, Cheung kidnapped Li XX and his driver and demanded and obtained a ransom of HK$1,030,000,000.

4. In April of 1977, defendant Cheung Tse-keung and others planned the kidnapping of Mr. Kwok in China—Guangzhou, Shenzhen, Dongguan. Cheung and Wu put up HK$ 2.2 million as expenses. At 6 p.m. on December 29, 1977, Cheung and other defendants kidnapped Kwok. After Cheung Tse-keung demanded and obtained HK$ 6,000,000,000 from the Kwok's family, the victim was released.

Given these facts in the case, there is no doubt that Cheung Tse-keung had committed criminal offenses in China and the PRC court had properly assumed jurisdiction in the case. Specifically, Article 24 of the PRC Criminal Procedure law provides:

> A criminal case shall be under the jurisdiction of the People's Court in the place where the crime was committed. If it is more appropriate for the case to be tried by the People's Court in the place where the defendant resides, then that court may have jurisdiction over the case.

However, the question remains as to whether or not the PRC court overreached its jurisdiction in taking over the adjudication of a case where both the conduct and the consequence of the criminal act of kidnapping happened in Hong Kong. More particularly, whether the PRC court has breached the spirit of the Basic Law of Hong Kong—allowing Hong Kong to be an autonomous and independent legal entity[53]—in its haste to assume jurisdiction of a case that happened mainly in Hong Kong. In support of this argument, one would readily observe that in the "Big Spender" case all crimes should not be treated equally for determining jurisdiction purpose. Conspiracy to kidnap, smuggling of arms and ammunitions, and illegal trading of explosives are all preparatory offenses to the main and completed offense of kidnapping. Thus, it can be argued that the preparatory offenses have merged with the completed offenses for determining jurisdictional purpose. In this regard, while Article 22 of the PRC Criminal Procedure Law provides that "Preparation for a crime refers to the preparation of the instruments or the conditions for a crime" is a crime in the PRC, the NPC has never intended "preparatory offenses" to be as serious as the completed offense. In fact, NPC made clear that preparatory offences should be "given a lighter or mitigated punishment or be exempted from punishment."[54]

Viewed in this light, it can be argued that with cases of cross-border crime, including that of the "Big Spender" case, preparatory crimes should not be tried in the jurisdiction where the initial "conduct" of the preparatory crime occurred (here China) but where the ultimate "consequences" of the final crime were felt (here Hong Kong).[55]

This position is buttressed by PRC's long-held position, before the Basic Law, in allowing cross-district (*huan qu*) crimes in China to be tried where the major crime occurred.[56] This is particularly the case when the NPC did not intend for the PRC Court to preempt the Hong Kong courts' criminal jurisdiction with the promulgation of the Basic Laws of Hong Kong.[57]

This position, compellingly argued by Hong Kong advocates, must ultimately be judged against international practices as applied to PRC context.[58]

## Position of International Law

According to the well-established position of international law, the penal jurisdiction of a country can be established based on five general principles:

> first, the territorial principle, determining jurisdiction by reference to the place where the offense is committed; second, the nationality principle, determining jurisdiction by reference to the nationality or national character of the person committing the offense; third, the protective principle, determining jurisdiction by reference to the national interest injured by the offense; fourth the universality principle, determining jurisdiction by reference to the custody of the person committing the offense; and fifth, the passive personality principle, determining jurisdiction by reference to the nationality or national character of the person injured.[59]

The position of common law is that crimes are local in effect and punishment. Each sovereign authority has undisputed jurisdiction over crime committed within its territory.[60] Collaterally, it has no interest to control and otherwise competent jurisdiction to prosecute extraterritorial crimes.[61] In this regard, Lord Macmillan opined:

> It is an essential attribute of sovereignty of this realm, as of all sovereign independent States, that it should possess jurisdiction over all persons and things within its territorial limits and all causes civil and criminal arising within these limits. This jurisdiction is exercised through the instrumentality of the duly constituted tribunals of the land.[62]

The territorial principle not only allows a State to prosecute and punish criminal acts within a State but also criminal conduct, a part of which occurred outside the State in any jurisdiction.

The territorial principles are well-established principles in international law as well as criminal code in many jurisdictions. In international law, American Law Institute (ALI), *Restatement (Third) Foreign Relations Law of the United States* (1987) provides in Section 403: Basis of Jurisdiction to Prescribe[63]: "Subject to Section 403, a state jurisdiction to prescribe law with respect to (1) (a) conduct that, wholly or in substantial part, takes place within its territory . . ."[64] In domestic penal code, the American Law Institute, *Model Penal Code*, Section 103, Territorial Applicability provides: "(1) Except as otherwise provided in this Section, a person may be convicted under this State of an offense committed by his own conduct or the conduct of another for which he is legally accountable, if: (a) either the conduct which is an element of the offense or the result which is such an element occurs within the state; or . . . (d) conduct occurring within the State establishes complicity in the commission of, or an attempt, solicitation or conspiracy to commit, an offense in another jurisdiction which is also an offense under the law of this State."

The British view on extraterritorial reach of State court is that the State can assert jurisdiction over persons or event where any element of an event takes place within its territory.[65] The "objective territorial principle" allows a State to punish criminal activities within the territorial limit of a State, even though some elements of the crime took place elsewhere.[66] The "subject" territorial principle allows a State to punish criminal activities commencing in its territory, even though the final element might have occurred abroad.[67]

"The jurisdiction of the nation within its own territory is necessarily exclusive and absolute. *It is susceptible  to no limitation not imposed by itself.* Any restriction upon itself, deriving validity from an external source, would imply a diminution of its sovereignty to the extent of the restriction . . . All exceptions, therefore, to the full and complete power of a nation within its own territories, must be traced up to the consent of the nation itself."[68]

## Notes

1.    There are many books and articles written about Basic Law; there are very few of them on issues relating to conflict of law, still less on legal problems involved in cross-border crimes. See "The Basic Law: A Bibliography of the Hong Kong Transition," *HKLJ* 27, no. 2 (1997): 251–60. In 1988, *The Journal of Chinese Law* devoted a whole issue to a "Symposium on the Hong Kong Basic Law," *The Journal of Chinese Law* 2, no. 1 (Spring 1988): 1–195, but none of the articles specifically address the issue of conflict of criminal law. For English language articles on legal issues in cross-border crime, see H. L. Fu, "The Relevance of Chinese Criminal Law in Hong Kong and its Residents," *HKLJ* 27, no. 2 (1997) 229–247; Zhao Bingzhi, "Issues in Criminal Law across the Taiwan Strait," *Journal of Chinese Law* 229 (1983): 227–51; Roda Mushkat, "Jurisdictional Issues in a "Highly Autonomous Region" – the Case of Hong Kong," *International and Comparative Law Quarterly* 42 (1993): 11–47.

    For Chinese articles, see Liu Guoxiang, "Legal Problems in Handling Criminal Cases Involving Hong Kong by Mainland Public Security Organs and Post-1997 Strategies," *Gongan Yanjiu* [Public Security Studies] 51 (1955): 32; Zhang Tao and Chen Weidong, "Discussion of Jurisdiction Authority over Criminal Cases Involving Hong Kong" ["Lun xiekang xingshi anjian de guanxia quan"], *Studies in Law* [Faxue Yanjiu] 3 (1992): 35–41; Li Xinjiang, "Legal Issue on Basic Law of Hong Kong and Crime Involving Hong Kong" ["Shang-Kang jiben fa yu xie-kang xingshi falu wenti"], *Politics and Law* [Zhenfa Luntan] 6 (1990): 65–69; Chen Chen Hongyi, "Principles of Handling Conflicts of Law between Hong Kong Special Administrative Region and Mainland China," *Wide Angle Monthly*, December 16, 1986; Nan Tian, *One Country Two Systems: Legal Issues* (1997), chap. 5, "The Conflicts and Resolution of Hong Kong Criminal Law and National Criminal Law"; Huang Jing, *Research on Inter-regional Conflict of Law* [Quji Congtufa Yanjiu] (Shanghai: Xuelin chubanshe , 1991); Liu Guoxiang, "Current Legal Issues in Handling Criminal Cases Involving Hong Kong by Mainland Public Security Organs and Post 1997 Strategies" [Dangqian yu neidi gongan jiguan banli xie kang xingshi anjian zhong cunzai de falu wenti ji 1997 hou de duice'] *Public Security Studies* [Gongan Yinjiu] 51 (1997), 55–7; Zhao Bingshi and He Xingwang, "Research on Judicial Cooperation Issues between Mainland China and Hong Kong and Macau Special Administrative Region" ["Zhongguo neidi yu Kang-Ao tebian xingzhengqu de xingshi xiezuo wenti yanjiu"], *Legal Scholars* [Faxuejia] 95, no. 2 , 47–56 (Professor H. L. Fu has cited this article in his article, "The Relevance of Chinese Criminal Law," 232, at footnote 16. He translated the second author—"He Xingwang"—as "*Hao* Xingwang" and the title of the article as "Legal Co-operation between Mainland China and Hong Kong and Macau Special Administrative Regions"), Zhao Bingzhi and Sun Li, "Research into Legal Issues Implicating HKSAR and Mainland" ["Shang-Kang tebian xingzhengqu yu neidi jiang huxie xingshi falu wenti yanjiu"], *Chinese Legal Science* [Zhongguo faxue] 4 (1993): 123; Zhu Seng-yuan, "A Discussion on Repatriation of Criminals under "One Country Two Systems" ["Lun "yiguo lianzhi" tiaojian xia song tufan de zhidu"], *Guangdong Legal Science* [Guangdong Faxue] 93, no. 4: 132; Liao Zeng yun, "Study of Criminal Judicial Assistance across the Strait" ["Lian-an xingshi sifa xiezuo yanjiu"], *Studies in Law* [Faxue Yanjiu]; Zhao Bingzhi and Qian Yi, "Discussion of Cross-Border and Cross-Region Crime and Punishment Principles" ["Lun kuaguo kua diqu fanzui ji qi zhengzhi yuanze"], *Legal Scholars* [Faxuejia] 93, no. 3: 139; "Mainland Court Adjudicating Hong Kong Resident's Cross-Border Crime, Legal Scholar Suggested the Using of Hong Kong Criminal Law," *Hong Kong Economic Journal*, November 17, 1998; Qu Fu, "'One Country Two Systems' and Chinese Legal System," *Wide Angle Monthly*, November 1996, 39–45; Fan Zhongxing, "The Judicial Relationship between the Central Government and Special Administrative Region," *Wide Angle Monthly*, July 1997, 84–89. *Wide Angle Monthly*, June 1997, 85–91; Albert Chen, "The Conflict of Law between Mainland China and Hong Kong," in *Renquan Yu Fazhi* [Human Rights and the Rule of Law], ed. Albert Chen and Johannes Chan (Hong Kong: Wide Angle Press, 1987); Zhao Yongchen, *Guojia Xingfa Yu Sifa Herzuo* [International Criminal Law and Judicial Co-operation] (Beijing: Beijing Law Press, 1994).

2. Chen Hongyi, "Principles of Handling Conflicts of Law." ("A more complex problem, regards crimes concerning Hong Kong and mainland, how to co-ordinate the courts' jurisdiction and criminal law from the two places.")

3. Roda Mushkat, *One Country Two International Legal Personalities* (Hong Kong: Hong Kong University, 1997), chap. 2, 44–84. Chapter 2 originally appeared as "Jurisdictional Issues in a 'Highly Autonomous Region'—the Case of Hong Kong," *International and Comparative Law Quarterly* (1993): 11–47.

4. Fu, "The Relevance of Chinese Criminal Law "; H. L. Fu, "Comment: The Battle of Criminal Jurisdictions," *HKLJ* (1998): 276.

5. Mushkat, *One Country Two International Legal Personalities*, 44.

6. Criminal Law of the People's Republic of China. (Adopted at the Second Session of the Fifth National People's Congress on July 1, 1979, promulgated by Order No. 5 of the Chairman of the Standing Committee of the National People's Congress on July 6, 1979, and effective as of January 1, 1980.)

7. See English translation in *Criminal Law and the Criminal Procedure Law of the People's Republic of China* (Beijing: Foreign Language Press, 1984), 5–49. Article 3 (1) (2) of PRC Criminal Law (1979) provides in pertinent part: "[t]he law is applicable to all who commit crimes within the territory [including 'abroad a ship or airplane'] of the People's Republic of China." PRC lawmakers further extended her criminal jurisdiction to cover extra-territorial matters by adopting the 'objective territorial principle' in Article 3(3), which deemed a crime to have been committed in China when "either the act or consequences of a crime takes place within the territory of the People's Republic of China."

8. Article 4 of the PRC Criminal Law is applicable to PRC citizens who have committed the following crimes inside or outside of PRC territory: (1) counter-revolutionary crime; (2) counterfeiting national currency and valuable securities crime; (3) corruption; (4) accepting bribe; (5) disclosing State secrets; and (5) posing as State personnel to deceive, and (6) forging official documents, certificates, and seals. In this regard, a PRC Supreme People's Procuratorate has asserted the "power to prosecute officials working for mainland enterprises in Hong Kong [and Macau]" for corruption in Hong Kong. See Connie Law, "Mainland Can Prosecute Chinese Officials in HK," *SCMP*, September 27, 1994, 6.

9. Article 5 of the PRC Criminal Law is applicable to PRC citizens who have committed crimes outside of PRC territory, which is punishable by a minimum of three years.

10. Mushkat, *One Country Two International Legal Personalities*, 44.

11. Depending on definition, most, if not all, criminal sanctions are ideological in nature and content. See generally, Robert Paul Wolff, *The Rule of Law* (New York: Simon & Schuster, 1971), esp. Richard Barnet, "The Twilight of the Nation-State: A Crisis of Legitimacy", 221–43. (National leaders use ideology to maintain power and secure control.)

12. HKSAR court jurisdictional matters were taken up at the joint meeting of the legal experts on March 15, 1987.

13. Martin C. M. Lee, "A Tale of Two Articles," in *The Basic Law and Hong Kong's Future*, ed. Peter Wesley-Smith and Albert H. Y. Chen, 309–24 (Hong Kong: Butterworths, 1988). At the thirteenth meeting of the third

subgroup (October 31, 1987, to November 2, 1987) in Guangzhou, a proposal touching upon conflict of law was raised but dropped: "Proposal 3 sought to exclude from the jurisdiction of the courts of the SAR relating to . . . (5) the basic responsibilities of Chinese nationals towards the state (such as cases of treason and the like)." This indicated some desire to maintain extraterritorial jurisdiction by the PRC in subversive conducts affecting the State. Ibid., 321.

14. Special Group on Law to the Basic Law Consultative Committee. Final Report on Conflict of Laws, Extradition, and other Related Issues (passed by the Executive Committee of the Consultative Committee for the Basic Law of the Hong Kong Special Administrative Region on June 12, 1987).

15. The proposal was in reaction to the following question: "What coordinating arrangements should be made concerning the criminal jurisdictions of the courts of the HKSAR and mainland China in order to safeguard double jeopardy in cases where both Hong Kong and a mainland Chinese court might claim jurisdiction?"

16. Ibid., 2. The Report also raised the issue of criminal jurisdiction based on "protective principle" as in the case of National Security Law and Anti-Subversion Law. See report on "Jurisdiction of the HKSAR courts and Applicability of National Laws of Hong Kong." (Unless otherwise specified in the Basic Law, PRC Criminal Law does not apply to Hong Kong.)

17. The Draft Basic Law of the Hong Kong Special Administrative Region of the People's Republic of China, Consultation Report (Vol. 5)—General Report on the Articles—(The Consultative Committee for the Basic Law of the Hong Kong Special Administrative Region of the People's Republic of China (October 1988) (Passed by the twenty-second Meeting of the Executive Committee of the Consultative Committee for the Basic Law of the Hong Kong Special Administrative Region of the People's Republic of China.), 174.

18. Article 18 of the Draft Basic Law provided in pertinent part: "The Hong Kong Special Administrative Region is vested with independent judicial power, including that of final adjudication. . . . Courts of the Hong Kong Special Administrative Region shall have jurisdiction over all cases in the Region, except that the restrictions on their jurisdiction imposed by Hong Kong's previous legal system shall be maintained . . . Courts of the Hong Kong Special Administrative Region shall have no jurisdiction over cases relating to defense and foreign affairs, which are the responsibility of the executive acts of the Central People's Government . . ." The final Article 18 provides in pertinent part: "The laws in force in the Hong Kong Special Administrative Region shall be this law, the laws previously in force in Hong Kong as provided for in Article 8 of this law, and laws enacted by the legis-lature of the Region. National laws shall not be applied in the Hong Kong Special Administrative Region except for those listed in Annexed III to this law. The laws listed therein shall be applied locally by way of promulgation or legislation by the Region."

19. Fu, "The Relevance of Chinese Criminal Law ."

20. Differences of views on such an important and sensitive subject—how to structure PRC–Hong Kong–Taiwan–Macau relationship—is uncharacteristic of PRC legal scholarship, which up until now have all been orchestrated

to express Party line. Uniformity of view is maintained and justified partly because the Party speaks the ultimate historical–scientific truth and partly because Party solidarity and discipline must be maintained to foster control and education of the mass. The lack of consensus might reflect a more liberal and enlightened view about academic scholarship, i.e., within limits, academics are allowed to openly debate legal and policy issues.

21. Zhao Bingzhi, "Zhongguo neidi yu Kang-Ao tebian xingzhengqu de xing-shi xiezuo wenti yanjiu," *Legal Scholars* [Faxuejia] 95, no. 2: 47–56. Zhao Bingzhi and Sun Li, "Research into Legal Issues Implicating HKSAR and Mainland" ["Shang-Kang tebian xingzhengqu yu naidi jiang huxie singshi falu wenti yanjiu"], *Chinese Legal Science* [Zhongguo faxue] 4 (1993): 123; Zhao Bingzhi, "Issues in Criminal Law across the Taiwan Straits," *Journal of Chinese Law* 3, no. 2 (Fall 1989): 227–50 esp. 227. For a more general discussion, see Zhao Bingzhi and Qian Yi, "Discussion of Cross-border and Cross-region Crime and Punishment Principles" ["Lun kuaguo kua diqu fanzui ji qi zhengzhi yuanze"], *Legal Scholars* [Faxuejia] 93, no. 3: 139.

22. http://www.info.gov.hk/chinfo/cheung-c.htm

23. S. C. Grenville Cross (Director of Public Prosecution), "Letter: Criticism over the Big Spender Case Unfair," *SCMP*, November 4, 1998. Li Shaoqiang (former chairman, Local Prosecutors' Association), "Balancing Law and Circumstances in Cross-border Crime Cases," *Hong Kong Economic Law Journal*, November 4, 1998, 12. Stephen Wong (Acting Solicitor General), "SAR Should Not Interfere with Mainland Judicial Process." The publishing of two articles on the same day by HKSAR government officials were not likely to be accidental. They registered a coordinated and concerted effort of the Justice Department to "weight in" on a fiery public debate running amok over the propriety of HKSAR (lack of) actions and opinions over the "Big Boss" case. A bit of context for the readers is in order. Before this time, Hong Kong public officials, particularly those from Department of Justice, rarely felt the need to defend their position in public, for three reasons. First, before the handover on July 1, 1997, the government justice officials were held accountable less to the people directly and more accountable to their professional, administrative, and political bosses indirectly. Second, public administration was beyond the understanding of the public. Policy (legal) issues were a matter of discussion and debate between experts and among professionals. Third, legal and justice officials were bound by law and not driven by public opinion or popularity contests. The year 1997 changed the way how HKSAR functioned.

24. Another question can be raised concerning the propriety of any claim of jurisdiction by the PRC, i.e., by international law standards whether the PRC criminal law jurisdiction (PRC Criminal Law, Article 6) is over-reaching.

25. Malcolm N. Shaw, *International Law*, 4th ed. (Cambridge: Cambridge University Press , 1997), 452.

26. "Whether the position of the Secretary for Justice with respect to the Cheung Tse-keung's case is based on sufficient legal grounds and was carried out dutifully according to the law?" Wong.

27. "What kinds of principle should we adopt to balance the conflicting expectations between the people from Hong Kong and mainland over judicial jurisdiction?" Wong.

28. The chief executive of SAR has taken up this position: "Legally, they can be tried in China because they have violated Chinese laws . . . we in Hong Kong 'one country, two systems' must respect legal procedures inside China. Our legal system is not at all under threat," *SCMP*, November 12, 1998.

29. Professor Chen Hung-yee, Dean of Hong Kong University Faculty of Law, adopts this position. Jimmy Cheung, "Grey Areas over First Legal Move," *SCMP*, November 9, 1998.

30. International law sanctioned "the territorial principle" as "one aspect of sovereignty exercisable by a state in its territorial home." D. P. O'Connell, *International Law* (1979): 823–31.

31. There appears to be little disagreement over this legal issue, i.e., China has "territorial" jurisdiction over that part of the (preparatory) offense committed in China. The debate at issue is which part of the many offenses leading up to the kidnapping of Li should be tried in China. Simply put, should China be able to try all offenses just because she has jurisdiction to try some. Chris Yeung, "The Case that Threatens Our Autonomy," *SCMP*, November 14, 1998. (Representative from the Hong Kong Bar Association, Roony Chan, suggested that putting aside the kidnapping charge, Hong Kong residents who were charged with robbery or firearms offenses in China should be returned to Hong Kong to face trial and justice.)

32. Charlotte Parsons and Angela Li, "Big Spender's Family Wins," *SCMP*, November 14, 1998. (The secretary for justice also concurred with this assessment. "First of all we have to examine whether mainland courts have jurisdiction to try this case and we feel that mainland courts have jurisdiction to do so.")

33. Moving the "Big Spender" case to be tried in Hong Kong was the major issue, both for the defendant's lawyers and Hong Kong opinion leaders. Ceri Williams, "Fresh Attempt to Move Case," *SCMP*, October 27, 1998. (Mr. Ivan Tang, Hong Kong lawyer for Cheung Tse-keung, questioned the legal basis for conducting the trial of a Hong Kong resident in the Mainland when most of the alleged crimes had been committed in the HKSAR.)

34. There was a noticeable shift of position in this regard, over time. Before the verdict, both the secretary for justice and the secretary for security were adamant against the repatriation of Cheung Tse-keung to Hong Kong for whatever reasons—prosecution or sentencing. After the verdict, the secretary for security softened the stance to one of willingness to consider extraditing the eighteen Hong Kong residents in the "Big Spender" case to stand trial in Hong Kong after they have served their sentences in China, and if it was not too late, e.g., no death or life sentence being imposed.

35. *Apple Daily*, October 25, 1998, A2, A4.

36. On November 3, 1998, the LegCo Security Committee held a closed-door meeting with the secretary for security, secretary for justice, Deputy Commissioner of Police Wong Chan Kwong, Senior Assistant Solicitor General Wong Hong Hing, and Senior Assistant Counsel, DPP, Li Ding Kwok. The Chairperson James To was satisfied that (1) there was not enough evidence to charge Cheung Tse-keung in Hong Kong and (2) the HKP had done what they could in investigating the case. The main reason given for lack of evidence was a lack of cooperation from the victim. The secretary for security decided, on compassionate grounds, not to prosecute the victim

for noncooperation. Coerced testimony was also considered not reliable. "Leco Members Agreed with Officials' Explanation, Hong Kong Government Lack Sufficient Evidence to Prosecute Cheung Tse-keung," *Hong Kong Economic Journal*, November 11, 1998. However, it is also clear that the "Big Spender" case was brought to the attention of the HKP and thoroughly investigated. Chris Yeung, "1996 Kidnap Rumor Led to Police Inquiry: Pattern," *SCMP*, October 20, 1998. (The last Governor of Hong Kong, Christ Pattern, confirmed that he asked the secretary for security to make an inquiry of a kidnap "rumored" around town only to be informed that "they (police) couldn't establish whether or anything happened." This is a slightly different version of the "Big Spender" investigation process and result (some evidence, one or more witnesses, nothing happened?) than admitted to by the secretary for security or the HKP (no report, noncooperative victims, no witness). The secretary for security did not say that she could not establish a crime, only that she did not have sufficient evidence to arrest and mount a successful prosecution. Government officials further confirmed that they had approached Mr. Li Kar-shing and Mr. Walter Kwok in May 1997 for information. Both Li and Kwok declined to discuss the case. The Security for Security did not make clear when she had information about a possible crime being committed. Then Governor Christ Patten denied ever having any "confirmed" information and knowledge. "The Police Felt They Have Done What They Could in Gathering Evidence," *SCMP*, November 9, 1998. Audrey Parwani, "Police Morale 'Hit by Lack of SAR Hearing,'" *SCMP*, November 9, 1998. ("Of course we are angry. We have been following this guy for ages and gathered so much evidence.")

37. Shaoqiang, "Balancing Law and Circumstances," 12.
38. It is an offense under Organized and Serious Crimes Ordinance to deal with property which he or she knows, or has reasonable grounds to believe, to be proceeds from an indictable offense. Parsons and Li, "Big Spender's Family Wins." (The police sought a restraining order from the court to confiscate $160 million in property, bank accounts, and vehicles. They seized $400,000 in cash and $2 million worth of valuables. The relatives were allowed to spend not more than $3,000 per week and restricted their legal bills to $50,000 (later raised to $120,000).
39. The Commissioner of Hong Kong Police made his intention known on August 18, 1998. Stella Lee, "Police Plan to Seize Assets of 'Big Spender,'" *SCMP*, August 19, 1998. Cheung's relatives were arrested for money laundering in September 1998 and appeared in court on October 9, 1998. One hundred sixty million in property, bank accounts, and vehicles were seized. Charlotte Parsons, "Big Spender Family Fights Clamp on Purse Strings," *SCMP*, October 10, 1998.
40. The police were asked to seek a new restraining order if and when they had more evidence. Parsons and Li, "Big Spender's Family Wins."
41. Shaoqiang, "Balancing Law and Circumstances," 12.
42. Cross, "Letter: Criticism over the Big Spender Case Unfair."
43. Ibid.
44. Throughout the public debate over the "Big Spender" case, the PRC authority has been unusually quiet. The clear impression one gets is that she did not want to be a part of the debate and let the record speak for itself.

When there was a need to make China's voice heard, China did so by proxy, i.e., through legal scholars and pro-PRC media. One PRC observer suggested that this reflected PRC's deliberate policy of not interfering in Hong Kong's internal affairs. Qiang Xuejun, "The Grey Area between China and Hong Kong Gradually Appears," *Hong Kong Economic Journal*, November 18, 1998.

45. Guangzhou Intermediary Court (the Court) conducted a lengthy press conference—"Guangzhou municipality intermediary court situation briefing session" ("Guangzhoushi zhongji renmin fayuan qinghuan jieshshao hui")—to explain to the public and the press its decision in the "Big Spender" case. The press conference was attended by the Court President Li Go, Deputy President Huang Min, Presiding judge Shi Anqi, and judicial officer Wu Chan. The symbolic significance of this event should not be underestimated. The PRC Court felt the need to explain their action, without being asked. This was a sure sign of legal maturity, e.g., transparency and accountability, not only to Chinese people, but also (or more so) to Hong Kong people. "Presiding Judge Asserted Once Again That Mainland Has Judicial Authority," *Ming Bao Daily News*, November 13, 1998, A4.

46. It is not clear why being arrested in Mainland China by itself justified the attachment of criminal jurisdiction in the Cheung case, other than for prudential reasons, i.e., ease of gathering evidence.

47. It is not clear why the uncovering of criminal evidence, e.g., proceeds of crime, contributed to the claim of jurisdiction.

48. "Special Topic: Hong Kong People under the Legal Net of Dictatorship," *Jiuxi Nian Dai Monthly*, July 1986, 42–56. ("In the mainland, how many Hong Kong people were executed?" From 1981 to September, 1983 105 Hong Kong offenders were arrested for smuggling of goods, drugs, and people. Within the ranks were 14K members and fugitive from justice in Hong Kong. From January 1983 to November 1983, the Shenzhen police uncovered 4,900 cases of smuggling by Hong Kong people with 70 people arrested. In January of 1983, the Shenzhen court sentenced three Hong Kong people [one to death, one death suspended, one for fifteen years] for conspiring with ten Mainland criminals to smuggle watches, electronic calculators, silver, nylon bags, and female undergarments. The problem was with the uneven quality of justice, i.e., corruption, arbitrariness, and harshness.)

49. Chen Hongyi, "Principles of Handling Conflicts of Law."

50. The Basic Law Drafting Committee was much concerned with the issues relating to conflict of law, including whether National Security Law or Anti-subversion law would or should apply to HKSAR; whether PRC officials, such as soldiers would be subjected to Hong Kong law, and lastly how criminal cases implicating concurrent jurisdictions were to be settled. Final Report on Conflict of Laws, Extradition, and Other Related Issues (passed by the Executive Committee on June 12, 1987, to the Basic Law Drafting Committee). (The committee adopted a clear line rule. Criminal cases involving both Hong Kong and China should be settled on the basis of the territorial principle, i.e., where the crime occurred.)

51. PRC and Hong Kong SAR Basic Law (Draft) Consultation Document. Fifth Consultation Report (5th Volume) (PRC and SAR Basic Law Consultative

Committee, October 1988.) (Article 94 cannot settle cross-border crime issues. Extradition agreement has to be negotiated.)

52. Ibid.

53. See The Draft Basic Law of the Hong Kong Special Administrative Region of the People's Republic of China, Consultation Report (Vol. 2)—Special reports. The reports on "The Relationship between the Basic Law and the Chinese Constitution and the Relationship between the Basic Law and the Sino-British Joint Declaration" and "One Country Two Systems" and "A High Degree of Autonomy" (The Consultative Committee for the Basic Law of the Hong Kong Special Administrative Region of the People's Republic of China [October 1998]). The report made clear that the return of Hong Kong resolved "the question of the sovereignty of Hong Kong" in "territorial sovereignty" terms, i.e., HKSAR is an inalienable part of the PRC. However, HKSAR is to be delegated with much power to govern herself under the principle of "zero sum game," i.e., power given to HKSAR would not be available to the PRC.

54. That is to consider the preparatory offenses, as with attempt crimes, being merged with the final criminal act.

55. This is basically the argument of Ms. Audrie Yu, Chairman, Hong Kong Bar Association, at the PRC—HK Law Seminar on "Legal Issues in Cross-border Crimes: Looking into the Future" on November 27, 1998, cosponsored by Chinese Law Program, Chinese University of Hong Kong, and French Centre for Research on Contemporary China in Hong Kong. The author was the co-chair of the event.

56. PRC Criminal Procedure Law (1979), Article 20.

57. *SCMP*, November 6, 1998. Margret Ng "Right to Autonomous Law." ("To give real assurance, it must be made clear that a person can only be prosecuted in Hong Kong for what he has allegedly done in Hong Kong . . . Article 18 provides that PRC law shall not apply in Hong Kong unless included in Annex III. Article 19 provides that Hong Kong courts have jurisdiction over all cases in Hong Kong. Article 22 precludes mainland authorities from interfering with matters which the SAR has power to deal with on its own.") Her argument though logical and persuasive from the Hong Kong perspective, failed to take into account PRC's central argument, i.e., PRC court is following PRC Criminal Law as informed and validated by international law and practices.

58. The application of international law to domestic problem is strongly resisted by the PRC. The Five Principles of Peaceful Coexistence entrenched in the PRC Constitution (1982) included a provision of "non-intervention" into a nation-state's domestic affairs. But, the PRC does not object to looking at foreign experience as a building block for her own legal principles. Fu, "The Relevance of Chinese Criminal Law," 232. (International law and practice on criminal jurisdiction is considered to be relevant and persuasive authority, even in the Hong Kong context.) In the case of Hong Kong, its own legal system incorporates British features and international standards. The thesis is that if PRC position is acceptable by common or international law standards, it should be accepted by HKSAR.

59. "Harvard Research on International Law: Jurisdiction with Respect to Crime," *American Journal of International Law* 29, suppl. 1 (1935): 435, 445.

60. *R. v. Governor of Belmarsh Prison*, ex parte Martin [1885] 2 All ER 548, Court of Appeal (All crimes are local. The jurisdiction over the crime belongs to the country where the crime is committed . . .)

61. Francis Wharton, *A Treatise on the Conflict of Laws* (Rochester, NY: The Lawyers Cooperative Publishing Company, 1905, orig. pub. 1872), Chapter XQ: "Criminal Law." The territorial principle if pushed to the limit would allow if not invite criminals to commit crime in one country and seek haven in the next, i.e., forum shopping.

62. Compania Naviera Vascongado v Steamship "cristina" [1938] AC 485, House of Lord.

63. According to Section 401 of the Restatement, jurisdiction to prescribe means "to make its law applicable to the activities, relations, or status of persons, or the interests of persons in things, whether by legislation, by executive act or order, by administrative rule or regulation, or by determination of a court."

64. In imposing "external limitations" on a country's jurisdiction to prescribe conducts, the ALI sought accommodation: "Territoriality and nationality remain the principal bases of jurisdiction to prescribe, but in determining their meaning rigid concepts have been replaced by broader criteria embracing reasonableness and fairness to accommodate overlapping or conflicting interests of states . . ."

65. *Lord Diplock in Treacy v. Director of Public Prosecutions* [1971] AC 537.

66. *R. v. Sansom* [1991] 2 All ER 145 and *Liangsiriprasert v. US Government* [1990] 2 All ER 866.

67. Martin Dixon and Robert Mccrqudale, *International Law*, 2nd ed. (London: Blackstone Press, 1991 ).

68. Marshall, C. J., in *The Schooner Exchange v. M'Faddon*, 11 U.S. (7 Cranch) 116, 136 (1812).

# 7

# Policy Analysis

## Introduction

The correct analysis of any public policy issue ultimately rests on a frame of reference, underscored by fundamental value postulates and informed by basic factual assumptions. Hence, the satisfactory resolution (settlement) of the "Big Spender" debate ultimately rests on the adoption of a proper frame of reference in response to the question: "How should a functional political relationship between PRC-HKSAR be structured and an administratively workable solution to cross-border crimes be arrived at under the rubric of 'one country, two systems' formula?"

A functional political PRC–HKSAR relationship is one that is:

1. Faithful to the original political settlement structured under the PRC Constitution and Hong Kong Basic Law, i.e., "one country, two systems."
2. Able to stand the test of time, i.e., evolving political circumstances and social developmental needs of the PRC versus HKSAR.
3. Capable of reconciling clashing political values and converging national identities of two radically different political economies.

An administrative workable solution to PRC–HKSAR cross-border crimes is one that is capable of achieving the articulated purposes and in line with established process of the PRC versus HKSAR criminal justice systems.

### Correct Analysis versus Satisfactory Resolution of Policy

It is postulated here that a "satisfactory" resolution of a public issue does not necessarily follow from a "correct" analysis of the (constitutional, legal, political, and social) issues in the case.

By "correct" analysis, I mean a policy analysis[1] process that involves the following steps:

1. Intelligence gathering—data and potential problems and opportunities are identified, collected, and analyzed.

165

2.   Identifying problems.
3.   Assessing the consequences of all options.
4.   Relating consequences to values—with all decisions and policies, there will be a set of values which will be more relevant (for example, economic feasibility and environmental protection) and which can be expressed as a set of criteria, against which performance (or consequences) of each option can be judged.
5.   Choosing the preferred option—given the full understanding of all the problems and opportunities, all the consequences and the criteria for judging options.[2]

In fact, in most cases, a "correct" analysis process does not generate the most "satisfactory" resolution of a public policy issue. The reason being, a "correct" analysis, as a rational choice process, drives at the *optimal* overall cost–benefit disposition of an issue from one of the contending parties' perspective. "Satisfactory" resolution calls for a *suboptimal*, if not even *minimal*, acceptable settlement of a dispute, through give and take of all parties to a dispute.

The major obstacle in any policy debate is not (only) about obtaining "correct analysis," but in achieving a "satisfactory" resolution of the issues on hand. "Correct analysis" is based on values masked as logic. "Satisfactory resolution" is based on interests expressed as feelings. Values are seldom negotiable, with logic presented as unassailable. Interests are compromisable, with feelings often inaccessible.

### Settling the "Big Spender" Debate—A Frame of Reference

The protracted debate over "Big Spender" case is a debate over frame of reference.[3]

An acceptable frame of reference for "Big Spender" debate should elevate the level of public discourse as it recasts the direction, nature, and content of arguments, to seek accommodation from all stakeholders in the "Big Spender" debate: the PRC versus HKSAR versus Hong Kong people.

In resolving the "Big Spender" case, it is not advisable to insist on adopting an "analytical" framework that has the effect of pulling the PRC and HKSAR apart; one country before two systems, or two systems at the expense of one country. Ultimately, any satisfactory resolution of the "Big Spender" case could not be had by ignoring the "feelings" of the PRC versus HKSAR, such as insisting on legal autonomy on the part of the HKSAR or insisting on political domination of the PRC.

It is argued by this author that HKSAR should not enter the debate insisting on fixed, absolute, and inviolable position, e.g., Hong Kong must be isolated and protected from all PRC influences. HKSAR should enter the debate based on flexible principles, and be prepared to give and take[4] to achieve the central purpose and ultimate aim of "one country, two systems" as the proper frame of reference.

Similarly, PRC political–legal authorities should not insist on exercising criminal jurisdiction over the Cheung case just because it has the right to do so under the PRC Criminal Law.

Instead, the PRC authorities should exercise jurisdiction over the "Big Spender" case if and when it best serves the purpose of uniting the PRC and HKSAR under one roof, i.e., realizing the ultimate purpose of "one country, two systems."[5]

## Purpose of Basic Law—"One Country, Two Systems"

On the surface, the "Big Spender" case is about making sense of the Basic Law, i.e., how to give meaning to an ill-defined principle of "one country, two systems" and how to interpret the amorphous phrase of "a high degree of autonomy." In reality, the challenge is about shaping and defining an evolving political relationship. In practical terms, the Basic Law is about structuring and maintaining a working relationship between two radically different criminal justice systems that are joined by culture, separated by history, and united by destiny.

Deng never intended for the "one country, two systems" formula to keep PRC–HKSAR apart, forever. It was meant to be a stopgap measure to grandfather the old and nurture the new in Hong Kong. The ultimate objective is for HKSAR to be reintegrated with the PRC, her motherland, gradually, incrementally, and as smooth as evolving circumstances allow. Viewed in this light, "one country, two systems" was a pragmatic solution to solve a "historical" problem. Hong Kong would be integrated with China in an incremental way without affecting the stability and prosperity of Hong Kong, e.g., the PRC was not yet ready to assume the administration of Hong Kong, and prejudicing the legitimate rights and expectations of all parties, e.g., Hong Kong people who were used to British rule. Fifty years were set originally to allow for incremental but inevitable changes in Hong Kong. Adjustments were expected on both sides. Sacrifices and accommodations must be made to the harsh reality of transfer of sovereignty, first legally and politically, in time socially and culturally.

The basic assumption of Deng was that the PRC and HKSAR would get to resemble more and more of each other, e.g., the Shenzhen SEZ looks and operates more like Hong Kong than anywhere in China now than ever before.[6] Likewise, Hong Kong would absorb more and more "new immigrants" from China, including their work habits, lifestyle, and culture.[7] In this regard, the political relationship between PRC–HKSAR was never meant to be, and should not be, a fossilized one.

In day-to-day practice, this means forcing the PRC and HKSAR to coexist with each other under one roof ("one country, two systems"). They are compelled, by force of circumstances, to work with each other to deal with common problems and concerns, e.g., the "Big Spender" case. Viewed in this light, cross-border crime disputes are structural in nature and enduring in kind; much like odd couples forced to share confined living space.

## Rule of Law Approach not Helpful

This part of the chapter is devoted to the exposition of a single proposition, i.e., the taking of a "rule of law" approach to the analysis and resolution of cross-border disputes is not helpful for Hong Kong and China, on the journey to reintegration, for three reasons. First, the exact meaning of the Basic Law, e.g., "high degree of autonomy," was not determined with certainty when formulated and not determinable with exactitude when applied.[8]

Second, the "Big Spender" case is a debate over interests and argument over policy, and not law.

Third, the "Big Spender" case is a contest over values and fight of politics, and not law.

The "Big Spender" debate over the meaning of Basic Law and criminal jurisdiction masks a deeper conflict over political ideology and criminal justice philosophy. In all, cross-border crime disputes are disputes between strategic partners with different interests and divergent values, and having to cooperate with each other to deal with emerging cross-border crime problems. Practically speaking, it is about seeking independence within an interdependent national polity in an international world order.

## The Indeterminacy of the Basic Law

The political elite and legal professionals in Hong Kong would have had the public believe that the "Big Spender" jurisdictional dispute was solely a dispute about the correct interpretation and application of the Basic Law.[9] Specifically, a fair reading of "a high degree of autonomy" in light of its legislative purpose and Article 18 of the Basic Law in accordance with the spirit of the "one country, two systems" would have resolved the debate in Hong Kong's favor.[10] In this way, proponents of the "rule of law approach" in Hong Kong, e.g., Margret Ng and Audriea Yu, would have interpreted the Basic Law in classical and positivistic terms.[11] They searched to "discover" the meaning of the Basic Law within the black letters of the Basic Law.

The classical interpretative approach is informed by the following fundamental propositions about the nature of law: law represents *consensus*; law is settled *truth*; law is *determined and determinable*; and law is *fixed*. All these propositions do not accurately characterize the Basic Law when conceptualized and as applied. For example, the Basic law is not determined and not determinable in a number of ways.

First, the Basic Law drafting process was marked by conflicts not consensus. Disagreements were built into the document. People agreed to disagree in order to force closure to a historical problem. As a result, it is only natural that there is more than one interpretation to the Basic Law.

Second, the Basic Law was designed as a living Constitutional document. It speaks in general and universal terms. In this way, the Basic Law makes allowance for creative interpretation of a yet-to-be formed the PRC and HKSAR relationship.

It is the central thesis of this book that interpretation problems over the Basic Law cannot be solved once and for all, as the Hong Kong opinion leaders and legal professionals would have Hong Kong people believe. For example, since its adoption, the phrase "high degree of autonomy" cried out for more exhaustive clarifications and refined definition. The negotiating parties have failed to provide clarifications for three reasons: First, the "inkblot"[12] quality of the phrase made possible a meeting of the (divergent) minds and allowed the parties to agree to disagree.[13] Second, the Basic Law was designed as a "living" Constitutional document. The "one country, two systems" was meant to be a creative, self-generating, as well as an ever-adaptive principle. The phrase "a high degree of autonomy" was adopted to make possible anticipated changes. Finally, the open texture of the Basic Law created anxiety, frustration, and desperation, as the negotiating parties looked ahead to a promising but uncertain future, namely how to *integrate* two systems of government that have nothing in common with each other.

What is the meaning of "high degree of autonomy"? How much degree of "autonomy" suffices as being autonomous? The Basic Law will not be able to provide a satisfactory answer to these kinds of "legal" questions. The temptation to use categorical rule (in practice referred to as "bright line rule") in order to capture a complex relationship and resolve complicated problems is great. However, the use of categorical rule to settle a relationship problem is ill-advised. It just serves to cover up the messy problem, with a nice and neat legal pronouncement.

The forced relationship between two incompatible partners—Hong Kong versus China—invites contentious and continuous dispute over the entitlement of rights—who is to decide what? The dispute over the political identity of self, disguised as conflicts over legal rights, would continue unabated until such time these two radically different legal systems merged with each other, or when the two political systems worked out all their differences.[14] This is not possible as long as the PRC insists upon her political sovereignty[15] and Hong Kong defends its administrative autonomy.[16] In the mean time, interpretation issues over the Basic law will multiply, endlessly.

### The "Big Spender" Case is about Interests and Policy, not Law

The proposition that the "Big Spender" case is about interests and policy, not law, is supported by two arguments. First, cross-border crime cases necessarily involve the balancing of competing interests—"autonomy" versus "comity"—in an increasingly interdependent world of cross-border and transnational crimes. Second, a State's claim of criminal jurisdiction automatically implicates the proper exercise of police power to secure various State interests, i.e., to advance the safety, health, and welfare of the people.

### Autonomy versus Comity

Legal issues involved in cross-border crimes, either between two regions in a State or between two countries in the international community, implicate problems of self-determination (sovereignty/autonomy/ independence) and collaterally nonintervention in domestic affairs by others.[17] In the present context, the ultimate question is how much sovereignty a political State or an autonomous administrative region can expect or be allowed to enjoy in the face of pressing problems of cross-border crime[18] arising as a result of growing interchange of people, goods, money, and ideas.[19] The "Big Spender" case served to bring all these issues into sharp focus in the form of a "conflict of jurisdictions" debate.

Traditionally, the State is independent, sovereign, and equal.[20] However, in reality, no legal qua political system is totally isolated from or otherwise unaffected by its neighbors.[21] Artificial geo-political or State boundaries, naturally developed, culturally fortified, historically affirmed, and habitually observed are not able to stop the constant interchange of materials, people, and ideas—generally activities between people.[22] Modern advances in communication (electronic highways), transportation (supersonic jets), and business structure (multi-international corporation) only help to break down State barriers even more. (New advances alter the traditional concept of distance; with electronic mail everyone is a next-door neighbor.)[23] New international trade agreements, e.g., European Union and NFTA, further make traditional concept of national border meaningless.[24] As a result, crimes have increasingly become international and borderless[25] or deterritorialized.[26] "[N]ational borders are becoming increasingly obsolete and irrelevant to criminal activities."[27] In order to deal with such cross-border crimes effectively, State police and court jurisdiction must reach beyond their tradition borders, i.e., become extraterritorial.[28] Alternatively, nation-state (the PRC) or administrative unit (HKSAR) must be prepared to surrender "sovereignty" or "autonomy" for better crime control. This has grave consequences for the traditional notion of political sovereignty and legal jurisdiction of a State.[29] Instead of insisting upon a zero-sum game, i.e., total political independence or mutually exclusive legal jurisdiction, the State must learn to accept nonzero sum solutions, i.e., cooperation and coordination of international efforts.[30]

In the case of PRC–Hong Kong, as a result of change of sovereignty, the once clearly separated political sovereign entities are fast breaking down; with their common border becoming more porous, in real terms indefensible and at time imperceptible.[31] The PRC economic reform made Shenzhen an open town, accessible to traders, investors, and tourists, and criminals. The returning of Hong Kong to China made Hong Kong a new home for millions of Chinese immigrants and China a second home for tens of thousands of north-bound workers and retirees, including fugitives from justice. The growth of commercial activities and ease of travel between the two places contributed to the explosion of cross-border crimes, calling for renewed assessment of the traditional concept of border control and sovereign integrity.[32]

In this regard, the ultimate "policy" question begging for an answer is, how much is the HKSAR (officials, elites, and people) willing to allow Hong Kong criminals (also Chinese nationals) be punished under a socialist (the PRC) criminal justice system in order to promote better cooperation in crime control between the PRC and Hong Kong? In theoretical terms, how much "autonomy" HKSAR is willing to give up in return for more order and security for both the PRC and Hong Kong?

## Prudential Exercise of Police Power

In international law, the right to exercise criminal jurisdiction is commonly recognized to be based on "territorial principle" or "nationality principle" or "protective principle." The "territorial principle" is based on protection control over "area." The "nationality principle" is based on protection control over "people." The "protective principle" is protection control over "impact" of an event. These principles are based on a still larger principle, i.e., the State has a right to protect-control matters of "interest" to the State in terms of security, order, welfare, and morality. Actually, all basis of criminal jurisdiction can now be reducible to one: the "protective principle" over legitimate State interest. As aptly observed by Christopher L. Blakesley:

> [P]rotective jurisdiction can be exercised whenever the State's vital interests are damaged or challenged, even if the crime is committed outside of and its consequences have no direct effect within the State's territory. In many cases where the court exercise criminal jurisdiction, couched in terms of territorial principle, they are actually based upon protective principle, and vice versa.[33]

The ultimate debate is over what counts as a legitimate State interest for a State to assume jurisdiction, e.g., is it right and proper for a State to penalize thoughts? While it is always true that a State has the infinite power to declare jurisdiction by fiat as sovereign, its self-asserted jurisdiction is also subjected to the constraint, and at times negation, of international law, which is defined by power and influence.[34] The imposition of broad principles and absolute rules in support of exercise of criminal jurisdiction is for the purpose of facilitating the ease of justice administration, which has little to do whether in any case jurisdiction should have been exercised. That is to say that the exercise of jurisdiction based on principles and rules in concrete cases might not be justified, having considered the competing or conflicting interests at stake. The exercise of criminal jurisdiction under "one country, two systems" should be based on prudential consideration, not categorical imperative. Given the importance of such decisions, they should be deliberated rationally and not arrived at automatically. In this regard, H. L. Fu, a law professor at Hong Kong University, was in favor of waiver of jurisdiction if the circumstances call for it:

> In dealing with the issue of concurrent jurisdiction, primacy might be assigned to either the SAR or the mainland courts, depending on the nature of the offence. Accordingly, one side might have the primary right to exercise criminal jurisdiction over certain offences and in normal circumstances should be accorded it. But the primary right might be waived. Where a case is considered as particularly important by the side without primary jurisdiction, that side could request the other side to waive its jurisdiction and to give sympathetic considerations to such a request. Any waiver of criminal jurisdiction would be conditional. If one side failed to exercise its jurisdiction, that is there was no prosecution, then the waiving side could resume the jurisdiction.[35]

This clarification is necessary to provide a proper analytical foundation to determine conflict of criminal law cases.

## Discussion—Lessons Learned

The question to be addressed is how to provide a framework of analysis in criminal law cases implicating HKSAR and PRC jurisdictions.

This book takes as a starting proposition that the "rule-bounded" jurisdictional rule, e.g., all cases happening in or with consequences to Hong Kong, should be tried in Hong Kong, ill-serving the "one country, two systems" design which affords the Hong Kong people a high degree of autonomy and self-determination. The idea of self-determination requires the Hong Kong people and HKSAR officials to decide for themselves on a case-by-case basis whether to assume jurisdiction, with no fixed principle or absolute rule.[36] The Hong Kong decision makers are expected to decide conscientiously, reflectively, and painstakingly having due regard for balancing Hong Kong's (local—individual—short term) interests as well as PRC's (national—collective—long-term) interests.

As observed, the proper disposition of the "Big Spender" case requires a policy–political debate, not just by following a legal one. It requires balancing of competing interests—securing independence in an interdependent world—rather than imposing absolute rule and insisting on inalienable rights. This observation, if taken seriously, requires a shift of paradigm by adopting a different frame of reference, i.e., change of mindset (thinking nationally instead of provincially) and method of analysis (following Coast's "economic of law" instead of Kant's "categorical imperative"). In so doing, it moves the debate from the realm of "established" law, "absolute" rights, and "categorical" principle to the realm of "integration" of values, "changing" of utilities, and "balancing" of interests, when possible, and where it properly belongs.[37]

The practical, result-oriented, and pragmatic approach to resolving legal issues involved in cross-border crimes in the PRC–HKSAR context was first extensively argued in *Columbia Journal of Chinese Law* in 1989 by Professor Zhao Bingzhi of the Law Department of People's University, and then the Deputy General of the Criminal Law Institute of China, who proposed that:

> In particular, due to the extended period of hostilities between the two sides and different governmental and legal systems, continued exchanges inevitably produce various legal problems. Of particular concern to each side are problems associated with criminal prosecution of non-residents and criminal jurisdiction over residents in each other's territory. The solution involves applying the law *fairly and reasonably* and requires that social order and *interests of both sides* are reasonably safeguarded. Such a solution will promote continued exchanges.[38] (Emphasis mine).

Zhao's "fair and reasonable" judicial doctrine, while flexible, is not without its guiding principles.[39] It rests on the fundamental premise that in solving "one country, two systems" disputes: "political and ideological considerations should be subordinate to the guiding principle of maintaining contacts and eventual unification"[40] and an equally compelling belief that such apolitical and nonideological approach has the best chance of improving "the handling of criminal problems involving Taiwan, help safeguard the interests of the people of the two sides, and help promote reunification . . ."[41] More simply put, interests from national reunification, not ideology of political separation is the approach.

The "fair and reasonable" judicial doctrine when applied requires the consideration of extralegal, policy (rational–unification), or personal (emotional–compassionate) factors in the prosecution and punishment of cross-strait criminals.

For example, as a policy matter to promote uninhibited travel between the PRC and Taiwan, "on March 14, 1988 the Supreme People's Court and the Supreme People's Procuratorate jointly issued a proclamation[42] stating that, as Taiwan residents returning to the PRC to visit relatives and to travel help promote the exchange of people and commerce, and thus help accomplish reunification, no crime committed by Taiwan residents in the mainland before the founding of the PRC will be prosecuted."[43]

For example, for compassionate reasons, on June 3, 1988, Mr. Chen Jianbin, vice-presiding judge of the Criminal Court of the Supreme People's Court, stated that PRC courts would treat bigamy resulting from forced separation of spouses due to PRC–Taiwan hostility as different from voluntary remarriage. Forced separation was understandable and would not be treated as criminal bigamy.[44]

Professor Zhao was not alone in advocating a pragmatic approach to address the legal issues involved in cross-border crimes. Professor Wang Chin-wen of the Law Research Institute at the Chinese Taiwan Cultural University also proposed the adoption by the PRC and Taiwan "especially established law" ("special law") to solve some of the existing legal problems between the two sides . . . one of the legislative aims of this "special law" is to incrementally bring about substantive unification of the legal norms of the two sides.

> Moreover, within the structure of "special law" norms, the two sides must investigate and revise the parts of their respective laws which have an *illusory effect* and are merely *political symbolism* in order to accurately reflect the reality of political subdivision of mainland China and Taiwan.[45] (Emphasis mine).

## The "Big Spender" Debate is Over Values and Politics, not Law

At the heart of any cross-border crime legal debate, including the "Big Spender" case, is a criminal justice policy debate denominated in more fundamental ideological and value terms.[46] "No matter what theory of law or political theory is professed, the inextricable bonds linking law and politics must be recognized."[47] Viewed in this light, the cold legal language and detached jurisprudential analysis serve only to hide deeper and broader differences in judicial qua political philosophy, as denominated by separate and distinct social qua moral values.[48] As aptly observed by McDougal and H. Lasswell:

> All systems (of public order) proclaim the dignity of the human individual and the ideal of a worldwide public order in which this ideal is authoritatively pursued and effectively approximated . . . the reference is to the basic features of the social process in a

> community—including both the identity and preferred distribution
> pattern of basic goal values, and implementing institutions—that are
> accorded protection by the legal process. Since the legal process is
> among the basic patterns of a community, the public order included
> the protection of the legal order itself, with authority being used as
> a base of power to protect authority . . .[49]

More simply put, conflicts between different criminal justice systems is a debate over ends—the shape of order and morality, and means—how best to achieve such order and morality.[50]

Throughout the "Big Spender" debate, various parties referred to the political and legal differences between the PRC and HKSAR as the basis for the strict enforcement of the "one country, two systems" principle in cross-border crime issues. These people observed that the PRC's criminal justice system is arbitrary, abusive, and inhumane, i.e., lacking in due process and human rights. That certainly explained why Hong Kong people were reluctant to have Cheung tried in China.[51] There is, however, no discussion on how such differences, especially in criminal justice terms, might have contributed to China's claim of jurisdiction over the "Big Spender" dispute in real terms.

Why did the PRC insist on trying the "Big Spender" case in China?[52] The answer rests with making sense of Cheung Tse-keung's case within a broader context of PRC history and culture, as manifested in her criminal justice philosophy and policy? Viewed in this light, the contentious arguments over who has the right to try the "Big Spender" masked differences of how criminals should be viewed and handled, historically, and culturally.

## The "Big Spender" Case in the Context of Chinese Culture and History

It is postulated here that notwithstanding the particularity of the "Big Spender" case, i.e., being one of the most sensational kidnapping cases in the annals of Chinese history, the disposition of the "Big Spender" case was driven by more entrenched legal culture and shared criminal justice values, i.e., visceral hatred of ruthless criminals and preference for substantive justice.

The crime control philosophy and policy of the PRC are very much influenced by historical Chinese thoughts and contemporary PRC philosophy on crime and punishment.[53]

First, traditionally, crime control starts with *prevention*. Prevention addresses early symptoms.[54] In terms of PRC criminal law, this means that early legal intervention is not only justified but also required. Chinese criminal law is not only concerned with reacting to "past crime" but also with anticipating "future crime." The Chinese criminal law is as concerned with criminal propensity as it is concerned with criminal impact. It is acknowledged that preparatory acts to a crime (e.g., conspiracy and attempt) pose discernable social harm and should be prevented. Depending on factual circumstances—intent of offender, probability of crime, and magnitude of harm—preparatory crimes can be as serious as the completed offense. For example, while a near-completed crime is treated more seriously than a preparatory offense, a preparatory offense by a hardened criminal is treated as more serious than a completed one by an occasional thief. China's approach is different from the common law, which views preparatory crimes as less serious than the completed crime based on the fact that completed crime creates more harm and retribution.[55] The completed criminal conduct is always of more concern. Given this difference in crime-control philosophy, the PRC's insistence on trying the "Big Spender" case in China is more understandable, if not wholly acceptable to the Hong Kong people. By engaging in a meticulously plotted kidnap conspiracy, Cheung Tse-keung being a habitual criminal posed a most serious threat to the Chinese society. It has challenged the dignity of the law and contributed to a culture of lawlessness. He was a prime target for control; the earlier the better. Arresting and prosecuting Cheung for preparatory offense made much sense. Punishing Cheung with death for planning, organizing, and directing the procurement of a large amount of explosives, arms, and ammunition was most necessary. The possession of explosives by Cheung was as serious as actually using them.

Second, crime control will not be successful without also addressing the *root causes* of crime, such as the moral degeneration of the individual[56] and criminogenic conditions of the environment.[57] As the PRC saw it, the problem with crime is a degenerated person and a criminogenic social environment. Cheung Tse-keung is a clear example. He was not afraid of the law and contributed to fostering a criminogenic culture. Hong Kong was not able to get to the problem by harboring or tolerating the problem. It was up to China to take those necessary remedial steps to forestall potentially more lawlessness ahead.

Third, traditionally, crime control starts with controlling the mind. The whole foundation of Chinese (Confucian) ethical order was based upon the ideal of self-cultivation. It was believed that "self-cultivation alone could solve all political problems and usher in the perfect society."[58] More specifically:

> Wishing to govern well in their states, they would first regulate their families. Wishing to regulate their families, they would first cultivate their persons. Wishing to cultivate their persons, they would first rectify their minds. Wishing to rectify their minds, they would first seek sincerity in their knowledge. Wishing for sincerity in their thoughts, they would first extend their knowledge.[59]

Turning to contemporary China, Mao associated learning and knowledge with the tendency to motivation. Thus, it is most important for the PRC to "control over the process whereby they (people) come to know and have belief." This then was the theoretical foundation of Mao's thought control. Thus, we see that from Confucius to Mao, bad ideas convert inevitably to bad actions; or crimes waiting to happen. It is important for the State to control thoughts and ideas as the origin of all (bad) things to follow. It is commonly accepted that preparatory acts are not bad acts before a crime, but the first act of a series of criminal acts. There is no reason in buying a gun without using it.

If punishment of preparatory acts is to be justified, it is done so because the ideas are now manifested as an external act, calling for control, and punishment. In this case, the PRC insisted to punish Cheung Tse-keung in China because he had already "intended" a vicious crime. If unchecked, Cheung's ideas would inevitably lead to serious crime. The "vicious mind," not the consummated crime itself, is deserving of punishment. Punishment created a deterrent in Cheung and the general public not to entertain bad thoughts.[60]

Fourth, traditionally, crime control in China pre-occurred with *character* conditioning.[61] More recently, PRC Criminal Law provides that criminals are to be reformed[62] if possible and extinguished if necessary. In the case of Cheung Tse-keung, he showed himself to be an evil person and career criminal beyond redemption. He showed that he had no respect for the law. He openly challenged the law in Hong Kong, a part of China. He had escaped justice before in Hong Kong. With the "Big Spender" case, he stood ready to test the limit of PRC legal system. He must not only be stopped; he must be terminated. Otherwise, he would be engaging in other more heinous crimes, to the detriment of the Chinese people.[63] Thus, Cheung was not punished for any of his criminal acts per se. He was executed for being a bad person.

Lest one be critical of PRC's position, criminal law in Western societies also penalizes for character, e.g., juvenile delinquents as status offenders. As a status offender, the juvenile delinquent is not punished for his or her act but for the fact that he or she is an immoral or incorrigible person. For example, the act of smoking may not be unlawful, but it reflected poorly on the moral (developmental) character of the juvenile. Thus observed, the PRC did not intend to overreach into HKSAR's criminal jurisdiction to extend her own, as much as she was using those criminal episodes in Hong Kong to forestall building up of a character profile for a criminal roaming at large in China.[64] Bad characters are potential risks and needed to be controlled. In this way, the PRC can rightfully claim that she was not punishing Cheung for his Hong Kong acts alone.

Fifth, effective crime prevention and control must be multifaceted, comprehensive, *integrated*, and *holistic*.[65] Traditionally, the individual, family, clan, community, and the State all have a role to play in preventing crime and controlling deviance in contemporary China. The PRC authority believes that crime control is not a one-person or one-agency task. Affirmatively, effective crime control requires mutual cooperation and coordination of crime control between the concerned, interested, and competent parties. Viewed in this light, the PRC in arresting, prosecuting, and executing a known criminal is contributing to HKSAR's law and order. The PRC has a moral obligation, if not even a legal duty, to rid HKSAR of a known criminal threat, which she was not able to deal with successfully. More specifically, in order for the PRC to play a useful and effective role in knitting together an integrated and holistic crime control net covering the bigger Hong Kong–PRC–Guangzhou region, the PRC must do her part in stopping people from plotting a crime inside China and committing it in Hong Kong or otherwise have Hong Kong fugitives escape into China. The integrated approach to crime control ignores traditional boundaries and focuses instead on functional responsibilities.

Sixth, traditionally and contemporarily, it is agreed that crime control can be best achieved through moral education as supplemented by *certain, severe, and speedy punishment*.[66] China feels that HKSAR is too soft on crime, which contributed to their criminal problem. The PRC, in arresting, prosecuting, and executing criminals in a fast, severe, and certain way, was assisting and not detracting from HKSAR's criminal justice system. (See Table 7.1.)

**Table 7.1**
**Traditional Social Control Philosophy/Ideal Compared: East (China)
versus West (the United States)**

|  | China | Hong Kong |
|---|---|---|
| Justifications for control | Reformation (offender) Restoration (social relationship) Reintegration (communal harmony)[67] | Retribution (to victim/ society)[68] Deterrence (individual/ society)[69] Rehabilitation (individual)[70] |
| Subject of control | Personal character[71] Internal thought Moral transgression | Social conduct External behavior Disorderly conduct |
| Method of control | Education—to reform | Punishment—to deter[72] |
| Strategy of control | Root of the problem Preventive—proactive | Manifestation of the problem Remedial—reactive |
| Site of control | Collective | Individual |
| Sources of control | Multiple layers Individual—family— neighbor—clan—State Multiple focus Psychological— physical—social economical—legal— political—cultural | Unitary system Judicial—legal |
| Nature of control | Informal—social[73] | Formal—legal[74] |
| Time of control | Proactive | Reactive |
| Assumption of controlled | Affective—social | Rational— autonomous[75] |

Chinese venerable social control thinking, as buttressed by more recent scientific formulation, calls for early intervention and speedy and severe reaction to crime.

Finally, following the legacy of traditional China,[76] the PRC prefers substantive justice to procedural justice.[77] This resulted (in part) from the fact that PRC justice officials labored under a Communist ideology which proclaimed itself to be scientific, thus truth must be derived from facts, and followed a political leadership which advocated pragmatism (Deng) and instrumentalism (Jiang) to problem solving, thus end is deemed more important and means.

In the case of the "Big Spender," it is most important to bring Cheung Tse-keung to justice in China, instead of honoring Cheung and HKSAR's jurisdictional-procedural claims, because the overwhelming facts of the case pointed to Cheung's guilt. In point of fact, most Hong Kong people wanted him to be brought to justice, with or without the blessing of the law.[78]

## Some Final Thoughts on Settlement Method and Work Style

Methodologically, how should cross-border issues be solved? Legislatively? Judicially? Administratively? Incrementally on a case-by-case basis? Comprehensively by adopting a national law? Substantively, how might such and other proposed solutions violate the letter of the "Basic Law," the spirit of "one country, two systems," or the fundamental principles under the PRC Constitution?

Most people familiar with the "Big Spender" dispute are well aware of the substantive legal and constitutional issues in the debate, but few are as concerned with issues of settlement methodology and work style.

The methodology used to deal with problems relating to cross-border crime has practical implications. For example, for a long time, cross-border crime issues between the PRC and HKSAR were resolved at an administrative level using a case-by-case and ad hoc problem-solving approach. This is referred to as "informal working arrangement," i.e., adopting commonly accepted practices to deal with routine operational problems between PRC public security and HK police.[79] Though not formally negotiated between the heads of government, there are nevertheless functional arrangements between HKP and PRC police in dealing with cross-border crimes. For example, instead of formal extradition, HKP would inform the PRC-MPS Security that a person(s) who is wanted is in China. The PRC-MPS would then arrest and deport the wanted person to the HKP at Lowu PRC–HKSAR border.

This kind of "informal working arrangements" are recommended for solving cross-border crimes without an agreement because: (1) they are functional in solving operational problems; (2) they are practical in dealing with day-to-day problems as a matter of course to the satisfaction of both PRC police and HKP; (3) they allow for creative adaptation of current working relationship, e.g., INTERPOL, to solve structural problems, e.g., extradition of fugitives to Hong Kong without a formal rendition agreement in place; (4) they allow for bold experimentation and incremental experiential learning as "one country, two systems" avail themselves; (5) they move the debate over the purpose and process of "one country, two systems" to a discussion of concrete steps on how to deal with cross-border crimes; and (6) they move the conflict of law issues from emotional debate and contentious arguments to one of rational discourse and cooperative discussion.

Work style can be a subtle, but effective, impediment to cross-border cooperation between the PRC and HKSAR. All along, the public was given the impression that the failure to reach a judicial assistance agreement resulted from substantive disagreement over key issues alone, e.g., dispute of waiver of capital punishment. However, the lack of progress over agreement might also have been due to a difference in work style. Hong Kong's problem-solving style, borrowing from the West and living out the colonial experience, has been a top-down and positivistic approach. The PRC, thinking in scientific and dynamic terms, likes to solve problems experientially and incrementally in a "scientific" manner—adopting a suboptimal tentative solution before embracing a final solution. It was Deng Xiaoping, the putative father of Chinese economic reform, who championed the use of pragmatism ("I care not if a *cat* is *white* or *black* so long as it catches the mice"), experientialism ("feeling the stone in crossing the river"), and scientism ("speak truth from facts") in solving China's emerging reform issues and problems.[80]

This clarification of settlement methods and work style is necessary to move the debate from a sterile legal analysis of what HKSAR "legal autonomy" means to a dynamic political discussion on how under "one country, two systems" the PRC versus SAR relationship should be fashioned in real terms.

## Notes

1.  Policy analysis involves "determining which of various alternative policies will most achieve a given set of goals in light of the relations between the policies and the goals." Stuart S. Nagel, ed., *Policy Analysis Methods* (Commack, NY: Nova Science Publishers, 1999).
2.  Ian Thomas, ed., *Environmental Policy: Australian Practice in the Context of Theory* (Sydney: Federation Press, 2007), 3–4.
3.  Whereas the Hong Kong advocates called for a "correct" analysis of the problem in ideological terms, i.e., complete legal autonomy for Hong Kong, the PRC sought a "satisfactory" solution to practical problems, i.e., cross-border crime cooperation.

4.    The frame of reference debate also points to a still larger difference in thinking pattern and style between the East and West in general and PRC and Hong Kong political elites in particular. See "News Magazine on Anson Chan, the Chief Secretary for Hong Kong" TVB-Pearl, November 11, 1999, Sunday, 10–11 p.m. (According to a retired senior Hong Kong official—Tso Kwang Wing—the strained working relationship between Anson Chan Fang On-sang, the Chief Secretary, and Tung Chee-wah, the Chief Executive, resulted, in part, from two different work styles and thought patterns as reflecting two governing traditions—one Chinese (Tung) and one British (Chan). See Zhang Li, an influential columnist in Hong Kong, has openly lamented that the absolute and dichotomist thinking style is not the best way to deal with PRC–HK differences. "Do not be Absolute," *Hong Kong Economic Journal*, January 9, 1999, 5. (The world is not made up of absolutes. To view it as such is asking for trouble, citing "yin-yang" dialectic of "yijing" school of thought.)

5.    The best possible solution for HKSAR is to assume jurisdiction, but divest venues for trial, and to have Cheung tried in HK courts based on PRC Criminal Law. This was the arrangement when the British took over Hong Kong in 1841. See Chapter One of Kam C. Wong, *Policing in Hong Kong* (UK: Ashgate, 2012).

6.    "Shenzhen + Grand Disco, is Taking Business from Hong Kong," *Next Magazine*, Issue 461, January 8, 1999 (In terms of night life, Shenzhen is getting to be more and more like Hong Kong with its bars, clubs, and discos. As a result, more and more people are going to Shenzhen to have a good time). See also Clarence Tsui, "Kicking Back in Shenzhen," *SCMP*, Sunday-Agenda, November 10, 1999. (Shenzhen has long been recognized as Hong Kongers' *bete noir* across the border. For many Hong Kong people, it is a place to visit, shop, and have fun. For some, it is home away from home—all five minutes away.)

7.    Danny Gettings and Quinton Chan, "Mainland Migrants to Soar by 10,000 a Year Deal Allows More Immigrants," *SCMP*, December 23, 1993 (Article 24 of the Basic Law allows Chinese children who have at least one parent who is a Hong Kong permanent resident to migrate to Hong Kong. There are 70,000–100,000 in such a category). Immigration of Mainlanders also resulted from cross-border marriages, imported labor (esp. professionals), and illegal immigrations. See "HK Husbands Less Appealing to Shenzhen Women," *SCMP*, December 30, 1998, 3. (According to Shenzhen's Civil Affairs Bureau, cross-border marriages have been declining from 1,069 in 1988 to 899 in 1990 to 555 in 1995 and 299 in the first eleven months of 1998.) "Editorial: Importation of Brains," *Ming Bao Daily News*, January 8, 1999, E.9. (HKSAR government plans to lift the restrictions on taking in Mainland experts this year.)

8.    This resembles the use of a "reasonable person's" test in tort law to ascertain a liability of tortfeasars or the application of "beyond a reasonable doubt" standard in criminal law to determine guilt. In both instances, the exact standard of legal responsibility cannot be determined in certainty, or is determinable in exactitude. What is "reasonable" in both instances has to be given substance in accordance with community standards and prevailing social/moral norms (via jury). The use of "a high degree of autonomy"

also recalls another famous U.S. Supreme Court decision in *Brown v. Board of Education*, wherein the Court asked the various States in the Union to implement the decision of the Court to desegregate the school systems with "all due deliberate speed." How much speed is required in desegregating State schools is open-ended, and is made contingent on political, economic, and social conditions in various States at the point of time.

9. Nowhere is this more apparent than the debate between Margret Ng and Grenville Cross. Margret Ng "Right to Autonomous Law," *SCMP*, November 6, 1998. ("Article 18 provides that PRC law shall not apply in Hong Kong unless included in Annex III. Article 19 provides that Hong Kong courts have jurisdiction over all cases in Hong Kong. Article 22 precludes mainland authorities from interfering with matters which the SAR has power to deal with on its own."). S. C. Grenville Cross (Director of Public Prosecution), "Letter: Criticism over the Big Spender Case Unfair," *SCMP*, November 4, 1998. (The Basic Law provisions did not preclude the PRC courts from exercising jurisdiction over the "Big Spender" case.)

10. On the other hand, the judicial officials in China confidently asserted their right to try the "Big Spender" case under the PRC Criminal Procedure Law. Specifically, a literal interpretation of Article 6 of the PRC Criminal Procedure Law would vindicate the PRC's legal position.

11. Margret Ng is a Barrister and LegCo member (law constituencies) while Audrey Yu is the Chairman of the Hong Kong Bar Association; both have a vested personal and professional interest to defend the "rule of law" on which their ultimate social, political, and professional authority rests.

12. The "inkblot" was used in Rorschach test as a psychological projective test of personality in which a subject's interpretation of ten abstract designs (the "inkblot") is analyzed as a measure of emotional and intellectual functioning and integration. *American Heritage Dictionary*, Second College ed. (Boston, MA: Houghton Mifflin Company, 1982), 662R, 1071L.

13. There are other sources of disagreement. Since legal concepts, like the idea of "autonomy," are human constructs and not related to human experience, perfect mutual agreement is impossible. J. C. Smith, "The Unique Nature of the Concept of Western Law," *The Canadian Bar Review* XLVI, no. 2 (1968): 191–225. William Gleysteen, Carter Administration, National Security Council, US–China Evaluation. C-Span, December 25, 1998, 2 a.m. (In negotiation with China since 1970 over the normalization of relations, the language of the treaty was left deliberately vague to provide for mutual agreement.)

14. It should also recognize that the term "one country, two systems" was never meant to be a fixed conception of how the relationship between the PRC and HKSAR should "always" be characterized. It is to be an ever-evolving concept to be determined by the changing relationship between the two people. This is the same argument over a living Constitution. It is never meant to foreclose the development of the people. As Hong Kong moves toward 2047, the difference between Hong Kong and China will become lesser and lesser. China will become more and more like Hong Kong, e.g., toward a market economy, and Hong Kong will become more like China, e.g., toward a more socialistic community. The people, way of life,

institutions of government, and culture of the two places would become more and more alike.

15. United Nations Charter, 1945, Article 2: "The Organization and its Members, in pursuit of the Purposes stated in Article 1, shall act in accordance with the following Principles:...7. Nothing contained in the present Charter shall authorize the United Nations to intervene in matters which are essentially within the domestic jurisdiction of any State..."

16. M. Davis, *Constitutional Confrontation in Hong Kong* (Oxford: Oxford University Press, 1989), 136–37. (The Joint Declaration and the Draft Basic Law accepted the ambiguity over political sovereignty [in the PRC] versus effective sovereignty [in Britain now with Hong Kong].)

    See The Draft Basic Law of the Hong Kong Special Administrative Region of the People's Republic of China, Consultation Report (Vol. 2)—Special reports. The reports on "The Relationship between the Basic Law and the Chinese Constitution and the Relationship between the Basic Law and the Sino-British Joint Declaration" and "One Country, Two Systems" and "A High Degree of Autonomy" (The Consultative Committee for the Basic Law of the Hong Kong Special Administrative Region of the People's Republic of China [October 1998]). The report made clear that the return of Hong Kong resolved "the question of the sovereignty of Hong Kong" in "territorial sovereignty" terms, i.e., HKSAR is an inalienable part of the PRC.

17. "Sovereignty" implied absolute authority to make political choices within a State and over a people. Dan Philpott, "Sovereignty," *The Stanford Encyclopedia of Philosophy* (Summer 2010 Edition), Edward N. Zalta, ed., http://plato.stanford.edu/archives/sum2010/entries/sovereignty/

18. It is of interest to note that while extraterritoriality is condemned everywhere, "US Extra-territorial Jurisdiction: The Helms-Burton and D'amato Act," *International and Comparative Law Quarterly* 46, no. 2 (1997): 378–91, cooperation in anticipation of possible jurisdiction conflicts is promoted everywhere. "Extradition and the European Union," *International and Comparative Law Quarterly* 46, no. 4 (1997): 948–57. (The trend worldwide is to cut down national barriers in facilitation of fighting cross-border criminals. For example, the Justice and Home affairs Council of the European Union has recently concluded two conventions to simplify and improve extradition. Convention on Simplified Extradition Procedure between Member States of European Union, was adopted on March 10, 1995 (1995) O.J. C78/1. Convention Relating to Extradition between the Member States of the European Union, adopted September 27, 1996 (1996) O.J. C313/11. P. 948.

19. Wang Changyin (Editor-in-Chief), *Analysis of Criminal Cases Involving Foreigners and Hong Kong and Macau in the Shenzhen Special Economic Zone* [Shezhen Jingji Tequ She-wai She-Kang- Aou Xingshi Anli Pingxi] (Beijing: Renmin fayuan chubanshe, 1990).

20. *Oppenheim's International Law*, ed. R. Y. Jennings and A. D. Watts, 9th ed. (London, 1992), Vol. 1, 52. See also H. Hinsley, *Sovereignty*, 2nd ed. (1986) (each independent State is sovereign within its territory), 225.

21. Hinsley, *Sovereignty*, 222 (Historical circumstances and present conditions may preclude the effective exercise of sovereignty).

22.	"Good Fences," *Economist*, December 19, 1998, 19–24. ("Borders are arbitrary abstractions, economic impediments, and surprisingly intractable."). Kevin Maney, "Economy embraces truly global workplace," *USA Today*, December 31, 1998, B1–B2 (Historian Stephen Ambrose observed that time and distance have been under constant and unrelenting assault since 150 years ago. With the invention of the railroad and telegraph then and the rise of information highway and virtual space now, the world is getting to be smaller with the crumbling of international barriers. For example, the Russian Central Bank defaulted on its debt on August 27, 1998. It caused the U.S. stock markets to lose 4.2 percent of its value.) See also John Helliwell, *How Much Do National Borders Matter?* (Washington, DC: Brookings Institution Press, 1998) (Borders between States could be opened or closed but mind and habits are harder to take down.)

23.	Alvin Toffler, *The Third Wave* (New York: Bantam Books, 1980).

24.	A. Jamieson and others, "Economic Liberalization and Cross-border Crime: The North American Free Trade Area and Canadian's Border with the U.S.A.," *International Journal of the Sociology of Law Part II* 26, no. 3 (1998): 285–321. (NAFTA forced the police, custom, and immigrant officials to revisit the traditional notion of national border in favor of a "virtue border" where functional police activities can take place, e.g., at airline counters.) Ibid., 307.

25.	Jamieson and others, "Economic Liberalization and Cross-border Crime," 285–321.

26.	Brian Tkhuck and Yvon Dandurand, "Recent International Efforts to Address Transnational Crime," Paper Presented at the International Conference on Crime and Criminal Justice in a Borderless Era, Ritsumeican University, Kyoto, Japan, November 2, 1998, 2.

27.	Ibid.

28.	M. Anderson and M. den Boer, eds., *Policing Nation across National Boundaries* (London: Printer, 1994).

29.	Malcolm N. Shaw, *International Law*, 4th ed. (U.K.: Cambridge University Press, 1997), 99. ("Interdependence and the close-knit character of contemporary international commercial and political society ensures that virtually any action of a state could well have profound repercussions upon the system as a whole and the decisions under consideration by other state.")

30.	See Bruce Broomhall and Allan Castle, "Action Against Transnational Organized Crime: Tackling Money Laundering in the Context of Institution-Building in the Asia Pacific," Paper prepared for The International Centre for Criminal Law Reform and Criminal Justice Policy (Vancouver, BC, Canada) international conference on "Responding to the Challenges of Transnational Crime" Courtmayer Mont Blanc, Italy, September 1998.

31.	"Mainland Custom Already Taking up Measures to Welcome the Use of the New "tungxing zheng" [Passage Permit]," *Ta Kung Pao* January 9, 1999, A12 (Beginning January 15, 1999, the PRC MPS has decided to use "Hong Kong-Macau Residents Commuting to and from Mainland Passage Permit" [Kang-Ao Juwen Laiwan Neidi Tongxing Zheng] instead of the current "Hong Kong-Macau Compatriot Returning Home Permit" [Kang-Au

Tongbao Huixiang Zheng] which effectively allows Hong Kong people to come and go into China at ease without prior endorsement or delay.)

32.	Changyin, *Analysis of Criminal Cases.*

33.	Christopher L. Blakesley, "United States Jurisdiction over Extraterritorial Crime," *Journal of Criminal Law and Criminology* 73 (1982): 1109. I came to this observation quite independent of Blakesley assertion.

34.	Ethan A. Nadelman, "The Role of United States in the International Enforcement of Criminal Law," *Harvard International Law Journal* 31 (1990): 37. (States are increasingly willing and able to exercise extraterritorial jurisdiction and as a result to increase needs to protect against transnational criminality and enhanced capacity to enforce one's jurisdiction claim.)

35.	H. L. Fu, "The Relevance of Chinese Criminal Law in Hong Kong and its Residents," *HKLJ* 27, no. 2 (1997).

36.	Here, I take notice of the importance of "rule of law" to secure Hong Kong people's rights and freedom. But, in the same breath, I also caution against over-reliance on the "rule of law," which in the ultimate analysis might deprive Hong Kong people of the right to self-determination, and with it denied Hong Kong the possibility of transcendental growth and self-renewal as a political entity.

37.	The trading of the right to control one's action (sovereignty) in return for certain assured outcome (order) is the basic assumption under the rational choice theory of human action. See Chapter 4 to James Coleman, *Foundation of Social Action* (Cambridge, MA: Harvard University Press, 1990). This is also the justification for the formation of a political community, e.g., UN. In the international arena, "comity" and "reciprocity" are the biggest inducements for the surrendering of sovereign right. The argument here is that just because Hong Kong has the right to "autonomy" (given by the PRC), it does not mean that this right cannot be traded for higher goods in the best (or better) interests of the Hong Kong people in the mix or in totality.

38.	Zhao Bingzhi, "Issues in Criminal Law across the Taiwan Straits," *Journal of Chinese Law* 3, no. 2 (Fall, 1989): 227–50, 227. For a more general discussion, see Zhao Bingzhi and Qian Yi, "Discussion of Cross-border and Cross-region Crime and Punishment Principles" ["Lun kuaguo kua diqu fanzui ji qi zhengzhi yuangze"], *Legal Scholars*[Faxuejia] 93, no. 3: 139.

39.	In more detail, there are four operative principles informing the proper exercise of judicial discretion in crime involving residents of Taiwan: (1) "PRC should take into account the long division between the two sides and adopt a lenient attitude in order to warm relations and to promote continued exchange"; (2) PRC criminal laws apply to Taiwan residents' violation in the PRC as well as in Taiwan; (3) conflict of laws between the Mainland and Taiwan is merely one between different jurisdictions inside one nation; (4) "in criminal cases involving Taiwan residents that may impede exchange and reunification, the PRC judiciary, to the extent feasible, should take jurisdiction and hear cases regardless of whether the crime is committed in the PRC or Taiwan. Bingzhi, "Issues in Criminal Law across the Taiwan Straits," 229–50.

40. Ibid., 229.

41. Ibid., 248.

42. Zuigao Renmin Fayuan, Zuigao Renmin Jianchayuan: "Guanyu Buzai Zhisu Qutai Renyuan Zai Zhonghua Renmin Gongheguo Chengli Qian de Fanzui Xingwei de Gonggao," 1988 *Zhonghua Renmin Gongheguo Zuigao Renmin Fayuan Gonggao* 16.

43. Bingzhi, "Issues in Criminal Law across the Taiwan Straits," 231.

44. "Guanyu Renmin Fayuan Chuli Shetai Minshi Anjian de Jige Falu Wenti," 1988 *Zhonghua Renmin Gongheguo Zuigao Renmin Fayuan Gonggao* 17.

45. Wang Chih-wen, "A Model for Solving Legal Problems between Taiwan and the Mainland," *Journal of Chinese Law* 3, no. 2 (Fall, 1989): 251–56, 255.

46. H. C. Black, *Black's Law Dictionary*, abridged 5th ed. (St. Paul, MN: West Publishing, 1983). (The classical definition of politics being: "the individuals of a state seek to determine or control its public policy.")

47. Shaw, *International Law*, 11.

48. R. Dwokin, *Taking Rights Seriously* (Cambridge, MA: Harvard University Press, 1977).

49. M. McDougal and H. Lasswell, "The Identification and Appraisal of Diverse Systems of Public Order" *AJIL* 52 (1959): 10–11.

50. Chen Xing-liang, *Xingfa Zhexia* [Criminal Law Jurisprudence] (Beijing: Zhongguo zhengfa daxue, 1992), 2. (Criminal law is about securing order and promoting morality.)

51. Some people argued that it is precisely the reason why Hong Kong people preferred to have Cheung investigated, prosecuted, and tried in China. The HKP was keenly aware of the cost involved in bringing Cheung to justice in Hong Kong. Successful law enforcement is a function of resources. Investigating and prosecuting a criminal with millions dollars of net worth requires the commitment of disproportionate amount of human as well as material resources. The police were also aware of the legal difficulties involved, in negotiating for Cheung's return. Legal rights for (confirmed) criminals translated into more (made-work) for the police. The people of Hong Kong wanted order restored and justice done, expeditiously and economically. In the case of Cheung Tse-keung, both order and justice required sweep, certain, and severe punishment of a known criminal—this could only be achieved in China.

52. Most Hong Kong people, especially lawyers, have failed to recognize that the dispute over jurisdictions is not only about law but also about policy. This is especially so in China where law is the handmaiden of policy driven by politics. Just because the PRC has undisputed legal jurisdiction over portion of Cheung's overall criminality, this did not mean that the PRC should exercise such jurisdictional rights. The PRC could as easily extradited Cheung over to Hong Kong, as she had done so many times before. (We do not know the factual circumstances of the other cases, especially the nature of crime, nationality/residency of offender, place of offense. However, we can surmise that the decision to transfer criminals hinged not only on law but also policy, if only it is for comity as in international practice.)

53. "Judicial Process and One Lawyer's Bold Stand," *Caijin*, April 22, 2011. http://english.caing.com/2011-04-22/100251590.html; Hua L. Fu, "Criminal

Defence in China: The Possible Impact of the 1996 Criminal Procedural Law Reform," *The China Quarterly* 153, no. 2 (1998): 31–48.

54. Feng Shuliang, *Zhongguo Yufang Fanzui Fanglue* [Chinese Crime Prevention Strategy] (Beijing: Falu chubanshe, 1994), 67–76.

55. In common law, attempts were punished as misdemeanors. Most states in the United States provide for reduced punishment for attempt. For example, The MODEL PENAL CODE, Proposed Official Draft (1962) Section 6.06 made an attempt, solicitation, or conspiracy to commit a felony of the first degree, and a felony of the second degree. Sanford H. Kadish and Monrad G. Paulsen, *Criminal Law and Criminal Procedure* (Boston, MA: Little Brown, 1975). The common law punished preparatory crime less and consummate crimes more in part because society seeks retribution for completed offenses. H. L. A. Hart, *Punishment and Responsibility* (Oxford: Oxford University Press, 1969), 129–31.

56. Confucius said: "From the emperor down to the common people, all without exception, must consider cultivation of the individual character as the root. If the root is in disorder, it is impossible for the branches to be in order . . ." *Sources of Chinese Tradition*, 115.

57. Guanzhi observed: "When people are rich, they will be contended at home and treasure their families. If they are contended at home and treasure their families, they will respect their superior and avoid crime. If they respect their superior and avoid crime they will be easy to rule." See Shuliang, *Zhongguo Yufang Fanzui Fanglue*, 72.

58. W. M. Theodore De Bary and others, *Sources of Chinese Tradition*, vol I (New York: Columbia University Press, 1963), 114 (hereinafter *Sources of Chinese Tradition*).

59. Ibid., 115.

60. This is commonly referred to as punishment for "thought crime," made famous by George Orwell, *Nineteen Eighty-Four* (New York: Signets Classics, 1961, orig. 1949). For modern-day renewal, see Scott Thill, "Punishing Thought Crime: Would New Bill Make *You* a Terrorist? Meet the Violent Radicalization and Homegrown Terrorism Prevention Act," *Alter Net*, January 17, 2008, http://www.alternet.org/rights/73991/

61. Confucians believed in the malleability of man. The Communists subscribed to the idea that "All history is nothing but continuous transformation of human nature" and the "central function of government will be treated as the transformation of the social natures of the citizen." See Donald J. Munroe, *The Concept of Man in Contemporary China* (An Arbor, MI: University of Michigan Press, 1977), 9–13. The preoccupation of the Communists with personal character as a means of crime control also has a political origin. Until recently, i.e., after 1982, the Communists classified people according to immutable personal background or class status, e.g., "hei wu lei"—landlords, rich farmers, counterrevolutionaries, bad elements, and rightists. These groups were discriminated against. "Farewell <Family Background Doctrine>" *Ta Kung Pao*, December 12, 1998, A4 (Effective from January 1979, the children of "hei wu lei" were allowed to enter school, apply for job, and enter the army without discrimination.)

62. Reformation started by admission of guilt and assumption of responsibility. The PRC police preached: "Leniency to those who confess; severity to

those who resist." When Bao Ruo-Wang, a political prisoner of Mao, met with his captors, he was told: "In front of you are two paths: the one of confessing everything and obeying the government, which will lead you to a new life . . ." Bao Ruo-Wang and Rudolph Chelminski, *Prisoner of Mao* (New York: Coward, McCann & Geoghegan, 1973), 73. See also David Balyley, *Forces of Order: Police Behavior in Japan and the United States* (Berkeley, CA: University of California Press, 1976), 140 (Japanese believe that apology is the first step toward personal reform, repairing of relationship, and reintegration to communal life.).

63.  The PRC, as a paternalistic parent (motherland), must stand ready to protect her own people, as a moral imperative.

64.  Another example is helpful. This is the case of habitual criminals' status. In the United States, one can put people in jail for life, if found to be beyond redemption, e.g., three strike law.

Kenneth Mentor, "Habitual Offender Laws: Three Strikes and You're Out." Department of Sociology and Criminal Justice, University of North Carolina Pembroke. http://kenmentor.com/papers/3strikes.htm

65.  *Sources of Chinese Tradition*, 115. Kenneth J. Peak and Ronald W. Glensor, *Community Policing and Problem Solving* (Upper Saddle River, NJ: Prentice Hall, 1996), 88–92. (After an analysis is done on a "crime problem," governmental agencies and community groups have to be engaged, either as guardian or as controller, to keep control of a problem. The point to note here is that criminal acts, large and small, are used as signifiers of incipient problems of crime.)

66.  The best way to control people is to use benevolence and punishment at the same time. The idea is captured by the phrase: "Dezhu xingfu" (Primarily use benevolence as supplemented by punishment). See "Kongyou de Falu Shixiang" (The legal thoughts of Kongyou), Liu Hai-nian and Yang Yi-fang, *Zhongguo Gudai Falu-shi Zhishi*[Knowledge in Chinese Legal History] (Helungjian: Helungjian remin chubanshe, 1984), 56–64.

67.  Erving Goffman provided a useful framework for the analysis of this "reformative-restorative-reintegration" justice model. Goffman observed that when expectations and norms are broken in the public place the rule breaker and victim engage in a series of highly ritualistic "remedial exchanges" for the purpose of reestablishing social relationship between the offender and victim. The process involves the offender providing an innocent excuse or sincere apology for the transgression to show personal remorse (reformation) in order to reestablish the broken relationship. Erwin Goffman, *Relations in Public* (New York: Harpers, 1971), chap. 4, 95–187.

68.  Andrew von Hirsch, *Doing Justice* (New York: Hill and Wang, 1976), 6 ("We take seriously Kant's view that a person should be punished because he deserves it.").

69.  Ted Honderich, *Punishment* (Middlesex, England: Penguin Books, 1984). (General prevention (citing Bentham) ought to be the end of punishment.)

70.  Norval Morris, *The Future of Imprisonment* (Chicago, IL: University of Chicago Press, 1974), xi. (Rehabilitative programs in prisons must be expanded and improved.)

71. "The determined scholars and the man of virtue will not seek to live at the expense of injuring their virtue. They will even sacrifice their lives to preserve their virtue completely." *The Analects*, Book XV, Chapter 7.

72. Honderich, *Punishment*. (General prevention (citing Bentham) ought to be the end of punishment.)

73. H. E. Pepinsky, "The People v. the Principle of Legality in the People's Republic of China," *Journal of Criminal Justice* 4 (1973): 51–60; "Reliance on Formal Written Law, and Freedom and Social Control in the United States and the People's Republic of China," *British Journal of Sociology* 26, no. 3 (1975): 330–42. (The United States relies upon formal legal control because of weak community structure occasioned by social, geographical, and occupational mobility. China uses informal communal social control because of relatively stable community structure.)

74. Ibid.

75. Bentham, "An Introduction to the Principles of Morals and Legislation (1789)," *The Utilitarians* (New York: Anchor Books, 1973) (Mankind governed by utilitarian calculus.)

76. Liang Zhiping, "Explicating "Law": A Comparative Perspective of Chinese and Western Legal Culture," *Journal of Chinese Law* 3 (1989): 55–91. (The term law in the West, e.g., Latin: *jus, lex* [French: Droit, Loi; German: Rescht, Gesetz; Italian: Diritto, Legge; Spanish: Derecho, Ley], means justice and rules, respectively (57, no. 1), while Chinese character for law, *fa*, stands for punishment, i.e., avenging a wrong (61). The traditional concept of law in China has grave impact on her legal culture: "Law was never perceived as a means of preserving rights, freedom and justice . . . Law was punishment." [89] More significantly perhaps is the fact that law was mainly used and perceived as a tool to impose order and secure obedience, not to guarantee right and promote challenge to order.)

77. Randall Peerenboom, "China and the Rule of Law: Part I," *Perspectives* 1, no. 5 (2000): http://www.oycf.org/Perspectives2/5_043000/china_and_the_rule_of_law.htm

78. In imperial China, morality informed law and law gave expression to morality. This is called "Confucianization of the law." Ch'u Tung-tsu, *Law and Society in Traditional China* (Paris and The Hague: Mouton, 1961). For literature on Confucianization of the law, see "Zhonghua faxi tedian tanyuan [The Research into the Origin of the Characteristics of the Chinese Legal System]," in Zhang Jinfan, *Zhongguo falu shi lun* [Discourse on Chinese Legal History] (Beijing: Falu chubanshe, 1983), 11–25; "Zhonghua faxi de xingcheng ji qi tedian" [The Formation and Characteristics of Chinese Legal System], in *Zhongguo gudai falu-shi zhishi*, Op. Cit., note 6, *supra*, 6–24, 12–13; Chen Gu-yuan, *Zhongguo fazhi shi* [Chinese Legal System History] (Beijing: Zhongguo shuju, 1988), 53–61; Qian Daqun and Xia Jinwen, *Tang lu yu Zhongguo xianxing xingfa bijiao lun* [A Comparative Study of Tang Lu and the Current Criminal Law in China] (Nanjing: Jiangsu renmin chubanshe, 1990), 31–42.

79. See Chapter 5, "Cross-Border Cooperation: HK versus the PRC," *supra*.

80. Chapter One, Kam C. Wong, *Police Reform in China* (New York: Taylor and Francis, 2011).

# 8

# Final Reflections

### Introduction

This book has thus far focused on describing the legal proceedings, public reactions, historical contexts, legal analyses, and policy analyses of the case. The remaining part of this chapter is reserved for the discussion of lessons learnt, particularly, what has the "Big Spender" case informed us about Hong Kong's legal institution and culture, or how mature is the rule of law in Hong Kong.

### Rule of Law in Hong Kong

The "Big Spender" case came at a time when the Hong Kong public and business leaders were increasingly concerned with the rule of law in Hong Kong[1] for specific reasons detailed below.

First, the politicians complained that the judicial officials had failed to perform their legal duty in enforcing the law in an even-handed manner. For example, the Secretary for Justice Elsie Leung Oi-sie has refused to prosecute Ms. Sally Aw Sian, the owner and Executive Director of Sing Tao News Group, for her alleged involvement in a circulation fraud case at the Hong Kong Standard.[2] Ms. Aw, a local deputy to the Chinese People's Political Consultative Conference, was named as a co-conspirator but not charged in the case.[3] There were clear and convincing evidences pointing to a conspiracy to defraud as unveiled by the ICAC and as determined by the Director of Public Prosecution, Mr. Grenville Cross.[4] Ms. Aw told the ICAP in a videotaped interview that she had given her staff the green light to go ahead with the plans to inflate circulation figures of Hong Kong Standard by printing more newspapers and selling them to bogus sister companies created for the purpose.[5] The secretary for justice failed to explain her decision to the public promptly and reasonably,[6] in spite of repeated invitations to do so.[7] This led Chairman of Bar Association Mr. Ronny Tong to state: "An explanation is needed to allay the suspicion or fears of people as

193

to whether everyone is equal before the law"[8] and Democratic Party legislator Albert Ho Chun-yan to observe: "If the explanation is not a reasonable one, on the face of it, I think Miss Leung has been biased towards Ms. Aw."[9]

Second, Hong Kong businessmen complained of bureaucrats destroying the settled expectation of law by over-regulation. For example, in an open letter (full page ad.) to the Hong Kong public, the karaoke owners complained that the Housing Department overregulated what had been a properly and sensibly regulated industry—by Urban Council, by Fire Service Department, by Police Department, by Housing Department, by District Council, and by Environmental Department. This has led to the closing down of many karaoke businesses, leading to 5,000 people becoming unemployed and losing upward of HK$1 billion.[10]

Third, investors complained about politicians destroying the rule of law. For example, billionaire Li Kar-shing openly proclaimed that he and other foreign investors declined to invest $10 billion in Hong Kong because the investment climate was destroyed by the politicians—particularly the respect for the rule of law had been grossly undermined by the politicians.[11] Li's concern arose as a result of a Democratic legislator, Chen Wai-ye, organizing contracted property purchasers to pressure the land developers not to take legal action against buyers who defaulted on their contracts as a result of economic downturn.[12]

Fourth, the general public was losing confidence in the legal system. Hong Kong was being increasingly politicized. The Hong Kong University Social Science Survey of 1,550 showed that for the second half of 1998, Hong Kong people's confidence in the rule of law registered 6.8/10, a decline of 0.17 point. In a random phone survey by a local newspaper of 522 people (over 3,703 calls) to the question "Do you agree with Li Kar-shing that some of the political party destroy Hong Kong's business environment?" 39 percent (203) agreed, 24 percent (127) disagreed, and 37 percent (192) had no opinion.[13]

Fifth, the foreign investors are increasingly concerned with the rule of law in Hong Kong. For example, the Hong Kong American Consulate, an otherwise reserved and careful public speaker, openly questioned the autonomy and independency of Hong Kong's legal system in a speech delivered at the Hong Kong Chamber of Commerce on January 25, 1999, citing in particular the failure of the secretary for justice in pursing the "Big Spender" and "Hong Kong Standard" cases.[14]

## Impact of "Big Spender" Case

The "Big Spender" case will have a defining impact and enduring influence on Hong Kong's legal landscape. That is to say, there will be a "Big Spender" legacy in Hong Kong. As the first test case over Hong Kong's "legal autonomy," the case helps to set the agenda, defines the issues, and shapes the discourse for years to come. Many issues are at stake: What is the reach of PRC criminal law jurisdiction? How should conflicts in the two Chinese jurisdictions be resolved? As we have already seen, as a test case, the "Big Spender" case accentuated the legal issues and aroused public debates. In so doing, the case clarified ambiguous positions and revealed vested interests.

However, more is at stake. The "Big Spender" case is not only a test case over the meaning of law; it is a litmus test on the legal culture of the Chinese and the Hong Kong people. How the case was handled revealed much about Hong Kong people's disposition and attitude toward the law. In this regard, it is instructive to observe, as pointed out before, that neither the Hong Kong justice officials (as agents of legal institutions) nor the general public (as embodiment of legal culture) showed much appreciation for "letter" and "spirit" of the rule of law. There were a number of telltale signs.

## Failure to Investigate Crimes

First, the two most senior justice officials of HKSAR—the secretary for security and the secretary for justice—were often found espousing dubious, if not even wrong,[15] opinions of the interpretation and application of the law.[16]

The secretary for security stated that a crime victim report is required to prosecute a crime.[17] The HKSAR issued this public statement on the handling of Cheung Tse-keung's case:

> The Police have initiated investigation into the alleged crimes despite that the victims had not made a report. However, they have not reached the state where they can launch a prosecution. The Police are continuing their investigations, and a HKP officer has been sent to attend the trial to gather any information that may help in the bringing of charges in Hong Kong.[18]

The secretary for security further explained the HKSAR's position with this public statement:

> Regrettably, the persons who were involved in the case never reported to us, they never provided us with direct evidence, how

can we use kidnapping charge as basis for rendition. That is why this case does not concern rendition as a result of kidnapping.[19]

While the secretary for security's statement was literally correct, i.e., no crime report—no investigation—no prosecution—no extradition, it was not legally so. The statement did not reflect Hong Kong law. More significantly, the Hong Kong people have a right to expect HKP to enforce the law and investigate crimes whether reported or not. In this regard, the Police Force Ordinance Chapter 235, Vol. 15, Laws of Hong Kong specifically provides in Section 10: "The Duties of the police force shall be to take lawful measures for—(1) preserving the public peace; (2) preventing and detecting crimes and offences; (3) preventing injury to life and property; (4) apprehending all persons whom it is lawful to apprehend and for whose apprehensive sufficient grounds exists."

Under the above provision with the Police Force Ordinance, when a crime has been committed (law violated) the police have a legal duty to investigate and prosecute, if sufficient evidence can be found. This is the case notwithstanding the lack of direct evidence due to non-cooperation of (consensual) victims or reluctant witnesses. In actual fact, the victim as a material witness can be forced to give evidence under Hong Kong law. Criminal Procedure Ordinances, Chapter 221, Section 91, provides penalty for misprision of a felony.[20]

The clear example is victimless crime, e.g., use of illegal drugs or assisted suicide. By definition and in practice, victimless crime[21] has no complainant[22] and few witnesses.[23] The sole issue for Mrs. Ip, Secretary for Security, in this case is whether a crime has been committed in Hong Kong. Legitimate question can and should be raised about the secretary for security's lack of understanding/appreciation of her legal duty to enforce the law in the public's interest, beyond the subjective desire of the victim, alone.[24] There were ample reasons to suspect that the secretary for security was not keen in bringing Cheung to the court of justice in Hong Kong. Whatever the reasons, the public have a right to be skeptical.

## Surrendering of Hong Kong Justice Autonomy

Doctrinally, "one country, two systems" contemplates the functioning of Hong Kong versus PRC criminal justice system side by side, independent of each other, with Hong Kong enjoying a high degree of autonomy and China not interfering with Hong Kong internal justice administration. To this end, Article 12 of the Basic Law makes clear: "The Hong Kong Special Administrative Region shall . . . enjoy a high degree of autonomy and come directly under the Central People's Government" and Article 18 states "National laws shall not be applied in the Hong Kong Special Administrative Region except for those listed in Annex III to this Law." To realize the above Constitutional design, Article 14 of the Basic Law provides: "The Hong Kong Special Administrative Region shall be vested with independent judicial power, including that of final adjudication."

Turning to PRC Criminal Law, Article 6 provides: "This Law shall be applicable to anyone who commits a crime within the territory and territorial waters and space of the People's Republic of China, except as otherwise specifically provided by law" and Article 7 provides: "This Law shall be applicable to any citizen of the People's Republic of China who commits a crime prescribed in this Law outside the territory and territorial waters and space of the People's Republic of China; however, if the maximum punishment to be imposed is fixed-term imprisonment of not more than three years as stipulated in this Law, he may be exempted from the investigation for his criminal responsibility."

In defense of HKSAR surrendering Cheung to PRC criminal justice system for investigation, prosecution, and execution without a fight, the secretary for justice argued that in Article 7 of the PRC Criminal Law[25] the term "territory" (*ling yu*) means "jurisdiction." This novel interpretation allows the secretary for justice to include Hong Kong crimes by Chinese citizens within PRC criminal jurisdiction, notwithstanding Article 18 (2) of the Basic Law.[26] Thus construed, Article 7 is applicable to Cheung (a Chinese citizen) committing kidnapping in Hong Kong, but escaping to China.[27]

This "purposive" construction is strained, counter-intuitive, and highly unconventional but arguably helps in advancing the ultimate purpose of "one country, two systems."[28] Beyond the fact that the Hong Kong justice officials are precluded by the PRC Constitution and Basic Law to interpret PRC Criminal Law, the interpretation was not supported by well-established Chinese legal text and authority. It certainly violated established cannons of legislative interpretation. In this regard, the Dean of Law School in Hong Kong, an eminent Chinese Law authority and a cross-border crime specialist, observed that the government's interpretation was incorrect. A Senior Research Fellow on Chinese Law, himself a former editor of a leading Chinese law journal, disagrees with the government's position. Mainland Chinese scholars find the interpretation indefensible.[29] Martin Lee has called this preposterous. Legal columnists suggested that the interpretation rendered by the secretary for justice served other ulterior motives. If our senior justice officials could not be trusted to interpret the Basic Law and PRC Criminal Law objectively and correctly, when they are in conflict, without fear or favor, our legal institutions cannot long last intact—"one country, two systems" will fail in its essential purpose of keeping Chinese versus Hong Kong legal system apart.[30]

### Compromising Rule of Law

Hong Kong senior justice officials did not see fit to acknowledge their mistakes in their apparent erroneous interpretation and application of the law. They chose to defend their indefensible position instead. In the case of the secretary for security, her position has shifted from not being able to prosecute without the cooperation of the kidnap victim to suggesting that there may not be enough evidence in the case anyway. In the case of the secretary for justice, the position has shifted from "territory" meaning "jurisdiction" in Article 7 of the PRC Criminal Law, making all Chinese nationals, including Hong Kong residents, subject to PRC Criminal Law, to making PRC Criminal Law applicable only to certain type of cases, i.e., when PRC citizens—residents—commit crimes in Hong Kong. The defensive maneuvering and skillful posturing gave the impression that there was no fixed meaning to law and more ominously law means what the officials want it to mean.

More serious than not acknowledging their mistakes, the senior justice officials appeared to "use" the law, after the fact, to justify policy decision arrived at earlier, i.e., to prosecute the "Big Spender" case in China, notwithstanding the Basic Law. The senior justice officials conceded to the assumption of criminal jurisdiction by the PRC courts without raising some of the more fundamental and controversial issues, i.e., how to handle cross-border crime cases, the likes of "Big Spender, implicating concurring and conflicting criminal jurisdiction? The use of the law to justify prior arrived at justice policy decision or to support political position of the PRC and HKSAR government is against the letter as well as the spirit of the rule of law. It most certainly compromised the duty of the justice officials in upholding the law and answerable only to the law.[31]

The performance of the HKSAR justice and security officials in this incident cannot help but serve to undermine the reputation of

Hong Kong as a "rule of law" city[32] and erode public confidence in the integrity of the legal system. A legitimate question is now being raised: "Whether Hong Kong's 'rule of law' can be preserved with the legal mentality of Hong Kong high officials being this way."[33]

Overall, it appears that the senior justice officials were less solicitous of the rights of the Hong Kong people (to try the "Big Spender" case in Hong Kong) as they were concerned with arguing for the right of China to try the case.[34] During the whole ordeal, not a single HKSAR official suggested that Hong Kong had the right to try a part of the "Big Spender" case in which the PRC court had no jurisdiction, i.e., kidnapping. The officials were also not keen in asking the PRC to repatriate Cheung to stand trial in Hong Kong or to serve his sentence in Hong Kong.[35] A noted Chinese law expert from China, Zhang Xin, associated with the Chinese University of Hong Kong, best captured such a public concern:

> When Hong Kong officials are confronted with conflict of laws issues between Hong Kong and the Mainland, would they first consider the Basic Law or would they follow Mainland officials in considering national law, which has no application to Hong Kong? This is the question of the most concern to the Hong Kong people. Regrettably, on the question of jurisdiction, the secretary for justice and secretary for security clearly prefer to consider national law cited by the Mainland officials, rather than consider whether such laws should apply to Hong Kong or firmly stand by and apply the Basic Law (to Cheung's case).[36]

More troublesome was the fact that the PRC might have conceded jurisdiction when asked.[37] Professor Zhao observed that:

> When law enforcement agencies in Taiwan, Hong Kong, or Macao request the PRC's cooperation in the apprehension and extradition of criminals, PRC judicial organs should actively cooperate so that the criminals can be apprehended and extradited to the appropriate law enforcement agencies. If law enforcement agencies of Taiwan, Hong Kong, or Macao do not request cooperation in apprehension or extradition, PRC law enforcement agencies could directly prosecute such crimes.[38]

While the statement was made in the context of a concurrent jurisdiction debate, as with the "Big Spender" case, however it was clear that the PRC judicial authority was not given an opportunity to entertain the request from HKSAR.

## Unequal Justice Administration

There was some evidence, arguably speculative, in this case pointing to the fact that the "Big Spender" case was treated differently from other kidnapping cases because the father of the kidnap victim, Li Kar-shing, was a rich, powerful, and influential person in Hong Kong.[39] Mr. Li was able to procure the assistance of the ex-Commissioner of Police as his security advisor who might have used his extensive connections in the HKP to effectuate the outcome of the case.[40] Mr. Li was also able to seek the personal intervention of President Jiang Zemin. Whether the central government was ever involved in the case, e.g., by giving direction to Hong Kong political authority, will never be known. After all, certain areas are still off limit to legal research, e.g., the role Chinese Communist Party played in judicial and Procuratorate appointments; the function and operations of the Party's legal–political committee; and how the Party members in the court and Procuracy resolve the conflict between legal mandate and Party directives.[41] However, according to reliable information, the central government's involvement in the "Big Spender" case was more than confirmed.[42]

Historically, the judicial branch of the PRC government was under the leadership and control of the Communist Party, in the person of the Party secretary. Xu Jia-tun, the former director of News China Agency, Hong Kong, confirmed that there was a "rumor" that Jiang appointed Wu Jintao and Wei Jianxing to form a special work group to oversee the prosecution of the case. Xu Jia-tun further confirmed that in the 1980s, when he was serving as Jiangsu Province Party secretary, important criminal cases, e.g., death sentence cases, must be approved by the provincial head who is also the political–legal committee secretary. Thus, it appears that this important capital case must have received the approval of the Political–Legal Committee Secretary, Wei Jianxing's, approval,[43] if not even Jiang himself.[44]

Li's plea to Jiang might have converged with other Hong Kong people's plea to the central government for help to secure law and order in Hong Kong.[45] On July 2, 1998, President Jiang came to Hong Kong to inaugurate the new airport. While in Hong Kong, Jiang took the opportunity to comment on the necessity to keep law and order in check in Hong Kong. Coincidentally, a higher official from the MPS, Zhu Entao, also suggested that the execution of Cheung was a textbook case of how Hong Kong and the PRC could effectively work together in fighting (cross-border) crime.[46]

## Politics, not Law, Decides

In their zeal to defend Hong Kong's "legal autonomy," the advocates for "one country, two systems" and defenders of Hong Kong people's rights were prepared to ignore the law and disregard the facts. Margret Ng and others were worried about the encouragement from China without investigating the facts. A cursory review of how cross-border crimes between the PRC and SAR were dealt with shows that China had been more than willing to help Hong Kong in arresting her wanted criminals. This cooperative spirit was not reciprocated. The "Hong Kong" advocates were willing to overlook or under-represent China's jurisdiction over criminal acts committed in China in favor of advancing Hong Kong's legal independence cause. Furthermore, they seem to argue that even if China has concurrent criminal jurisdiction over Cheung, she should "respect" Hong Kong's jurisdiction as more dominant by extraditing Cheung to Hong Kong for prosecution.

The willingness to bend the rules, twist the facts, and ignore China's right to promote (preserve?) Hong Kong's legal system is honoring the rule of law in its breach. A culture of rule of law starts by following rules and respecting rights, even if the following of law is detrimental to ones self-interest, in the immediate case and in the short run.

Lastly, there appeared to be a gross disparity between the legal culture of the general public and those shared by the legal professionals and politics. In the defense of Hong Kong "legal autonomy" in asking for the return of Cheung Tse-keung to Hong Kong, the representatives from the Hong Kong Bar Association and Hong Kong LegCo members all did so in the name of the public. However, the people on the streets showed very little sympathy for Cheung Tse-keung. They were more concerned with achieving substantive justice, i.e., executing Cheung Tse-keung wherever he could be found, than be concerned with procedural justice, i.e., fair trial for Cheung or "legal autonomy" for the SAR. The justice officials from the SAR government deemed following policy was more important than abiding by the law. The Hong Kong people were more concerned about substantive justice (executing Cheung) than worrying about procedural justice for Cheung or legal autonomy for themselves.

The "Big Spender" case tells the Hong Kong people two things about their criminal justice system in general and their justice officials in particular. Their law enforcement officials were less interested in enforcing the law than protecting the privacy and sensitivity of the rich. The justice officials were less interested in defending Hong Kong people's right and sanctity of the law, than using law to justify cases tried in China for political or policy reasons.

## Feeling versus Thinking Justice

The "Big Spender" case also tells us two things about Hong Kong people's legal culture. In disposing of Cheung, the Hong Kong people were more pragmatic than legalistic, and inclined to want to "feel" than "think" about justice. They were less concerned about the "rule of law" as a process as they were interested in securing a "just outcome" in substantive terms. The Hong Kong political elite and legal professionals were less interested in maintaining the letter and spirit of the Basic Law as they were concerned about maximizing Hong Kong's legal autonomy, with or without the blessing of the law.

The "Big Spender" case was played out in the arenas of culture and politics, not rationality and law.

## Notes

1. Cliff Buddle, "When the Rule of Law is Paramount," *SCMP*, January 26, 1999. (There are increasing concerns that HKSAR officials—from chief executive to secretary for justice—do not understand the importance of the rule of law for Hong Kong.)
2. Angeli Li, "Prosecutor Silent on Aw Decision," *SCMP*, November 18, 1998. (Earlier, the secretary for justice failed to prosecute Xinhua for failing to meet the forty days' reply rule as required by Hong Kong privacy laws, after Legislator Emily Lau Wai-hing asked to see any file Xinhua might have over her.)
3. May Sin-mi Hon, "Aw Case Evidence Inadequate," *SCMP*, March 25, 1998.
4. Li, "Prosecutor Silent on Aw Decision." (Mr. Cross refused to confirm or deny that he had made a case for prosecution in the Aw's case while the secretary for justice acknowledged that there had been a difference of opinion between her and Mr. Cross.)
5. Angela Li, "Case for Aw to Answer" in Court," *SCMP*, January 23, 1999.
6. See "Three Persons Found Guilty in the Hong Kong Standard Case and was Immediately Jailed, Judge Pointed Out that Hu Xian Conspired," *Hong Kong Economic Journal*, January 21, 1999, 2; "LegCo might Use Special Authority to Summon Leung Oi Sze," *Ming Bao Daily News*, January 23, 1998, A11. (Margret Ng, LegCo member (law constituents) wanted to call the secretary for justice to explain her refusal to prosecute in spite of clear evidence. Martin Lee, Chairman of Democratic Party, felt that the refusal to prosecute in light of clear evidence was not acceptable.)
7. Audrey Parwani and Cheung Yi, "Chairman Adds his Voice to Aw Outcry," *SCMP*, January 22, 1999. (Margret Ng, Chairman of the LegCo panel on administration of justice and legal services invited the secretary for justice to address the panel, but she declined.)
8. Ibid.

9. Magdalen Chow, "Furore over Sally Aw's 'Escape,'" *SCMP*, January 21, 1999. (A proper explanation was essential to restore the confidence of the public in the rule of law.)

10. "Excessive Regulation Destroying the Rule of Law Spirit and Investment Climate, Leading to Unemployment," *Apple Daily*, December 30, 1998, A19.

11. See "Li Kar-shing said the politicians intent to damage contractual spirit, suspended $10 billion dollars' project on account of change in political climate," *Hong Kong Economic Journal*, December 23, 1998, 3 (It is not good for Hong Kong if people are encouraged [by politicians] to ignore their contractual obligations.) The chief executive and chief secretary were quick to assert that the Hong Kong government was still very much a true believer in and a keen supporter of the rule of law and the contractual spirit. "Chan Fang On sang suggested that Li Kar-shing (comment) was not directed at the government, Tung Chee-wah responded with agreement and respect with contractual spirit," *Hong Kong Economic Journal*, December 24, 1998, 2. Hung Qing-tian, "Treasure the Only System in Hong Kong, Together Reconstruct the Society," *Hong Kong Economic Journal*, December 31, 1998, 22. (Li Kar-shing is worried about the rule of law and ruining of contractual spirit in Hong Kong. He is correct.) "Donation of $10 Billion," *Hong Kong Economic Journal*, December 28, 1998, 28. (While property tycoon Mr. Li complained about the lack of rule of law, he himself [bypassed the legal system] and complained to the central government [over his son's kidnap]).

12. For a summary of the events leading to Li Kar-shing's outburst, see "The Mystery of Li Kar Shing 'Getting Mad,'" *New Magazine*, issue 460, January 1, 1999, 42.

13. "Tung, Chan Pacify Li Kar-shing," *Ming Bao Daily News*, November 24, 1998, A4.

14. "Citing Hong Kong Standard and 'Big Spender' Case, Pointing to Lack of Judicial Independence in Hong Kong," *Oriental Daily News*, January 26, 1999, A20.

15. "Lee Chu Ming Debated Yip Lau Suk Yi," *Ming Bao Daily News*, November 8, 1998 (The chairman of the Democratic Party accused the secretary for security of being irresponsible in misinterpreting Art. 7 of the PRC Criminal Law. To say that Hong Kong is not a part of PRC's territory is simply politically incorrect.) Martin Lee, Chairman (a barrister), Democratic Party, in an interview with Michelle Han over the "Cheung Tse-keung's case," 9:45–10:00 p.m., December 9, 1998, CNN, Hong Kong, observed that the position of the secretary for security on no report–no crime thesis as not tenable. "Murder victims do not complain." He further observed that the conduct of the justice officials was inexplicable and showed signs of "bowing" to the PRC authority.

16. There is a more basic issue of whether the HKSAR justice officials had the Constitutional power—under the PRC Constitution or Basic Law—to interpret the language of the PRC Criminal Law and giving effect to it. More significantly, if they have no Constitutional right to do so, what is the legal basis of their opinion (however, informed and correct). More practically,

what is the legal recourse against such usurpation of interpretative authority.

17.	There was a subtle but significant shift in the secretary for justice's opinion on the issue of the victim's reporting requirement in the investigation and prosecution of a case. The position of the secretary for justice has shifted from: (1) no report–no investigation–no crime to (2) no report–no substantiated crime to (3) no report–no reliable evidence to prosecute.

18.	"Daily Information Bulletin—Government response to Cheung Tse-keung Case (English Only)," Sunday, November 1, 1998, htp://www.info.gov. hk/gia/general/199811/01/response.htm. While there is nothing wrong with failed investigation for lack of credible and sufficient evidence, but the secretary for security made clear that the lack of prosecution was due to lack of cooperation from the victims. This drew wide-ranging criticism from legal professionals, politicians, commentators, and academicians.

19.	Zhang Xin, "SAR should not "Refuse to Take Note without Complaint," *Hong Kong Economic Journal*, October 31, 1998.

20.	Misprision of felony is the concealment of a crime: "The offense of concealing a felony committed by another, but without such previous concert with or subsequent assistance to the felon as would make the party concealment an accessory before or after the fact." (H. C. Black, *Black's Law Dictionary*, abridged 5th ed. (St. Paul, MN: West Publishing, 1983), 518L. 18 U.S.C.A. Provides: "Whoever, having knowledge of the actual commission of a felony cognizable by a court of the United States, conceals and does not as soon as possible make known the same to some judge or other person in civil or military authority under the United States, is guilty of the federal crime of misprision of felony." See Goldberg, Misprision of Felony: An Old Concept in a New Context, *A.B.A. J.* 52 (1966): 148.

21.	Victimless crime is a misnomer. No crime is victimless. Individual drug use in private leads to deteriorated health for the population as a whole, with lower productivity and higher medical costs for society.

22.	While the drug users might not complain, the community residents would.

23.	Victimless crime is a misnomer. No crime is victimless. Individual drug use in private leads to deteriorated health for the population as a whole, with lower productivity and higher medical costs for society.

24.	The desire of the victim is often a major consideration on whether to prosecute in most criminal cases, such as rape victims or juvenile crime, but not the only one. A crime violates private (individual harm) and public (collective safety) interests.

25.	PRC Criminal Law states in pertinent part: "This law is applicable to offences provided under this law committed outside the territory (*ling yu*) of the People's Republic of China by a citizen of the People's Republic of China. . . ."

26.	"National laws shall not be applied in the Hong Kong Special Administrative Region except for those listed in Annex III to this Law. The laws listed therein shall be applied locally by way of promulgation or legislation by the Region."

27.	The HKSAR government's legal position is most clearly stated in a public statement issued by the Government Information Centre on November 11, 1998, http://www.info.gov.hk/chinfo/cheung-c.htm. See also the secretary for security's answer to LegCo on Wednesday (November 18, 1998): "according to her understanding of Article 7 of the Chinese Criminal Law, mainland courts have jurisdiction to try Chinese nationals who are residents in the mainland and who have committed offences outside the mainland." Margret Ng, "Endangered by Lack of Action on Suspect Law," *SCMP*, November 20, 1998.

28. Phone discussion with Peter Wong, Senior Assistant Solicitor General (policy) on November 20, 1998.

29. Zhang Xin, "The Content of "Lingyu" (Territory) in Chinese Law," *Hong Kong Economic Journal*, November 28, 1998. (The Secretary for Justice, Ms. Leung, after consulting Chinese legal expert, suggested that "lingyu" in Article 7 of the PRC Criminal Law means "jurisdiction" and thus apply to Chinese-Mainland criminals committing crime in Hong Kong. The secretary of justice failed to disclose the name of the Chinese expert and did not make known her supporting legal authority.)

30. At least two Hong Kong law professors, one from the PRC and the other from Australia, agreed with the government's position. See H. L. Fu, "Comment: The Battle of Criminal Jurisdictions," *HKLJ* (1998): 276. "A literal reading . . . Art. 7 (of PRC Criminal Law) would *not* and should not apply to Hong Kong. But this interpretation would defeat the purpose of the PRC criminal law, which aims to follow a Mainland resident wherever he goes."

31. Huang Jiang-tien, "Hong Kong Government Interpret National Law "to Serve Self Purpose ("weii suo xu")," *Hong Kong Economic Journal*, November 12, 1998.

32. "Ma Ying-jiu Hope to Inspect Hong Kong," *Ming Bao*, December 7, 1998. (Ma Ying-jiu, the newly elected Mayor of Taipei, wanted to learn from Hong Kong. Hong Kong's "rule of law" was considered to be far superior than that of Taiwan.)

33. Zhang Xin, "Further Discussion on Hong Kong Government's Attitude towards Jurisdiction," *Hong Kong Economic Journal*, November 21, 1998, 7. At the time, Zhang was a staff member with the Chinese Law Program, Chinese University of Hong Kong. The author is the Director, Chinese Law Program.

34. Xin, "SAR Government should not 'Avoid Responsibility because of no Report.'" (Even if the PRC has jurisdiction over the case, the Hong Kong government should not stand back without getting involved in protecting Hong Kong residents' right.) Wang Ziyan, "'High Degree of Autonomy' is not Bestowed by God," *Hong Kong Economic Journal*, November 9, 1998. (When the Basic Law was being drafted, a PRC official informed the author that the successful implementation of Basic Law and establishment of "one country, two systems" depended on Hong Kong people. The officials in Hong Kong were derelict in not fighting for Hong Kong in the Cheung's case.) Xin, "Further Discussion on Hong Kong Government's Attitude towards Jurisdiction." (Hong Kong justice officials have the responsibility to be concerned about whether Hong Kong residents received a fair trial in China. The thinking and actions of Hong Kong justice officials were not conducive to maintaining a rule of law in Hong Kong.) Zhon Zheng-tien, "Hong Kong should Pay Attention to Maintaining Distance with the Mainland," *Hong Kong Economic Journal*, November 23, 1998. (Many Hong Kong people repeatedly said that they do not want the central government to interfere

with Hong Kong affairs; however, they also tried very hard to anticipate central government's intent and preference and acted accordingly.)

35.  "Yip Suk-yi said that the death penalty issue should be dealt with according to situation, the government has difficulty in arriving at judicial assistance with the mainland," *Hong Kong Economic Journal*, December 4, 1998. The sudden change of position outraged liberal legislators who promised a "take no prisoner" fight ahead, including internationalizing the issue. (Martin Lee, Chairman, Democratic Party, would fight until the "end of the world" including internationalizing the issue if the waiver of the death penalty was not made a mandatory agreement of any rendition agreement with China.) Martin Lee was also concerned about the secretary for security making critical concessions before negotiation started. "Martin Lee is critical of Yip-Lau Suk-yi: on the transfer of fugitive arrangement, weakening one's stance without negotiation," *Ming Bao*, December 8, 1998.

36.  Xin, "Further Discussion on Hong Kong Government's Attitude towards Jurisdiction," 7.

37.  Zhao Bingzhi, "Issues in Criminal Law across the Taiwan Straits," *Journal of Chinese Law* 3, no. 2 (Fall, 1989): 238.

38.  Ibid., 239.

39.  The public has a right to be skeptical. After all, this was not the first-time rich and influential people close to the PRC leadership received favorable treatment from the secretary for justice. In the first case, the secretary for justice used her discretion not to prosecute the chairman of the Sing Tao/Hong Kong Standard press group for corruption, even though there was clear evidence of wrongdoing. The incident caused an uproar, but the secretary for justice was able to weather out the storm. There were suggestions then that justice was not blind.

40.  There is no valid documented evidence pointing to this connection. But, it was widely rumored. The involvement or lack thereof of the Ex-Commissioner of Police at the time was the least investigated subject in the whole "Big Spender" case. At least one movie on the "Big Spender" case implicated the ex-HKP Commissioner, albeit quick to disclaim any liability, by using different names for key players in the event. "Operation Billionaires" (CD released by Universal Laser & Video Co. Ltd. [Hong Kong]).

41.  Hong Shi, "Contemplation Resulting from 'fa mang' (Legal Blindless)," *Hong Kong Economic Journal*, November 21, 1998.

42.  Kam C. Wong's personal discussion with the informant having access to senior Chinese officials, November 23, 1998.

43.  *Yazhou Zhoukan* (The International Chinese Newsweekly), December 14, 1998, 38–39.

44.  Xu Jia-tun, "Party More Important or Law More Important?" *Hong Kong Economic Journal*, November 23, 1998.

45.  Zhong Zhengtian, "Hong Kong People should be Careful in Reflecting Views," *Hong Kong Economic Journal*, September 10, 1998 (A part of the Hong Kong people complained to the central government that Hong Kong's law and order was not good. This affected the confidence of the rich people in Hong Kong. This led the central government to take action to purge the "Big Brother" gang.)

46.  *Oriental Daily*, December 6, 1998, A2.

# Appendix

## Rule of Law versus Rule by the People: A Litmus
## Test for Hong Kong Legal Culture

The CFA judgment in the "right of abode" case will be long remembered in the annals of Hong Kong legal history for causing crisis; first a constitutional and now a social one. However, beyond causing unwelcome crisis, the "right of abode" case is a most welcome and timely litmus test for the legal culture in Hong Kong.

## A Litmus Test for the Legal Culture in Hong Kong

Between March 5–7 and May 3–4, 1999, the Faculty of Social Science, Chinese University of Hong Kong (CUHK), conducted two scientific telephone surveys entitled "Public's view on the HKSAR CFA's right of abode decision" (Survey I) and "Hong Kong people's assessment on the right of abode issue and performance of the Hong Kong government" (Survey II), respectively.

The surveys' findings are most revealing of Hong Kong people's legal culture in two ways. First, the surveys tell us something about Hong Kong people's knowledge and understanding of the law. Second, the surveys tell us something about Hong Kong people's identification with and commitment to the law.

## On Hong Kong People's Knowledge and
## Understanding of the Law

In order for the Hong Kong people to hold the law in high regard, they must first know and understand the law. From the surveys, it is clear that Hong Kong people have very little knowledge about or understanding of the important legal issues in the "right of abode" case.

A month after the right of abode decision, Survey I shows that most people in Hong Kong could not correctly identify some of the most important rulings in the CFA right of abode case. For example, only 32.4 percent of those surveyed correctly answered this question—"(2a)

According to the court's decision, mainland children born to parents before they become a Hong Kong resident can apply for the right of abode in Hong Kong?" Overall, the average correct answer rate to three "knowledge and understanding" based questions was only 33.6 percent. That is to say, two out of three people in Hong Kong did not know what the "right of abode" case is all about!

What is encouraging, however, is that there is a noticeable growth in knowledge or understanding of the legal issues in the "right of abode" case between Survey I (March 5–7, 1999) and Survey II (May 3–4, 1999). For example, the correct answer rate jumped from 32.4 percent to 48.4 percent on one of the "knowledge and understanding" question.

Two factors might have accounted for this overnight increase. First, the public was exposed to daily doses of "public" legal education on the "right of abode" case—on TV, from the radio, and in the press. Second, the public was made aware of the real impact and dire consequences of the decision by the HKSAR government. The "right of abode" decision is no longer an abstraction—it is a reality they have to live with, e.g., lower standard of living, more competition in the work place, etc.

The lesson is clear. Legal culture does not grow on trees! The cultivation of legal culture starts with educating the Hong Kong public to the relevance and importance of law on their social problems and personal well-being.

## On Hong Kong People's Fidelity to the Law

People's fidelity to the law, i.e., commitment to and identification with the law, is a necessary condition to any vibrant rule of law culture. In practice, people's fidelity to the law is manifested as the following of legal principles, instead of being driven by expedient or utilitarian considerations in the resolution of legal problems.

The surveys show clearly that Hong Kong people do not exhibit a strong identification and commitment to the rule of law.

To begin with, as a general proposition, the Hong Kong people respect the rule of law and accept judicial independence in the abstract.

*On the issue of respect for the rule of law.* In Survey I, when people were asked the question: "(17) Do you agree or disagree that the CFA should follow legal viewpoint in deciding cases?" an overwhelming 72.5 percent agreed. This shows that Hong Kong people hold the law in high regard.

*On the issue of acceptance of CFA's judicial independence.* In Survey I, when people were asked the question: "(4) Some opinions suggested that, the CFA right of abode decision is a manifestation of judicial independence. Do you agree with this view?" a clear majority of 66.4 percent agreed. This can be construed as an affirmation of the CFA's constitutional role and approval of its legal authority in the Hong Kong legal system.

However, notwithstanding their respect for CFA's judicial independence, a sizable majority (68 percent) of the Hong Kong public was of the opinion that the CFA's decision was wrongly made in light of its adverse economic consequences. This shows that the public, while respecting the independence of the CFA, were much more concerned with the potential social and economic impact of the CFA's decision.

The conclusion to be drawn is an unmistakable one: for the Hong Kong people legality is not as important as economics in the evaluation of the CFA performance in the "right of abode" case.

Hong Kong people's agreement with the CFA ruling deteriorated over time. In Survey II, an overwhelming majority, i.e., 77.4 percent, thought that the CFA made a wrong decision. Nothing has changed since the Survey I other than the fact that the secretary for security has released the estimated potential adverse impact of the right of abode decision to Hong Kong. The tentative conclusion one can draw is that Hong Kong people's fidelity to the law is a function of the economic and social impact of the CFA's decision.

More tellingly, Hong Kong people are not keen in obeying laws they disagree with. Survey II shows that instead of being committed to carrying out the CFA's decision "as is" with good faith and due diligence, most Hong Kong people think about changing or avoiding the CFA decision. A full 66 percent agreed with various "escape" measures—amending the Basic Law, seeking a PRC NPC-Standing Committee interpretation, having the CFA change its decision—in order to limit the rights of right of aboders. Only 34.1 percent are willing to bite the bullet and carry out the decision of the CFA in its entirety.

## Hong Kong People are Pragmatists and Utilitarian

Ultimately, Hong Kong people are pragmatists and utilitarians par excellence. They are more concerned with protecting their collective social welfare rather than interested in upholding legal principles or human rights. Thus, in Survey I, when people were asked to choose between judicial independence or social or economic development, the people surveyed picked the former over the latter by a wide margin, i.e., 55.5 percent preferred social and economic development over 44.5 percent who preferred judicial independence. In this regard, Survey I's finding was reinforced by Survey II which shows that Hong Kong people are much more willing to consider collective social welfare rather than legal principles or human rights in deciding the right of abode of the Mainland children.

Survey II-A10: "In deciding the issue of whether mainland children should enjoy the right of abode, legal viewpoint, human rights and society's interests as whole should all be taken into account, which of the above do you thing is the most important?"

|  | Frequencies | Effective Rate |
| --- | --- | --- |
| Legal viewpoint | 111 | 14 |
| Human rights | 107 | 13.5 |
| Collective social welfare | 577 | 72.6 |
| Do not know/hard to say | 92 | Missing values |
| Refuse to answer | 24 | Missing values |
| Total | 911 | 100 |

Sample: 792; missing sample: 116.

## Some Concluding Observations

What are the implications of the above legal culture research findings?

Most people assume that the people love the rule of law and their government officials have a tendency of abusing the law. However, what if the Hong Kong public's legal culture is less rulebound than utility driven.

Should the HKSAR government officials and politicians follow the election mandate and give the Hong Kong people what they want, i.e., rule by law, or should they impose on the Hong Kong people a legal culture they do not identify with, i.e., rule of law?

Viewed in this light, the real issue behind the current "right of abode" debate that needs to be debated and resolved is one of rule of law (legality) versus rule by the people (democracy).

# Index